SOCIALISM AFTER HAYEK

ADVANCES IN HETERODOX ECONOMICS

Fred S. Lee, University of Missouri–Kansas City, Series Editor
Rob Garnett, Texas Christian University, Associate Editor

Over the past decade, economists seeking alternatives to mainstream economic thinking—heterodox economists—have undertaken novel, integrative reformulations of their own theoretical traditions, including Austrian, Feminist, Institutional-Evolutionary, Marxian, Post Keynesian, Radical, Social, and Sraffian economics. Despite long-standing rivalries among these heterodox paradigms, a new wave of pluralism since the early 1990s has given rise to new conversations within and among them, fueled by a shared desire to overcome the limitations and hegemony of mainstream economics. To encourage this new generation of economic research, Advances in Heterodox Economics aims to publish books that promote fresh lines of heterodox work in economic theory, policy, philosophy, intellectual history, institutional history, and pedagogy.

Economics in Real Time: A Theoretical Reconstruction
John McDermott

Socialism after Hayek
Theodore A. Burczak

Socialism after Hayek

★

Theodore A. Burczak

THE UNIVERSITY OF MICHIGAN PRESS

Ann Arbor

2009   2008   2007   2006   4   3   2   1

A CIP catalog record for this book is available from the British Library.

Library of Congress Cataloging-in-Publication Data

Burczak, Theodore A., 1964–
     Socialism after Hayek / Theodore A. Burczak.
          p.   cm. — (Advances in heterodox economics)
     Includes bibliographical references and index.
     ISBN-13: 978-0-472-09951-1 (cloth : alk. paper)
     ISBN-10: 0-472-09951-5 (cloth : alk. paper)
     ISBN-13: 978-0-472-06951-4 (pbk. : alk. paper)
     ISBN-10: 0-472-06951-9 (pbk. : alk. paper)
     1. Socialism and society.   2. Hayek, Friedrich A. von (Friedrich
August), 1899– I. Title.   II. Series.
     HX542.B79   2006
     335—dc22   2006008019

Contents

Foreword

Stephen Cullenberg

Two dates, seventy-four years apart, serve as bookends to the twentieth century's many experiments with socialism. On November 8, 1917, Vladimir Lenin announced the formation of a new communist government in what was to become the Soviet Union, a government that ruled in one form or another until Christmas Day 1991, when Mikhail Gorbachev resigned and handed over power to Boris Yeltsin.

For many, the collapse of the Soviet Union represented the triumph of liberal capitalism and the end of a century-long debate over socialism and communism. Whether one was concerned about the viability of actually existing socialist countries, such as Yugoslavia, China, or Cuba, or the theoretical possibility of new forms of socialism in capitalist countries, such as Japan, France, or even the United States, suddenly the very idea and project of socialism seemed passé. The triumph of capitalism was widely proclaimed. The "End of History" was nigh, not as the inspired liberation of universal freedom of working people everywhere, as Marx and Engels had predicted in the *Communist Manifesto*, but, rather, as the coldly efficient ascendance of global neoliberalism.

Many reasons have been offered for the collapse of socialism, ranging from the inefficiency of planning in a large economy, to the lack of material incentives and rewards for innovation, to the overly statist and undemocratic nature of socialist politics, to the outside aggression and imperialist advances of capitalist countries. An alternative explanation, which I favor, focuses not so much on the failure of socialist economies along one or another dimension but, rather, on a failure of the socialist imaginary.

Socialism has long been identified not only with an end to economic exploitation, exclusion, and alienation but also with the end of business cycles, the eradication of poverty, ecological sustainability, and the abolishment of racial, gender, and sexual oppression. This socialist imaginary has placed impossibly heavy burdens on socialist projects everywhere. Socialism's burden has been that not too little but too much has been asked of it. No economic system can guarantee such a myriad of beneficial outcomes. Socialism can and should instead be defined "thinly," not as a modernist utopia, but as a project that seeks to end economic exploitation and exclusion through the transformation of class relations in production. Various types of socialism can and have coexisted with both democratic and nondemocratic political institutions, with environmental degradation and ecological sustainability, and with poverty and egalitarian distributions of income. What makes the socialist project different from others is that within it those who participate in the production of surplus are not excluded from the decisions about how it is to be used and distributed, regardless of the difficulty of the decisions and trade-offs that the disposition of the surplus requires.

The deconstruction of socialism's burden in many ways takes its theoretical cue from what is now known as postmodern Marxism. In contrast to more traditional forms of Marxism, postmodern Marxism casts a skeptical eye on intellectual or political projects that seek to find an overarching logic to history or to provide a rational foundation for individual or class behavior. Postmodern Marxism looks for moments of "dialectical surprise" in history, moments of contingency and uncertainty that cannot be predicted or contained. It is in this sense that postmodern Marxism shares an affinity with the work of Friedrich Hayek, a profound critic of classical socialism and a doyen of the conservative Right today.

The dialectical surprise in this book is how Burczak uncovers and then recovers what he calls Hayek's "applied epistemological postmodernism," and then shows how it can be used to rethink the socialist project in a new and unique way. Hayek was deeply critical of what he thought was the hubris and certitude of the classical socialist model. He felt that economic action (including the actions of government officials and professional economists) was characterized by uncertainty, error, and subjective perception—what he called "knowledge problems." These knowledge problems gave rise to other fundamental concerns for a socialist economy that many critics of socialism have pointed out: problems of incentives, information dissemination, and coordination.

Rather than dooming the idea of socialism, Burczak transforms Hayek's critique into a profound new way to think about socialism. By linking the Marxian focus on various forms in which surplus labor is performed, appropriated, and distributed to the Aristotelian capability theory developed by Amartya Sen and Martha Nussbaum, Burczak weaves a tapestry of a new model of socialism that is rich in its understanding of complex economies (and thoroughly informed by Hayek and the Austrian tradition of economics) while making visible many of the ethical concerns that have animated socialists for over one hundred years. This is heterodox economics at its best.

Acknowledgments

Over the years, I have incurred substantial intellectual debts that have compounded into this book. Stephen Resnick and Richard Wolff introduced me to the notion of postmodern Marxism. James Crotty and Douglas Vickers opened the door to the idea of radical subjectivism, via Keynes. Samuel Bowles and Herbert Gintis showed how to transform traditional economics into political economy. All were my teachers in the Economics Department at the University of Massachusetts—Amherst. The model of socialism in this book is partly animated by an imaginary conversation among Resnick and Wolff, and Bowles and Gintis. Peter d'Errico in the Legal Studies Department at the University of Massachusetts taught me much about legal realism. Resnick, Wolff, Vickers, and d'Errico served on the committee for my 1994 PhD dissertation, "Subjectivism and the Limits of F. A. Hayek's Political Economy," which raised the question about how a left-wing Hayekian economics would look. That question is finally answered, in a preliminary way, by this book.

Jack Amariglio, David Ruccio, Stephen Cullenberg, and George DeMartino have also been important influences on my thinking, through their contributions to economics and postmodernism (especially Amariglio 1990 and Ruccio 1991), a thin theory of socialism (especially Cullenberg 1992), and class justice and Nussbaum and Sen's capability theory (especially DeMartino 2003).

Over the past decade, I have enjoyed and profited from many conversations, e-mail exchanges, and published debates with the Austrian economists Peter Boettke, William Butos, Bruce Caldwell, Steven Horwitz, Israel Kirzner, Roger Koppl, Don Lavoie, David Prychitko, and Mario Rizzo. They have contributed to my understanding of Austrian Economics, Hayek, and the possibility of a post-Hayekian socialism. I thank each without in any way implicating them for the socialist ideas in this book.

There are also time debts that must be acknowledged. First, Denison University's Robert C. Good Faculty Fellowship program and the Office of the Provost provided a semester's leave and a course reduction that gave me time to complete the book. Second, my family—Cathy, Jack, and George—were patient when my attention was regularly drawn away from them to Hayek and socialism.

My largest debt is to Rob Garnett, whose commitment to pluralism and heterodox economics and whose skills as an editor are in large part responsible for this book seeing the light of a published day.

Material in several chapters has been previously published. I thank the following publishers for permission to draw on and reprint that material:

Chapter 1 uses some material from "Focusing on Appropriative Class Justice: A Comment on DeMartino's 'Realizing Class Justice,'" *Rethinking Marxism* 16 (April, 2004): 207–9. It is reprinted with the permission of Taylor and Francis, http://www.tandf.co.uk.

Chapter 2 borrows from and expands "The Postmodern Moments of F. A. Hayek's Economics," *Economics and Philosophy* 10 (April 1994): 31–58. It is reprinted with the permission of Cambridge University Press.

Chapters 3 and 4 use parts of "The Contradictions between Hayek's Subjectivism and His Liberal Legal Theory," in *F. A. Hayek as a Political Economist*, ed. J. Birner, P. Garrouste, and T. Aimar. London and New York: Routledge, 2002, 183–201. This material is reprinted with the permission of Routledge.

Chapter 4 also draws from "A Critique of Kirzner's Finders-Keepers Defense of Profit," *Review of Austrian Economics* 15 (January 2002): 75–90. This material is reprinted with the permission of Springer Science and Business Media.

Chapter 6 reproduces, with some additions and clarifications, "Ellerman's Labor Theory of Property and the Injustice of Capitalist Exploitation," in *Review of Social Economy* 59 (June 2001): 161–83. It is reprinted with the permission of Taylor and Francis.

CHAPTER 1

Hayek, Marx, and Socialism

★

Classical socialism was a movement to replace the unplanned and exploitative institutions of capitalism with national planning, public ownership, and distribution according to human need rather than by the arbitrary capriciousness of the market. Its goals were to distribute economic resources broadly among the people in order to create the conditions for widespread, substantive freedom and to end alienating, exploitative labor processes. Socialism promised all people the resources to live a flourishing life, not just the market freedom to exchange, which offered no guarantee of a decent standard of living. This traditional socialist project was derived from Marx and Engels's dream of a future that would transcend the allocative and distributional anarchy of the market through the abolition of private property and the establishment of social ownership of the means of production and central planning.[1] Socialism, or perhaps its more advanced form of communism, would realize the human potential to harness productive forces to achieve a rational economic order, social justice, and real freedom for all.

Classical socialism had no larger enemy in the twentieth century than Friedrich Hayek. Born in Vienna in 1899, Hayek became a naturalized British citizen in 1938 and taught for many years at the University of Chicago as a member of the Committee on Social Thought. He won the Nobel Prize for Economics in 1974. In later years, he became the intellectual darling of the conservative movements in the United States and Britain. British prime minister Margaret Thatcher claimed Hayek as the intellectual progenitor of her policies to privatize the British economy and scale back the British welfare state. President George H. W. Bush awarded him the Medal of Freedom in 1992, the year of Hayek's death.

Because the Right has appropriated Hayek's thought in defense of small government capitalism, those of other political persuasions—including many heterodox economists—tend to dismiss Hayek's ideas as reactionary. But this dismissal is a mistake. Hayek's economics and social theory are based on what might be called an "applied epistemological postmodernism." His work is unified by a common concern: to understand the limited and socially constituted nature of human knowledge and to trace the implications of this radical epistemology for the theory of human action and social evolution. For Hayek, the knowledge of economic actors is beset with error, uncertainty, social prejudice, and subjective perception. So, too, is the knowledge of government officials. And so is the knowledge of the economic theorist. It is precisely Hayek's postmodern skepticism about the attainability of objective knowledge and his corresponding rejection of a scientistic understanding of society that place the biggest obstacles in the way of the defense of classical forms of socialism based on government planning or government control of the market. Socialists and other advocates of government activism in the economy ignore Hayek's insights at their intellectual peril.

Don Lavoie famously sums up Hayek's conception of the general human/economic problem as "the knowledge problem" (Lavoie 1986b, 5), concerned with how best to coordinate the actions of scattered individuals, each of whom is in possession of unique, partial, tacit, and potentially erroneous knowledge. In later chapters, I will reclassify this as "the factual knowledge problem." Hayek believes that market competition is the only effective solution to this problem. In his view, a private property, free market system establishes a structure of incentives that encourages individuals to utilize their unique perceptions and knowledge in a manner that fulfills others' needs and desires. If a society attempts to implement central planning with the hope of replacing the anarchic outcomes of the market with a rationally planned economy, it is bound to be disappointed by the inability of central planners to access and utilize individuals' subjective, situational knowledge as effectively as a private property, free market system.

In addition, Hayek's theory of knowledge leads him to reject all notions of distributive justice that might guide the construction of a welfare state to ameliorate the potentially disruptive effects of the market economy. For Hayek, people, especially government officials, cannot acquire an objective, unprejudiced assessment about the nature of a fair outcome and the definition of human need. There is, therefore, no uncontroversial definition of a just distribution of resources. Whenever government officials attempt to alter the distribution of income or wealth, they are imposing their subjective value judgments on others, rather than acting in the common interest. In other words, Hayek thinks that there is an ethical knowledge problem that stands in the way of a rationally constructed welfare state.

Given the factual and ethical knowledge problems, Hayek insists that real-world economists and government officials are inherently unable to acquire the knowledge that would be required to achieve any particular vision of economic order or social justice. Absent these possibilities, he argues that a market economy that facilitates the exchange of private property, regulated by the rule of law and evolved common laws, is the only institutional structure that can effectively promote cooperation among diverse, dispersed, and anonymous people and thereby advance the common good. Given the limits to human knowledge, the formal freedom provided by the rule of law and unimpeded market exchange is the best that modern societies can offer to their citizens.

Karl Marx, the father of modern socialism, also recognized the dispersion of human knowledge in a market economy. But, as Chris Sciabarra argues in his fascinating *Marx, Hayek, and Utopia* (1995), Marx viewed the dispersal of knowledge as a result of workers' alienation from the means of production, a transitory side effect of the property relations of capitalism. This stands in contrast to Hayek, who views the strictures on human knowledge as "existentially limiting," that is, as natural and transhistorical properties of human existence (Sciabarra 1995, 119). Sciabarra understands Marx to accept epistemic fragmentation as only a temporary feature of social development, to be overcome in a socialist or communist society. For Marx, development of the forces of production and cooperative work relations would allow tacit and dispersed knowledge to be articulated and integrated in consciously directed economic activity, thereby solving Hayek's supposedly permanent knowledge problems. Sciabarra calls this Marx's "synoptic delusion" (ibid., 46)—the idea that one can consciously design a new society to achieve social justice. Many interpreters of Marx have embraced and extended this premise to argue that a Marxian vision of communism or socialism could only be realized by a centrally planned economy. Sciabarra claims that Hayek's thought ultimately triumphs over Marx's—and free market capitalism over centrally planned socialism—because Hayek resisted the synoptic delusion while Marx and his followers did not.

For contemporary socialists, this raises fundamental questions. Is there any meaningful notion of socialism that can answer Hayek's epistemological critique? Can the goals of classical socialism be achieved without central planning and the abolition of private property? Can there be socialism after Hayek?

My aim in this book is to answer these questions in the affirmative by developing a "libertarian Marxist" conception of socialism, a socialism committed to forms of procedural and distributive justice that are central to the Marxian tradition and a socialism keenly aware of the factual and ethical knowledge problems emphasized by Hayek. One aspect of this project is to end the exploitation of labor. Marx believed this could be accomplished through "the ultimate abolition of the wages system" (Marx 1965, 79). One way to achieve this is by prohibiting the wage-for-labor-time exchange and requiring that joint forms of production take place in democratic, labor-appropriating firms. This would institute a Marxian/socialist type of procedural justice. Another aspect of the socialist project is to achieve a measure of distributive justice, as expressed by Marx's famous dictum that resources in a socialist society would be distributed according to need (Marx 1978). I will call on the Aristotelian capability theory of justice developed by Martha Nussbaum and Amartya Sen to suggest a set of welfare-promoting institutions that work toward some semblance of this goal. I will be especially concerned with identifying forms of distribution that would enhance the economic viability of workplace democracy and democratic appropriation. To this end, I will argue that the redistribution of wealth is more important to the post-Hayekian socialist project than is the redistribution of income. The resulting vision of socialism will join an Austrian emphasis on market processes as vital engines of knowledge production, social coordination, and human well-being to Aristotelian/Marxist notions of justice and human well-being, to give new meaning—and hopefully a new set of practical possibilities—to the term *market socialism*.

In sum, I will attempt to mix the wisdom of three heterodox traditions to create a new socialist stew. Each of these traditions contains insights not found in mainstream economics. Hayek and the Austrians provide a richer theory of market processes than the utility-maximizing, equilibrium approach of neoclassical economics. The Marxian tradition imparts a consequentialist understanding of class as a process of producing, appropriating, and distributing surplus labor that is rendered invisible by standard economic theories of the firm. The Aristotelian capability theory of justice enunciated by Nussbaum and Sen provides an intersubjectivist method to make interpersonal comparisons of well-being, a method that is sorely lacking in many contemporary forms of utilitarian theory, including Hayek's tradition of Austrian economics.

Yet none of these heterodox traditions alone is a sufficient guide for the future of socialism. Each needs to absorb certain concepts and criticisms from the others to maximize its own contribution to human betterment. Marxists need to understand the theoretical and practical importance of the Austrian theory of the market process in order to retain their relevance in the post-Soviet world. Hayekians need to understand that there are rigorous, defensible theories of social justice, such as Nussbaum and Sen's capability theory, in order to escape the relativistic libertarianism to which they are prone. And Nussbaum and Sen's capability theory must be enriched by a Marxian theory of class and an appreciation of Hayekian knowledge problems in order to achieve its potential as a normative framework for the promotion of freedom and human development. The goal of this book is to bring these three traditions together to propose a new heterodox perspective on the future of socialism.

POSTMODERNISM, MARXISM, AND HAYEK

Since I am highlighting the role of Hayek's epistemological postmodernism in his critique of centrally planned socialism, a brief discussion of postmodernism will be instructive, as it is a concept with many interpretations. Some people use the term *postmodern* to refer to a style or to a time period (Jameson 1984). I will use it here to refer to a particular mode of inquiry. A postmodern social theory is one that eschews reductionist (essentialist) and teleological reasoning and attempts a more dialectical, overdetermined understanding of social phenomena. This is opposed to essentialist genres of social theory, in which social outcomes are presumed to be reducible to a predetermined subset of causal agent(s). This broadly antiessentialist postmodernism takes a position against the modernist "notion of an autonomous rational subject and the related idea . . . of knowledge as representation" (Ruccio 1991, 500). In place of the autonomous subject, postmodernists employ concepts of decentered subjectivity. The concept of the decentered subject is intended to capture "the idea that subjectivity is not prior to but constituted by systems of language, power, and the other aspects of social life" (501). Since postmodernism rejects essentialist reasoning and the idea of knowledge as representation, it is often characterized as a belief in the social constitution of the individual and in the unattainability of objective truth and knowledge. The epistemological pessimism of postmodernism is related to the Hayekian knowledge problems and is the theme I am most interested in pursuing in this book, although I will also consider Hayek's dialectical theory of people and society.

Although Hayek was never an active participant in debates surrounding modernism and postmodernism, his methodological works are marked by a deep skepticism about the possibilities of objectively true knowledge (Hayek 1952, 1979a). He criticizes rationalist and empiricist epistemologies, and he extends his epistemological critique beyond methodological concerns to the descriptive, or scientific, understanding of knowing and acting human beings. The impossibility of objective knowledge lies at the heart of Hayek's subjectivist theory of human action and his concept of the market as a discovery process. These Hayekian notions of subjectivism and market process—ideas usually associated with the Austrian school of economics—trace one nascent postmodern position within economics. To be clear, in discerning the potential for a postmodern economics in Hayek's work, I am not claiming that this was his announced intention. Rather, this interpretation emerges from a reading of Hayek's texts that focuses on his epistemological views and his criticism of what he calls "constructivist rationalism," a theoretical perspective founded on the belief that people rationally choose their own histories and that "all social institutions are, and ought to be, the product of deliberate design" (Hayek 1973, 5). Hayek links constructivist rationalism to modernist or essentialist theories of human action, theories that reduce social outcomes to the choices of asocial rational agents, based on a "false conception of the human mind as an entity standing outside the cosmos of nature and society, rather than being itself the product of the same process of evolution to which the institutions of society are due" (ibid.).

There is a school of contemporary Marxian economic thought that has actively embraced many of these postmodern ideas. This school arose from the pathbreaking work of Stephen Resnick and Richard Wolff, who initiated what some have called the "Amherst school" of postmodern Marxism (Resnick and Wolff 1987).[2] Resnick and Wolff embrace both a postmodern epistemology that understands all human knowledge to be the product of a unique, complex, and open-ended socialization rather than as a mirror of nature, on the one hand, and, on the other, a postmodern ontology that understands the constitution and causation of social events to be the overdetermined product of various—perhaps an infinity of—natural and social forces. A central goal of Resnick and Wolff's reconfiguration of Marxism is to prune the vestiges of essentialism from Marxian thought. They reject the remnant of last-instance economic determinism and evolutionary teleology in traditional Marxism. One critic has labeled Resnick and Wolff's antiessentialist, nonteleological social ontology as "everythingism" (Carling 1990). While the intent of this label was pejorative, it captures the flavor of postmodern Marxism's perspective on the nature of reality, a perspective in which everything does, to some extent, depend on everything else.

Since it is impossible for human knowledge to capture all possible lines of causation of social events, Resnick and Wolff reason that every social theory must inevitably specialize, adopting a favored conceptual entry point into social analysis and seeking to trace, albeit partially and provisionally, its causal connections to the rest of the social totality. The entry point for postmodern Marxism is the concept of class. Resnick and Wolff carefully define class as the process of producing, appropriating, and distributing surplus labor. This idea of class is distinct from other, more commonly held notions of class that focus on the distribution of income, wealth, and power or the cultural habits of different groups of people. It also gives rise to somewhat nontraditional definitions of capitalism and socialism. Classical Marxism understands capitalism as a form of economy that combines widespread private property and more or less free markets to produce exploitation. Classical socialism, then, aims to abolish exploitation by replacing private property with social property and markets with central planning. For the postmodern Marxists, however, there is no one-to-one relationship between the presence or absence of private property, markets, and central planning and the existence of exploitative class processes (i.e., class processes in which the producers of surplus labor do not participate in its appropriation). Class exploitation can persist in the presence of central planning and socialized property. Resnick and Wolff argue, for example, that the Soviet Union did not eliminate exploitation. They regard the Soviet experience as an example of state capitalism, rather than socialism or communism (Resnick and Wolff 2002). The positive goal of postmodern Marxism is to use antiessentialist, nonteleological modes of analysis to understand the social construction and consequences of exploitative class processes and to envision and enact nonexploitative, socialist alternatives.

But do these postmodern Marxists really escape the synoptic delusion that Sciabarra sees in Marx? In principle, they do. Jack Amariglio and David Ruccio argue that postmodern Marxism resists the capitalism-as-irrational/socialism-as-rational dualism that characterizes modern radical social thought. They criticize the delusions of rational planning, claiming to find "no evidence that planning means stability and order . . . [or] implies a 'better' method to get at the 'true' needs of individuals and/or enterprises" (Amariglio and Ruccio 1998, 250). They even make the quasi-Hayekian claim that "the disorderliness [disequilibrium] of markets can (at certain times, in particular circumstances) lead to the satisfaction of social needs" (ibid., 251). From their postmodern perspective, disorder, decentering, and uncertainty are ubiquitous "facts" of social existence. The aspiration of rational economic planning to achieve social justice is thus directly called into question by postmodern Marxists. Yet Amariglio and Ruccio do not dismiss socialist planning tout court. Since postmodern Marxism retains the goal of eliminating exploitative class processes, they would support socialist planning if it "announced itself as nothing more than an activity in which the desires of exploited classes were given priority" (ibid.).

The Hayekian question would be whether even this qualified defense of planning could actually be realized, given the knowledge problems endemic to the human condition. Amariglio and Ruccio do not ask this question, because they (and postmodern Marxists generally) have paid relatively little attention to the link between postmodern epistemology and economic processes. In particular, they have yet to seriously investigate the positive complementarities between the market and class processes—for example, how private property and market exchange might serve as conditions of existence for socialist class relations within firms. In other words, they have yet to consider how the ideas of Marx and Hayek might work together to strengthen the case for certain forms of market socialism.

This lack of interparadigmatic learning is both acute and understandable, given the long-standing political animus between Marxists and classical liberals, such as Hayek. It is understandable on normative and methodological grounds as well, as Marxists are wont to imagine that social theories focused on individual (negative) liberty and choice-oriented subjectivity "serve to hide and perpetuate class injustice" (Wolff and Resnick 1987, 9). Yet this deafness is costly to Marxists, especially postmodern Marxists, given the nonessentialist epistemology and postmodern methodological individualism that lie at the heart of Hayek's economics. In ignoring Hayek, postmodern Marxists are in danger of eliding Hayekian knowledge problems in their theories of social organization. They are also perpetuating a spurious disjuncture between their notions of class justice and liberal notions of human freedom. As Cohen (1995) argues, Marxists can no longer afford to dismiss freedom and justice as "bourgeois" concerns. The old Marxist faith in a utopian future where material abundance would transcend these concerns is no longer very inspiring as material scarcities continue to challenge most of the world's population. Marxists should therefore engage in practical and ethical discussions of how their class-minded struggles might serve to enhance human freedom and vice versa. Reading Hayek, Nussbaum, and Sen alongside of Marx can help us to accomplish this.

The most serious attempt by a postmodern Marxist to construct a vision of socialism that accepts Hayekian knowledge problems, albeit implicitly, is Stephen Cullenberg's thin socialism. Cullenberg (1992) suggests that an important reason why people view socialism as a failure is because socialists have asked too much of it. Socialism has been understood as a utopia that would end the exploitation and alienation of labor; eliminate business cycles and poverty; abolish racial, sexual, and gender oppression; and establish more harmonious relations between people and the environment. Cullenberg proposes that we instead draw on Resnick and Wolff's reconstruction of Marxism, in which the primary goal of a Marxian socialism would be the abolition of exploitation, not central planning and the socialization of the means of production. Cullenberg's thin definition of socialism meets this goal by requiring that firms be democratically organized in the sense that workers would collectively appropriate the fruits of their labor.

Cullenberg's thin notion of socialism seems fully compatible with the private ownership of capital and free markets, circumscribed only by the prohibition of contracts for wage labor. His thin socialism implements a Marxian notion of procedural fairness—that those who work should also appropriate the product of their labor—that allows him to embrace firmly the goal of ending exploitation while he just as firmly rejects central planning and state ownership of the means of production. While Cullenberg does not address Hayek's arguments directly, he succeeds in articulating a notion of socialism that escapes Hayek's factual and ethical knowledge problems; that is, it avoids Hayek's critique of statist "social justice."

In this regard, however, Cullenberg's conception of socialism becomes too thin. By eschewing all consequentialist claims, his postmodern Marxian socialism would leave socialists with nothing to say about the distributive injustices of unmet basic needs and dramatically unequal allocations of wealth, income, and opportunities. A market economy populated by firms in which workers, rather than capital owners, democratically appropriate the fruits of production could easily yield undesirable inequalities of income and wealth distribution, inequalities that have long been a concern for socialists.

The question then arises whether it is possible to thicken Cullenberg's definition of socialism to include a commitment to distributive justice without jettisoning a concern for Hayekian knowledge problems. George DeMartino has taken some valuable first steps in this direction by proposing a rearticulation of postmodern Marxism within Nussbaum and Sen's theory of justice. In his excellent book *Global Economy, Global Justice* (2000), DeMartino uses Nussbaum and Sen's capability approach to develop some unique theoretical and policy proposals that might initiate a movement toward global economic justice. Perhaps even more significant for socialist theory, DeMartino shows how a Marxian concern to eliminate class injustice might be grafted onto Nussbaum and Sen's capability theory (ibid., 104–7). This attempt to wed class justice to the capability theory corrects a major defect of the otherwise fertile and progressive theory of justice offered by Nussbaum and Sen. In a subsequent paper, DeMartino (2003) takes these brief remarks and turns them into a well-developed framework for understanding and addressing class injustice.

DeMartino adopts Resnick and Wolff's tripartite definition of the class process as the production, appropriation, and distribution of surplus labor. On this basis, he argues that class justice has three dimensions: productive justice, appropriative justice, and distributive justice. This nifty reframing allows DeMartino to reconcile Marx's famous expression of productive and distributive justice—"From each according to his ability, to each according to his needs" (Marx 1978, 531)—to Marx's separate concern with appropriative justice: seeking an end to the exploitative appropriation of surplus labor by nonproducers. DeMartino asserts that we can see these three concerns as part of a larger agenda concerning class justice, an agenda whose normative foundation lies in the Aristotelian principle of capabilities equality.

DeMartino argues that productive class justice is related to the first part of the Marxian ethic, "From each according to ability." Since "[p]roductive class justice refers to the fairness in the allocation of the work of producing the social surplus," DeMartino maintains that producing according to ability is a possible form of realizing this aspect of class justice (DeMartino 2003, 8). This notion of productive class justice might also be extended to include Marx and Engels's vision of despecialized labor patterns in The German Ideology.

> "[I]n communist society, where nobody has one exclusive sphere of activity but each can become accomplished in any branch he wishes, society regulates the general production and thus makes it possible for me to do one thing today and another tomorrow, to hunt in the morning, fish in the afternoon, rear cattle in the evening, criticize after dinner, just as I have a mind, without ever becoming hunter, fisherman, shepherd, or critic." (Marx and Engels 1970, 53)

The open question is whether a complex society could ever regulate general production (through central planning?) to achieve this level of freedom and equity in the work of producing the social surplus. Perhaps market incentives can ensure that people produce according to ability. But if not, it is possible that Hayekian knowledge problems would make it impossible to achieve productive class justice. DeMartino does not address this issue.

DeMartino is more successful in using Nussbaum and Sen's capability theory to suggest how we might think about distributive class justice. He sees Nussbaum and Sen's notion of capabilities equality as harboring a complex, nonessentialist theory of distribution according to need, a theory that is compatible, to a large degree, with postmodern Marxism. In chapter 5, I will follow DeMartino's lead to show how the capability approach might help us to understand the nature of distribution according to human need and to respond to Hayek's procedural theory of justice. DeMartino's argument will lead us to ask about how various forms of distributive class justice might contribute to the achievement of appropriative class justice.

Regarding appropriative justice, DeMartino distinguishes between strong and weak definitions of appropriative justice. In the strong sense, appropriative justice would mean "appropriative rights are restricted to productive workers, however they be defined" (DeMartino 2003, 18). This strong definition is consistent with workplace democracy and with Cullenberg's thin socialism, as long as "productive worker" is defined to include all people who work in the firm. DeMartino, however, is more inclined to advocate what he calls a weak definition of appropriative justice, under which productive workers "are not excluded from fair and meaningful participation" in the appropriation of the surplus. As he points out, this weak form would be satisfied by institutional arrangements in which the entire community enjoys the right to appropriate the fruits of labor. While he does not spell out the exact nature of this communal appropriation, it is hard to imagine how it would not involve some sort of democratic government acting as the agent of appropriation. If that is the case, Marxian socialism would once again fail to confront the Hayekian knowledge problems inherent in economic administration by a central government.

In sum, DeMartino provides an attractive framework within which to think about class justice and the enhancement of human capabilities. Yet he, too—like the postmodern Marxian economics literature generally—neglects the knowledge problems that would attend to the institution of such a thickened socialism. To this extent, the postmodern Marxian literature has yet to provide an economically feasible, consequentialist case for socialism.

This book is born out of this lack. Its goals are to defend a strong form of appropriative justice consistent with democratic, labor-appropriating firms operating in a system of competitive markets (i.e., Cullenberg's thin socialism) and to advocate for socialist distributive justice against the Hayekian suspicion that such ideas lead us inevitably down a statist road to serfdom. Limiting the notion of appropriative class justice to DeMartino's strong definition precludes the possibility of communal appropriation by a central government. But it does not preclude the possibility of the entire community sharing in the rights to a distribution of the surplus product. In other words, there might be a role for the state to redistribute income or wealth to promote a more widespread satisfaction of human needs, or, in the language of Nussbaum and Sen, to strive toward equal capability to achieve vital human functionings. This possibility will also be explored as a possible component of a post-Hayekian socialism.

These "postmodern socialist" arguments are also inspired by a recent wave of innovative work within Austrian economics that, unlike Hayek's, wrestles explicitly with issues raised by postmodernism. Don Lavoie has made some of the most important contributions to this literature with his work on economics and hermeneutics (1986a, 1990). Other notable contributions include the work of Lavoie's students—Peter Boettke (1990), Steven Horwitz (1992), and David Prychitko (1995), among others—as well as the radical subjectivism of Ludwig Lachmann (1986), Koppl and Whitman's notion of "rational-choice hermeneutics" (2004), and Richard Ebeling's suggestion that we can see the market as a "hermeneutical process" (1986). A unifying thread in this postmodern Austrian literature is a Hayekian rejection of rationalist and empiricist theories of knowledge and the adoption of interpretive (perhaps even dialectical) epistemologies. The postmodern Austrians—like Hayek, but unlike the postmodern Marxists—apply these epistemological insights to their conceptions of human action and theories of the market process. I will discuss these ideas in more detail in chapter 2.

Regarding socialism, however, the postmodern Austrians remain uniformly opposed to it. In an article titled "Why Are There No Austrian Socialists?" Boettke answers his own rhetorical question on the premise that socialism must entail some sort of central planning (Boettke 1995b). Since central planning dispenses with profit incentives, Boettke reasons that socialism must be inferior to markets in regard to social coordination and wealth production. Similarly, Prychitko claims that Marxists cannot really be "*market* socialists"; they have to choose one or the other. As he puts it, any model of so-called market socialism that allows "capital goods markets tempered by indicative planning . . . ends up with a market-based, non-socialist, non-Marxist (albeit interventionist) system" (Prychitko 2002, 33). Prychitko reaches this conclusion because he interprets Marx's critique of alienation as necessarily a critique of the market, rather than a critique of capitalist work relations. In general, the antisocialist arguments of Austrian economists are based on unreconstructed images of socialism as central planning and Marxism as antimarket. They do not recognize the possibility of a postmodern Marxian vision of economics and a concept of socialism that is not confined to the traditional debate of market versus plan.

Perhaps the failure of postmodern Marxists and postmodern Austrians to engage in serious discussions of postcapitalism is a result of a hangover—celebratory on one side and dejected on the other—from cold war disputes over the viability of socialism and communism, particularly in the Soviet Union. There remains a tendency among economists in each group to view the other school's conceptual "entry point" (class for the Marxists, individual action for the Austrians) as a slippery slope toward a coercive, totalitarian evil (an overreaching, interventionist state or a ravagely exploitative neoliberalism). This book is animated by the belief that these worst-case fears are not pertinent to contemporary discussions of socialism and that Austrian and Marxian insights can and should be combined in the struggle for an ethically desirable and economically feasible socialism. As Lavoie aptly puts it, "it is time for these more liberal elements of the left and right sides of the old political spectrum to transcend the confines of these obsolete ideologies and work together to articulate a new vision of the free society" (Lavoie 1994, 283).

POST-HAYEKIAN SOCIALISM

Geoffrey Hodgson claims: "If socialism is to survive at all it must overcome its congenital *agoraphobia*—which means, literally, 'fear of markets.' It has to learn to inhabit open systems and open spaces" (Hodgson 1999, 61). With this I agree. An appreciation of Hayek's epistemological postmodernism and its relationship to the Austrian theory of the market process can help post-modern Marxists to overcome any residual market phobia, since they are otherwise eager to embrace open systems and open spaces. Post-Hayekian socialism must inevitably be market socialism; national economic planning is a dubious ambition for the future of socialism. At the same time, post-modern Marxism gives market socialism a reachable goal: the abolition of exploitative class processes. Abolition of exploitation and abolition of markets are not isomorphic objectives. Post-Hayekian socialism should also retain a concern for meeting human needs. The Aristotelian tradition as read through the overlapping eyes of Hayek, Marx, Nussbaum, and Sen can show us how. I again agree with Hodgson when he asserts, "if socialism is to be rescued from its theoretical and practical failures, then it has to be both a mixed economy and 'market socialism' in some genuine sense" (ibid., 17).

To develop this concept of post-Hayekian market socialism, I will begin by exploring the postmodern epistemology that underlies Hayek's critique of central planning and his advocacy of privately held property and competitive market processes. I will then critically examine Hayek's conclusion that a market economy regulated by the rule of law and evolved common laws (i.e., a "free market economy") is the institutional form most compatible with human ignorance, procedural justice, and human well-being. Hayek's conclusion, I will argue, cannot withstand the scrutiny of his own epistemological perspective. This opens the door to the possibility of a socialist theory of justice. Nevertheless, Hayek's insights about knowledge and markets will motivate a search for market socialist alternatives that do not depend on socializing the means of production or government control of the economy.

Chapter 2 outlines the postmodern moments of Hayek's social theory, particularly in his theory of knowledge. It links Hayek's hermeneutical methodological individualism to his defense of a market economy and critique of central planning articulated in the socialist calculation debate in the 1930s. The socialist calculation debate centers on the possibility that governments can effectively conduct national economic planning. Hayek argues that central planning is doomed to failure because it is impossible for government planners to access the knowledge necessary to direct resources to their most efficient use. This knowledge exists in an essentially fragmented form, in the minds of diverse and dispersed individuals. Hayek shows why government planners cannot obtain this subjective knowledge and why free market exchange is the only economic institution that can elicit the discovery and employment of subjective knowledge for the benefit of society. For many years, the conventional wisdom held that Hayek was wrong and that central planning could work. Today, most economists consider Hayek to have been right. Like Sciabarra, these economists also believe that Hayek effectively killed socialism. While I do not agree with this new conclusion, socialists would profit by studying Hayek's nuanced theory of the market.

Chapter 3 explains Hayek's procedural theory of justice and its dependence on an evolutionary conception of the rule of law as the appropriate regulator of a market economy. For Hayek, the rule of law establishes a fair process for the conduct of economic activity. He defends the market process guided by common laws consistent with the rule of law as the institutional framework most likely to improve the life chances of anyone chosen at random. This is because he sees a common law system as typically operating in the interests of no particular person. The common law process establishes a set of impartial, agreed-on rules. Chapter 3 describes how Hayek uses the rule of law and the common law to draw a line between appropriate and inappropriate government action regulating the market and, most notably, to preclude government attempts to achieve distributive justice.

Chapter 4 challenges these conclusions. It does so by criticizing Hayek on the basis of his own epistemological and normative principles. I will use the insights of the American legal realist tradition to show that the agreement about socially beneficial rules to govern the market that Hayek believes to be discovered by the common law may be largely imaginary. A major contribution of the legal realists is to show that agreements about social benefits and the common good do not exist as objective knowledge, waiting somewhere "out there" for judges to find it. If such agreements about the common good are possible, they must be created through a more participatory, democratic process. In addition, chapter 4 argues that the supposed impartiality that Hayek ascribes to a market economy guided by the rule of law may be illusory as well. It is likely the case, as critics of the market have argued for several centuries, that the market serves the interests of the wealthy more than those of the poor. The modern credit rationing literature will be employed to show that market economies can be systematically biased against the poor. The inability to obtain credit can prevent asset-poor individuals from being able to pursue opportunities that they uniquely and subjectively perceive. This possibility further reinforces the claim that the tacit agreement about the constitution of the common good that Hayek sees in the common law is a mirage.

Chapter 5 presents an alternative theory of justice that might guide the development of a post-Hayekian socialism, drawing from the works of Nussbaum and Sen and from Aristotelian interpretations of Marx. Many authors argue that Marx's thought harbors a theory of social justice in the tradition of Aristotle (McCarthy 1992; de Ste. Croix 1981). In *Capital*, Marx does occasionally acknowledge Aristotle approvingly (Marx 1976), and his 1844 manu-scripts (Marx 1964) clearly reveal an Aristotelian influence. This book accepts the Aristotle-Marx connection as unproblematic and does not argue for it in any detail. I am more concerned with seeing how well the particularly thorough account of social justice developed separately and jointly by Nussbaum and Sen can withstand the knowledge problems posed by Hayek and how it might motivate and inform a vision of socialism. One of the primary goals of good government, according to Nussbaum and Sen's approach, is to ensure that all people have the means to develop their capabilities to lead choiceworthy lives. A choiceworthy life is one that a person has reason to value, because the available choices allow a person to achieve the essential human functions consistent with human flourishing. Social justice therefore requires government to ensure, to the greatest degree possible, that all individuals have the means available so that they can choose to lead a flourishing life.

Chapter 6 develops an argument for democratic, worker-managed enterprises operating in a private property, market-based economy as an institutional structure that can achieve the Marxian goal of abolishing exploitation in economic processes that require group production. Workplace democracy ends exploitation by enabling workers to be the initial appropriators of the product of their labor. The argument for democratic self-management is based on an Aristotelian concern for how participation and dignity are important to achieve well-being. Chapter 6 thus links a normative argument for democratic self-management with Nussbaum and Sen's approach to justice developed in chapter 5.

Chapter 7 examines some market socialist proposals to achieve distributive justice in light of their ability to promote worker self-management and to escape Hayekian knowledge problems. Two approaches are considered: those advocating the redistribution of profit income and those supporting redistribution of wealth. The argument to redistribute profits is represented by John Roemer's proposal for an egalitarian redistribution of capital ownership via the institution of a coupon stock market: allowing individuals to purchase stock shares using only equally distributed coupons issued by the government for this purpose. The important question is whether Roemer's coupon stock market could potentially solve the financing problem of labor-managed firms in a way that fosters economic efficiency and preserves distributive justice. I will argue that it might not, that a coupon stock market may fail to enable extensive entry by start-up worker-managed firms. This conclusion leads to an investigation of wealth redistribution. In particular, I will examine Bruce Ackermann and Anne Alstott's (1999) call to institute what they term a "stakeholder society" that would redistribute wealth through wealth taxation and a substantial, once-in-a-lifetime cash grant to citizens at the age of majority. Chapter 7 concludes that wealth redistribution is more desirable than profit redistribution, because of the former's ability to promote the economic viability of worker self-managed enterprises in the context of rivalrous market competition and hence the construction of a post-Hayekian socialism.

In conclusion, chapter 8 brings together the arguments of chapters 5–7 to sketch an institutional structure consisting of democratic firms operating in a mixed economy of private property, competitive markets, and a set of welfare-promoting government institutions. Chapter 8 compares this vision of socialism to the participatory socialist planning model of Michael Albert and Robin Hahnel (1992) and to Samuel Bowles and Herbert Gintis's more congenial proposals for a postcapitalist society (1998). The vision of socialism developed in this book overcomes the antimarket bias of Albert and Hahnel's socialism and the antisocialist bias of Bowles and Gintis's market reform proposals, while not necessarily falling victim to Hayekian knowledge problems. It also speaks to the need for economics to return to the traditions of Hayek and Marx and to read them in a spirit of productive creativity elicited by the tensions between these two traditions. This is one of the important tasks that should occupy the future of heterodox economics.

CHAPTER 2

Hayek's Postmodern Economics

★

In the history of economic thought, Hayek's version of Austrian economics is often categorized as a branch of neoclassical economics. This categorization is misleading. Neoclassical economists understand economic outcomes to be the result of actions by and interactions among self-interested individuals who constantly seek to enhance their subjectively perceived well-being (i.e., utility) in the context of economic, social, and legal constraints that are known by these individuals with a fair degree of certainty. Neoclassical economists conceive the economy mechanistically, reducible to the behavior of maximizing individuals, and see the economic problem as a social engineering problem: how to improve resource allocation and aggregate well-being by adjusting constraints on individual action. Diverse socialists throughout the twentieth century, from Oscar Lange ([1936] 1966) to John Roemer (1994), have adopted this general approach to economic thinking. Much of the twentieth-century debate about the possibilities and limits of socialism has been couched in terms of the problematic given in part by neoclassical theory: how to change the economic, social, and legal constraints so that utility-maximizing individuals will act in a manner consistent with economic efficiency and social justice. Hayek, though, generally rejects this mechanistic approach to economic theory.

Hayek's criticisms of socialism are rooted in concepts and arguments that lie largely outside the problematic of mainstream, neoclassical economics. This is one reason that socialists consistently misunderstand and mischaracterize his work. He develops a postmodern individualism that rejects the mechanical, modernist individualism of neoclassical economics as well as classical socialism. His understanding of individual action fits much more comfortably within the hermeneutical tradition of social theory than with the reductionism of neoclassical economics. For Hayek, individuals have subjective perceptions not only of their own goals (i.e., definitions of well-being) but also of the constraints they face. There is therefore an irreducibly interpretive dimension to all human action. This point is frequently missed in the appreciation neoclassical economists express for Hayek's thought (see, e.g., Lucas 1981), as well as in contemporary socialist criticisms of Hayek (e.g.,

Roemer 1995). In addition, socialists generally fail to take seriously the policy implications of Hayek's postmodern individualism—the ways in which his attention to the fragmented nature and limits of human knowledge strengthens the case for markets against conceptions of socialism that give government officials an important planning role. To develop an effective case for socialist forms of economic organization in the wake of Hayek's arguments, it is necessary to grasp the various dimensions of his postmodern subjectivist economics.

POSTMODERN INDIVIDUALISM

To understand Hayek's contributions to economic theory, I will start by examining his advocacy of methodological individualism, since this poses a puzzle that is usually overlooked by Hayek's casual interpreters. On one hand, Hayek is known as one of the first economists to call for economics to return to its microfoundations. As early as 1931, he exhorted economists to explain economic outcomes in terms of individual action (Hayek 1931, 4). Like all theorists who call themselves methodological individualists, Hayek criticizes social theory that deduces individual action from an assumed apprehension of autonomous social structures. Nobel laureate Robert Lucas, who became famous in the 1970s for his reductionist approach to macroeconomics, applauds Hayek for his methodological individualism (Lucas 1981, 216). On the other hand, Hayek is critical of atomistic, reductionist social theory, which is also characterized as "methodological individualism." Lucas misses Hayek's criticisms of reductionism. The solution to Hayek's methodological puzzle lies in how his notion of subjectivism leads him to construct a methodological individualism that is nonreductionist and nonessentialist—that is, hermeneutic and postmodern.

To identify Hayek as a hermeneutic postmodernist is not uncontroversial. Bruce Caldwell believes that Hayek saw himself as constructing scientific foundations for his subjectivist perspective on the dispersed, diverse, and fragmented nature of human knowledge. The point of Hayek's work in psychology, Caldwell argues, is to give a scientific rationale to the view that when a person observes the world, whether for theoretical or practical purposes, that observation is always "interpretation, one might put it, all the way down" (Caldwell 2004, 249). Thus Caldwell (1994) describes Hayek as a "scientific subjectivist." While I do not disagree with Caldwell's assessment, I see no inherent conflict between Hayek's scientific aspirations and his nascent postmodernism. There is little doubt that we can interpret Hayek as having made important contributions to hermeneutical social theory, whether or not he intended them as such.

Hayek clearly intended his notion of methodological individualism to be a foil against the reductionist, Cartesian individualism commonly exhibited in neoclassical economics and the holistic social theory characteristic of traditional Marxism. In the essay "Individualism: True and False," Hayek carefully distinguishes his version of methodological individualism from the Cartesian approach (Hayek 1948d). He calls his view of individualism, descendant from the Scottish Enlightenment, "true" individualism, contrasting it with the "false" individualism of the Cartesians. False individualists, Hayek suggests, attempt to understand social phenomena in terms of isolated, self-contained individuals who are able, using their powers of reason, to create and sustain optimal institutions. He places social contract theorists, economic planners, and legal positivists within this tradition.

Hayek believes it is misleading to view individuals as separate from society. Because Hayek defines "true" individualism as "an attempt to understand the forces which determine the social life of man," he argues that "[t]his fact should by itself be sufficient to refute the silliest of the common misunderstandings: the belief that individualism postulates (or bases its arguments on the assumption of) the existence of isolated or self-contained individuals, instead of starting from men whose whole nature and character is determined by their existence in society" (Hayek 1948d, 6). He acknowledges that there are social influences on individual action, that humans are inherently social creatures. But, even so, Hayek insists "that there is no other way toward an understanding of social phenomena but through our understanding of individual actions directed toward other people and guided by their expected behavior" (ibid.). This is because true individualism denies the independent existence of social structures and hence their ability to determine human action. Hayek employs his notion of true individualism not to support the supposed integrity of the autonomous individual but to challenge the notion that pregiven social structures determine human existence.

The postmodern, classical liberal philosopher G. B. Madison reinforces this view. "The whole point of Hayek's methodological individualism," according to Madison, "is not to reduce the whole to the sum of its parts" (Madison 1990b, 49). Because the individual is always caught up in a social context, a context that influences understanding and agency, the possibility of such a reductionism is precluded. Madison believes that the purpose of Hayek's methodological individualism is "to remind us that those irreducible 'wholes,'" like society or culture,

> are nevertheless not *things*—ontological entities (such as a group mind) capable of exerting efficient causality on individuals and, thus,

of "explaining (in the scientistic sense) their actions"—but are, rather, as it were, *meaning-objects* which are not understandable apart from the categories of human understanding and agency, apart, that is, from the "individual." (ibid., 49–50)

In addition, Madison points out that Hayek's choice of the term *individualism* was more likely the desire to find a counterpoise to the term *socialism* than an expression of a rationalist, Cartesian worldview.

Apparent in Hayek's essay "Individualism: True and False" and more fully developed in his *The Counter-Revolution of Science* (Hayek 1979a) is Hayek's effort to articulate the notion that there is an irreducible role for interpretation as a guide to human action and, even more significant, that interpretative ability is determined neither by an all-encompassing reason nor by social structures. Interpretation is a subjective act of an individual caught within a social context. It is not a matter of apprehending the objective nature of the world. Thus Hayek's ambition to produce a theory of human action in which "wholes" do not exert "efficient causality" does not eliminate social factors as fundamental constituents of individual perception and behavior. By assigning a central role to socially constituted, subjective interpretation in his theory of human action, Hayek produces a nonessentialist theory of human agency. His subjectivism leads him to recast economics as a nonessentialist, hermeneutical social science.

THE CONSTITUENTS OF HUMAN ACTION

To grasp the nonessentialist, hermeneutic character of Hayek's methodological individualism, it is revealing to consider his explanations of subjectivism and the constituents of human action.[1] The opening proposition of Hayek's methodological individualism is that "every individual chooses and acts [often, but not always] purposively, i.e., in pursuit of his purposes and in accordance with his perception of his options for achieving them" (White 1984, 4). This accent on perception is coupled with the view that "the contents of the human mind, and hence decision-making, are not rigidly determined by external events" (O'Driscoll and Rizzo 1985, 1). Because the contents of the mind are not rigidly determined by external events, Hayek's understanding of purposive action is not equivalent to rational action, in that rational action involves the pursuit of an optimal course of actions, given an objective knowledge of potential economic opportunities. Rather, in Hayek's view, individuals act according to their subjective perceptions of opportunity.

Understanding the complex constitution of human perception is a major concern for Hayek. This led him to write an important book on psychology (Hayek 1952) in which he indicated the social aspects of individual perception. Hayek is quite clear that perception is not determined by the objective world. He does not believe that the senses or reason (or some combination of these) give the individual a window to the objective world. He assumes no direct correspondence between thought and reality.

> There exists . . . no one-to-one correspondence between the kinds (or the physical properties) of the different physical stimuli and the dimensions in which they can vary, on the one hand, and the different kinds of sensory qualities which they produce and their various dimensions, on the other. (Hayek 1952, 14)

Consequently, Hayek rejects the empiricist belief that true, objective knowledge can be built up from sensory perception. Instead, he argues that "[e]very sensation, even the 'purest', must . . . be regarded as an interpretation of an event in the light of the past experience of the individual or the species" (ibid., 166). People cannot experience things directly, because conscious sensory experience itself provides no way to classify sensations. The way in which people categorize sensations is contingent on the theories and mental rules that they use to guide their interpretations of the data: sensations are meaningless without interpretive devices, theories, and classification schemes by which they can be grouped, arranged, and contextualized in the mind.

Hayek also avoids the rationalist position that reduces the mind's interpretive capacities to given categories of understanding and the innate capacity of reason. Kant, for example, agrees with Hayek that people cannot obtain objective knowledge (or knowledge of things in themselves) and that knowledge cannot be derived from pure sensation. He also believes, like Hayek, that experience, to be meaningful, must be placed in context. Unlike Hayek, however, Kant believes that the categories people use to classify and understand sensation are "borrow[ed] from no experience" but are given attributes of the mind (Kant 1977, 36) and that the contextualization of experience is thereby produced through universal principles of reason. For Kant, reason "contains in itself the ground of ideas, . . . necessary concepts whose object cannot be given in any experience" (ibid., 70). These ideas of reason allow us to piece together the particulars of experience to reach a comprehension of how the world operates and how we should act in it. Reason thus transcends experience to give context and order to experience.

Hayek opposes the Kantian "distinction between sensory perception of given qualities and the operations which the intellect is supposed to perform on these data in order to arrive at an understanding of the given phenomenal world" (Hayek 1952, 166). He objects to the postulate of pregiven mental categories that sort, classify, and order sensory perception. Instead, Hayek believes "the apparatus by means of which we learn about the external world is itself the product of a kind of experience" (ibid., 165). Conscious sensory experience becomes "possible only after experience in the wider sense of linkages has created the order of sensory qualities—the order which determines the qualities of the constituents of conscious experience" (ibid., 167). The mind's classificatory apparatus is itself the product of past experience. He reminds his readers, though, that "[e]xperience can never teach us that any particular kind of structure has properties which do not follow from the definition (or the way we construct it)" (Hayek 1948b, 74). In other words, he resists the notion that experience will eventually move us closer to the truth of the objective world. Hayek rejects all attempts, empiricist and rationalist, to ground knowledge on objective facts or transcendent reason. His view that perception is not rigidly determined by external events is most consistent with the hermeneutic or postmodern position that perception is socially constituted, that is, determined by no single thing and influenced by many, perhaps infinite, things.

Throughout his work, Hayek describes many institutions and phenomena that influence perceptions. For example, he points to the structure of our language as "itself impl[ying] certain views about the nature of the world," and he argues that "by learning a particular language we acquire . . . a framework of our thinking within which we henceforth move without being aware of it" (Hayek 1967b, 86–87). He also emphasizes particular theories operating within a language as equally important constituents of perception. Theory helps to determine which of the potentially infinite perceived events are worthy of investigation, that is, which perceptions become facts for the investigator: "What make a number of individual phenomena facts of one kind are the attributes which we select in order to treat them as members of one class" (Hayek 1979a, 80). The selection of facts, Hayek goes on to argue, is contingent on the adoption of a particular classification scheme or theory: "the qualities which we perceive are not properties of the objects but ways in which we (individually or as a race) have learned to group or classify external stimuli. To perceive is to assign to a familiar category (or categories)" (ibid., 83–84).[2]

It is in the explanation of how perception is constituted by language and discourse that Hayek's hermeneutics are most apparent. On many occasions, Hayek emphasizes that in order to understand a different society, a theorist must learn the beliefs and concepts held by people in that society, since the meaning of their acts depends on those theories. It is impossible for outsiders merely to observe a foreign culture and understand the actions they witness.

> If . . . we had developed our modern scientific technique while still confined to a part of our planet, and then had made contact with other parts inhabited by a race which had advanced knowledge much further, we clearly could not hope to understand many of their actions by merely observing what they did and without directly learning from them their knowledge. It would not be from observing them in action that we should acquire their knowledge, but it would be through being taught their knowledge that we should learn to understand their actions. (Hayek 1979a, 106)

For example, Hayek suggests that if anthropologists repeatedly witnessed a chain being placed around the neck of some people in a foreign land, they could not tell whether those people were being rewarded or punished. No amount of measurement or modeling would enable the anthropologists to understand this action. Understanding the action is only possible by learning the meaning these people attribute to it (ibid., 50).

Location is also an important constituent of perception. According to Hayek, "there is beyond question a body of very important but unorganized knowledge which cannot possibly be called scientific in the sense of knowledge of general rules: the knowledge of the particular circumstances of time and place" (Hayek 1948h, 80). An individual's knowledge is both limited and enabled by the occupation of a unique economic location. What a person perceives to be an opportunity for gain and the means by which the agent believes this can be achieved are "facts" that everyone cannot know, because everyone occupies different spaces. For example, the ability to respond to a possible profitable opportunity depends on being in the right place to perceive the opportunity and on imagining a workable production technique to exploit it.

Hayek is not saying that each individual has special access to a particular spatial aspect of objective reality. Such a formulation of the impact of location on perception would suggest the possibility that an individual could undertake a rational search process to gather any information not ready at hand. Rather, Hayek describes the knowledge obtainable in a particular location as the "special knowledge of circumstances of the fleeting moment not known to others" (Hayek 1948h, 80). Occupying different spaces potentially opens the door to different perceptions. Nevertheless, the necessarily subjective nature of perception implies that if someone were to occupy the same location previously occupied by another—for instance, one manager replaces another in the same factory—the second occupier would not necessarily perceive the same production function and resource scarcities as did the first.

Time is another constituent of perception and human action, insofar as the passage of time engenders ever-changing expectations of the future. Human action is integrally connected to the anticipation of future possibilities (see Hayek 1948a). There are always elements of uncertainty and imagination in our decisions, since fulfillment or frustration of our objectives can only occur after a decision is taken—in the present—to follow a particular course of action. Satisfaction or regret occur in the future. Hence people's acts are guided not only by constraints and opportunities thought to exist but also by conjectures of what might come to exist. Since the passage of time will often change people's perceptions of what can happen, these shifting expectations of possible future outcomes are an important constituent of human action.[3]

Finally, a theme Hayek elaborates in his work on psychology is how unconscious, mental rules "govern our perceptions, and particularly our perceptions of other people's actions" (Hayek 1967e, 45). For example, a child can understand a smile and return the expression without being able to articulate the meaning of the smile. The child's understanding of the smile is an example of rule-guided perception. Hayek suggests that we learn these mental rules through a process of imitation and identification, and he reminds his readers that the "capacity to imitate someone's gait, postures, or grimaces certainly does not depend on our capacity to describe these in words" (ibid., 48). Rule-guided perception is important for Hayek because it indicates the limits to reason as the regulatory mechanism of mental processes. The rules guiding individual perception, as in the case of the child's understanding of a smile, are often implicit and cannot be described.

In Hayek's economics, the indeterminacy of the future both forces and frees people to make "real" choices, choices in which the range of potentially relevant opportunities, constraints, and possible outcomes cannot be known with certainty and must therefore, to some degree, be imagined. Although the notion that people act purposively based on their subjective perceptions and imaginations is repeated in different forms by nearly all Austrian economists who write on methodology, this postulate does not fully capture Hayek's explanation of the constituents of human action. For Hayek, "[m]an is as much a rule-following animal as a purpose-seeking one" (Hayek 1973, 11). Social rules play as central a role in affecting human action in Hayek's theory as do perceptions and purposes. He emphasizes the importance of rules, conventions, and institutions as guides to action when the consequences of action are unknown. Rules guard against what man "most fears, and what puts him in a state of terror when it has happened[:] . . . to lose his bearings and no longer to know what to do" (Hayek 1967d, 80).

Contrary to social theorists who seek the origin of rules in an original social contract struck among maximizing, self-interested people or as the efficient result of a bargaining process among rational individuals, Hayek believes that the "fact of our irremediable ignorance of most of the particular facts which determine the processes of society is . . . the reason why most social institutions have taken the form they actually have" (Hayek 1973, 13). Many rules "cannot be wholly reduced" to the actions of rational individuals (Hayek 1967d, 70).[4] Not only is it impossible to derive many rules from individual reason; it is not necessary to articulate certain rules in order to be able to follow them. For example, in order to stay afloat, swimmers breathe more deeply than pedestrians, even though they may remain unaware of their changed breathing patterns. People may know how to perform a certain action without knowing that (or being able to articulate that) their actions follow a certain rule: " 'know how' consists in the capacity to act according to rules which we may be able to discover but which we need not be able to state in order to obey them" (Hayek 1967e, 44). Thus, for Hayek not all human action is purposive and under the direction of conscious knowledge. Tacit, rule-bound knowledge is also an important guide to action.

In sum, Hayek develops a theory of human agency that is quite different from that found in textbook, neoclassical economics. Neoclassical economic theory typically posits autonomous, maximizing, rational, (perfectly) knowledgeable human agents who are able to choose the single, best course of action based on known objectives and constraints. The theoretical convention is to reduce social outcomes to the choices of these asocial, rational beings. Orthodox economists make few attempts to theorize the socially constituted nature of individual perception and action. In comparison, Hayek develops a rich theory of human action, one that captures the social aspects of agency while avoiding the functionalism of holistic theories. At the same time, his social theory is not reductionist either. Social outcomes, institutions, and rules cannot be reduced to individual choices and actions in Hayek's theory, because Hayek's agents are epistemologically limited and socially constituted. His discussions of subjectivism and the constituents of perception and on rule-following as well as purpose-seeking behavior produce a theory of human agency that, I believe, is aptly characterized as nonessentialist, or postmodernist. This nonessentialist theory of economic action is integral to Hayek's conceptualization of the market as a discovery process.

Hayek's theory of the market is the cornerstone of his economic liberalism, as he insists that markets are most conducive to freedom and the best facilitators of progress, which he defines as the potential for people to strive continually to explore new possibilities and to discover and create new ways of living. His economic theory begins with the concept of "dispersed information," a concept that partly captures the temporal and spatial aspects of economic agency. Because competitive markets allow and encourage entrepreneurs to explore potentially gainful opportunities—opportunities that are contingent on subjective perceptions and being in the right place at the right time—they are the best institutional structure to exploit the dispersion of uniquely and subjectively held economic knowledge. "If we can agree that the economic problem of society is mainly one of rapid adaptation to changes in the particular circumstances of time and place," Hayek writes, "it would seem to follow that the ultimate decisions must be left to the people who are familiar with these circumstances, who know directly of the relevant changes and of the resources immediately available to meet them" (Hayek 1948h, 83–84). According to Hayek, "*wherever* the use of [market] competition can be rationally justified, it is on the ground that we do *not* know in advance the facts that determine the actions of competitors" (Hayek 1978a, 179). He celebrates markets because they foster the discovery and social coordination of new products, techniques, and preferences.

We can begin to comprehend Hayek's notion of discovery by contrasting it to the notion of individual choice in neoclassical economics. For neoclassical economists, individual choice is guided by mechanical calculations, the famous cost-benefit analysis encapsulated in the utility-maximizing model. In the neoclassical story, the individual acts to obtain a subjectively preferred market basket by choosing among a given set of market baskets attainable with income earned through production with a given production function and a known endowment of resources. The economic actor also knows the vector of all market prices, so that alternative market baskets "are *known* to be 'there[,]' . . . not *discovered* to be there" (Kirzner 1989, 10). Market prices, endowments, and productive techniques are all objective data available for the utility-maximizing calculation. Once knowledge of these "fundamentals" is obtained, the individual, in effect, has no real choice: rational agents must produce or purchase the one market basket that is optimal. For individuals who know their preferences, market choice is determined by the objective data. Thus the influential twentieth-century neoclassical economist Vilfredo Pareto was able to argue that once the economist obtained "a photograph of [the individual's] tastes," then "the individual may disappear" from economic analysis (quoted in Tarascio 1972, 415). For Pareto, technology and resource availability were objective factors. As Tarascio comments, "Pareto's conception of pure economics was that it involved a study of objective factors, i.e., the relationship between economic quantities, without reference to the individual (subjective factors)" (ibid., 414–15).

Neoclassical economics reduces market outcomes to given preferences (subjective data) and given technology and resource endowments (objective data). The market performs the task of articulating all of these "givens" into a state of equilibrium, an equilibrium that maximizes efficiency, that is, net gains from trade. Hayek, in contrast, insists quite forcefully that preferences, technology, and resource endowments are all discovered or created in the market process. Moreover, in a market economy, there is no shared interpersonal hierarchy of ends. So the market order cannot be said to maximize any aggregate measure of wealth or well-being. But even though the market does not produce any objectively definable optimum, Hayek believes that the market is valuable because "it may yet be highly conducive to the achievement of many different individual purposes" (Hayek 1978a, 183).

Hayek advances the claim, unusual for an economist, that preferences are not determined before an individual "goes to market." He argues that people's innate desires are few; Hayek mentions food, shelter, and sex. He sees most desires as culturally constituted: "It would scarcely be an exaggeration to say that contemporary man, in all fields where he has not yet formed firm habits, tends to find out what he wants by looking at what his neighbors do and at various displays of goods . . . and then choosing what he likes best" (Hayek 1967c, 315). The market creates a wide variety of goods people can sample to discover which goods they most prefer. Against those who argue that such a notion of preferences is inconsistent with consumer sovereignty, Hayek responds that "particular producers can [not] deliberately determine the wants of particular consumers" (ibid., 315). Although individuals may discover their preferences as the market process unfolds, they are not forced to purchase or desire any particular good. Consequently, no particular producer exercises power over any particular consumer.

For Hayek, the data neoclassical economists usually conceptualize as the objective basis for market decisions (i.e., technology, resource endowments, and market prices) are subjective and indeterminate in the same sense that preferences are. For instance, he argues, "which goods are scarce goods, or which things are goods, and how scarce or valuable they are—these are precisely the things which competition has to discover" (Hayek 1978a, 181). As Israel Kirzner explains in an extended commentary on the Hayekian notion of the market discovery process: "What an individual decides to do is the outcome, not necessarily of his given preferences and of the arrays of market baskets marked out by prices and budget constraints—but of what the individual *believes* to be the set of available opportunities" (Kirzner 1989, 12). Because beliefs about preferences, production functions, and resource availability are not determined by the data, because the data must always be interpreted, market "choice is the prototype of indeterminate action" (Lachmann 1986, 113). Choice is not determined by an optimal course of action that fulfills the most desires or preferences subject to known constraints. The effects of time, place, and perception on human agency may lead to choices that are incorrect or inefficient by the standards of neoclassical theory and that do not produce the satisfaction that individuals believed they would receive.[5]

What Hayek refers to as the activity of the "man on the spot" (Hayek 1948h, 83) commands center stage in his theory of the market as a discovery process. Kirzner and other subsequent Austrian economists call this activity entrepreneurship. In the market process, entrepreneurs test their hypotheses about what things consumers may wish to purchase and how these things might be provided at low cost. These hypotheses are based not on objective, universally accessible knowledge but on the individual seller's particular knowledge, which may be partly articulate and partly tacit and which remains always contingent on the seller's unique spatial and temporal location. If sellers are able to persuade potential buyers that their wares are attractive at the asking price, then the sellers' hypotheses will yield a profit. Otherwise, the seller will be forced to test a new hypothesis. A private property, free market system establishes a structure of incentives that encourages individuals to utilize their unique perceptions and knowledges in a manner that fulfills other people's needs and desires.

The incentives of monetary profit and hazards of monetary loss that exist in a market economy serve to create an agreement among sellers of productive factors, producers, and consumers about which goods are scarce, which technologies might be appropriate, and which goods are pleasing. For Hayek, the chief benefit of the market is that it facilitates a competitive process that allows dispersed individuals to discover whether their subjective perceptions of economic opportunity are warranted, given others' subjective preferences and perceptions. Having to pass the test of market competition facilitates the coordination of the actions of dispersed individuals who possess partial and subjective knowledge. The best way to interpret Hayek's notion of the market discovery process is not as a mechanism to uncover knowledge of objectively existing production possibilities and preexisting consumer preferences but as a type of dialogical process that creates an evolving set of intersubjective agreements and disagreements about efficient methods to produce ever-changing desirable goods. The lure of profit and the aversion to loss teach people which of their ideas about production and consumption make sense in a larger social environment in which they must rely on the efforts of others to satisfy their needs and desires. Market competition, one might say, creates a form of knowledge or truth about commodity values, productive techniques, resource scarcities, costs, and so on.

Rather than presenting market competition as a predictable process, Hayek depicts the market as a seething cauldron of unpredictable change, constantly remaking the world. To participate in a market economy is to partake in "a voyage of exploration into the unknown, an attempt to discover new ways of doing things better than they have been done before" (Hayek 1948e, 101). Yet a market economy is not chaotic in Hayek's view. Hayek maintains that market competition continually and spontaneously engenders order.

> Competition is essentially a process of the formation of opinion: by spreading information, it creates that unity and coherence of the economic system which we presuppose when we think of it as one market. It creates the views people have about what is best and cheapest, and it is because of it that people know at least as much about possibilities and opportunities as they in fact do. (Hayek 1948e, 106)

In a world in which people are epistemologically limited, socially constituted, rule following, and creative, we can understand the market process as facilitating the creation and subsequent use of new knowledge as well as the spontaneous coordination of actions guided by subjective perceptions.

THE SOCIALIST CALCULATION DEBATE

Hayek's process-oriented understanding of the market emerged out of his participation in what is known as the socialist calculation debate during the 1930s, particularly in his reaction to Oscar Lange's use of neoclassical economics to propose a model of market socialism (Lange [1936] 1966). Neoclassical economics has a long history in theories of socialist planning and market socialism, ranging from Enrico Barone (1908) to John Roemer (1994). Barone first demonstrated the formal similarity between a planned economy and a perfectly competitive market economy. He showed that both could be represented by a set of simultaneous equations representing the technical possibilities of production, costs, and consumer demands. His demonstration of the formal similarity between a planned and competitive market economy led some socialists to contend that a centrally planned economy would actually be more efficient than real-world, imperfectly competitive market economies. A central planning board could collect information on the demands, scarcities, and production possibilities of various goods and services and could use this information to solve a system of simultaneous equations that would determine the optimal production and distribution of goods and services much more effectively than would an undirected market economy populated by firms with market power.

Proposals to replace all markets with central planning came under the fire of Hayek and his fellow Austrian economist Ludwig von Mises in a sequence of books and articles published in the 1920s and 1930s (Hayek 1935; Mises 1920, 1936). Hayek does not contest Barone's demonstration of the formal similarity between a centrally planned economy and a perfectly competitive market economy, but he insists that Barone's work reveals the practical impossibility of a planned economy. There are two parts to Hayek's argument. First, he contends that a central planning board cannot possibly perform the millions of calculations necessary to replicate the allocative ability of the market (Hayek 1948g, 181–82). Second, even if the planning board could perform the necessary calculations, Hayek maintains that the planning board could never gather the information—about costs, technology, and consumer preferences—necessary to execute these calculations. There is no way, in Hayek's view, for a central agency to overcome the problems created by the dispersion of subjectively held knowledge. Hayek argues that knowledge of production possibilities, resource scarcities, and consumer demands does not exist as an objective set of magnitudes that can be bundled into convenient packets of information and channeled to central planners. These arguments clarify and extend Mises's earlier critiques of central planning.

In response to Hayek's and Mises's negative assessments of central planning, several economists, most notably Oskar Lange ([1936] 1966), acknowledged the difficulties posed by the complete replacement of markets by central planning. Instead, they advocated models of market socialism that preserved markets for labor and consumer goods, while abolishing private property in capital goods and other nonlabor means of production. In Lange's model of market socialism, the state would own the means of production, thereby eliminating the markets for real capital and for financial shares of those capital goods. But if the markets for labor and consumer goods were retained, allowing people free choice of occupation and in consumption, Lange thought that the allocative role of the central planners would be considerably simplified. Under such a scheme, central planners would not have to make all the calculations that Hayek believed were impossible to perform. Instead, the planners would only have to design a method to determine the various prices of capital goods, since the markets for these goods were eliminated, and to instruct managers of state-owned firms how to act, since market discipline on management was removed. If these problems could be surmounted, a market socialist system would offer the advantages of a more equitable distribution of income, control over the business cycle, and production for need rather than profit. Or so Lange argued.

To determine the prices of capital goods once the state assumed control of the means of production, Lange borrowed an idea from Fred Taylor ([1929] 1966), who previously had sketched a model market socialist system. Taylor proposed that the state could develop a series of "factor valuation tables" through an iterative process that would place rational values on the various means of production. The first step of this iterative process was for the socialist planning board to record the market prices of capital goods that had existed during the previous capitalist society. The initial factor valuation table, based on historical market data, would give the managers of state-owned enterprises a preliminary idea about the economic value of the capital goods they supervised. Managers would then be instructed to treat these prices and the market-determined prices of labor inputs as parameters for the purpose of calculating the costs of production.

Lange suggested that the central planning board, knowing the cost of labor and the cost of capital, could then impose two rules of production on the managers of state-owned firms. First, managers should be instructed to figure out the cost-minimizing combination of capital and labor for every level of production. Second, plant managers should ascertain the price of their output from the consumer goods market and then choose a level of production where output price equals the marginal cost of production; that is, firms should produce where price equals marginal costs, utilizing a cost-minimizing strategy, thereby mimicking the behavior of firms in the neoclassical theory of perfect competition.

The central planning board would continually monitor market and production conditions, looking for shortages and surpluses evident in the consumer goods markets and excess or inadequate supplies of capital resources, as reported by the plant managers. The planning board would react to any instance of disequilibrium by adjusting the prices in the factor valuation tables. After the factor valuation tables were updated, plant managers would be instructed to treat these new prices as the relevant data in determining their production costs and optimal production levels. This trial-and-error process would be repeated until the economy converged to a general equilibrium in which the average price of each consumer good equaled the minimum cost of its production and in which the factor valuation tables were adjusted to eliminate all excess supplies and demands for capital goods. In this way, Lange argued that a planning board could replicate the pricing and coordination functions of competition in capital goods markets (as well as the markets for other nonlabor factors of production).

What, then, would be the benefit of adopting this form of market social-ism? If Lange's model merely replicates market outcomes, then why go to the trouble of socializing the means of production and instituting a planning board? Lange thought there were several reasons. First, socializing the means of production would allow the equal distribution of income derived from capital. While the market would determine labor income, Lange pro-posed that social welfare could be maximized if capital income were distrib-uted equally to all citizens in the form of a social dividend. Second, the plan-ning board would determine the rate and composition of investment spending. This would alleviate the business cycle and institute a more ratio-nal rate of capital accumulation. Finally, the planning board could incorpo-rate external costs and benefits in the factor valuation tables, thus enabling market socialism to account more effectively than free markets for what Lange called "social overhead costs" (Lange [1936] 1966, 104).

Three characteristics of Lange's blueprint need to be highlighted in order to understand Hayek's critique. Each is derived from Lange's belief that the neoclassical, competitive equilibrium model was an appropriate description of a market economy. First, since the neoclassical model treats preferences and resource availability as givens and since Lange understood the neoclassi-cal equilibrium model to be an accurate representation of a market economy, he explicitly assumed that preferences and resource availability could be treated as givens by the planning board (ibid., 60).

Second, Lange's two production rules, that firms were to produce where price equals marginal costs and where average cost is minimized, depended on costs being objective variables readily observable by plant managers and central planners. In other words, Lange imagined that firms faced clearly identifiable production possibilities, as if technology were an objective given. Lange wrote that costs of production "are determined ultimately by the technical possibilities of transformation of one commodity into another, i.e., by the production functions." He believed that these production func-tions were like tangible blueprints and that plant managers could communi-cate knowledge of these blueprints to the planning board so that "adminis-trators of a socialist economy will have exactly the same knowledge, or lack of knowledge, of the production functions as the capitalist entrepreneurs have" (ibid., 61).

Third, Lange's model assumed that economic action was determined by objective data. In perfect competition as described by the neoclassical model, all economic actors are "price takers." Lange emphasized that "each individ-ual separately regards the market prices as given data to which he has to adjust himself," so that "[m]arket prices are thus parameters determining the behavior of the individuals" (ibid., 70). Under this model, as long as economic actors, especially plant managers, followed the appropriate optimizing rules, their courses of action were clearly defined. This notion is consistent with Pareto's belief that once an individual's (subjective) preferences are registered, the economist (or planner) need no longer attend to individual, subjective factors. For socialists working in the tradition of neoclassical economics—that is, socialists who treat prices as parameters and understand scarcity and technology as objectively definable—a socialist economy can be conceived without reference to the subjective, socially constituted nature of individual perception and action.

Hayek's critique of Lange's socialism is rooted at the most fundamental level, in their differing visions of the economic problem. For Lange, the economic problem is how society can best make the "choice between alternatives," that is, how society can best allocate given resources based on the prevailing pattern of consumer demand and the available production techniques. He understands these alternatives to be determined by objective facts. For Hayek, the economic problem is how to achieve economic order on a large scale among epistemologically limited individuals whose knowledge and circumstances are constantly changing. Hayek's subjectivism leads him to see "the economic problem of society [to be] mainly one of rapid adaptation to changes in the particular circumstances of time and place" (Hayek 1948h, 83). The ephemeral knowledge of economic opportunities contingent on time and place can never be " 'given' to any single mind" (ibid., 77) and thus is impossible to centralize. It is available only to the man on the spot, and what he sees or imagines may well be in error or inconsistent with others' perceptions and desires. Only the test of market competition can decide the "truth-value" of the entrepreneurial knowledge of the man on the spot. Hayek's conclusion is not that central planning is impossible but that it is likely to result in considerably lower standards of living, since government planners cannot elicit and exploit subjectively held knowledge as effectively as can a competitive market process.

Perhaps Hayek's insistence that dispersed, subjective knowledge cannot be universally shared or centralized will be clearer if we recall his claim that much of the knowledge guiding human action is inarticulate: that is, people know how to perform certain actions without fully comprehending how or why they are performed. Individual producers have firm-specific knowledge about production techniques and material suppliers that is difficult or impossible to transmit to a central authority, because this knowledge is in the form of habit, intuition, ingenuity, and personal contacts. Hayek explains:

[The centralization of knowledge] is an absurd idea even in so far as that knowledge is concerned which can properly be said to "exist" at any moment of time. But much of the knowledge that is actually utilized is by no means "in existence" in this ready-made form. Most of it consists in a technique of thought which enables the individual engineer to find new solutions rapidly as soon as he is confronted with new constellations of circumstances. (Hayek 1948f, 155)

Lavoie is especially convincing in arguing that the ability of the market to coordinate inarticulate knowledge is the key to understanding Hayek's subjectivist theory of the market process. From a subjectivist perspective that accepts the existence of inarticulate knowledge, "producers know more than they can explicitly communicate to others" (Lavoie 1986b, 9). Thus one characteristic of a private property market economy is that it provides individuals the incentive and opportunity to act on inarticulate, subjective perceptions of economic opportunity.

The existence of dispersed knowledge suggests to Hayek that private property owners, not a centralized agency, should be responsible for production. Since Hayek understands the economic problem to be the social coordination of individuals who are adjusting to local changes in data (the subjective knowledge of preferences, technologies, and resource scarcities), he insists that production and consumption decisions "must be left to the people who are familiar with these circumstances, who know directly of the relevant changes and of the resources immediately available to meet them" (Hayek 1948h, 83–84). He praises the exchange of private property in markets—guided by the incentives of profit and loss—as a process that can coordinate individual action and make social use of broadly dispersed knowledge that is intrinsically inaccessible to a planning authority. Only private ownership provides individuals with the incentives and control necessary to respond to the particular circumstances of time and place. Given Hayek's attention to the problem of dispersed knowledge, it is not surprising that he is critical of Lange's market socialism, a proposal Hayek claims to be "born out of an excessive preoccupation with problems of the pure theory of stationary equilibrium" (Hayek 1948g, 188).

Hayek offers several specific criticisms of Lange's model that further elucidate the implications of subjectivism and the notion of the market as a discovery process. First, Hayek notes that because Lange's planning board must fix prices for some period of time, prices cannot instantly change. If plant managers find themselves with a temporary surplus or shortage of inputs, they cannot respond by lowering or raising input prices to correct the situation. They have to wait until the planning board readjusts the factor valuation tables. Whereas prices in a competitive market can change immediately, prices in Lange's market socialism are not flexible to take advantage of these circumstances and thus cannot reflect "distinctions based on the special circumstances of time, place, and quality" (Hayek 1948g, 193). Consequently, a market socialist society will utilize less knowledge than a free market economy and will therefore be inefficient in a Hayekian sense.

Second (and closely related to his first criticism), Hayek maintains that under Lange's model, socialist managers will have little or no incentive to take advantage of unique circumstances within their firms that might reduce production costs. Lange does not recognize this problem, because he sees technological knowledge as objective knowledge that is visible to anyone who looks for it. In reality, it is not easy to monitor whether managers are actually following the planning board's instructions to produce at minimum cost. Lavoie comments: "It is only by assuming objectively known costs that the function that profit maximization fulfills under capitalism can plausibly be replaced with a pair of rules issued by the central planning board to plant managers. If costs are unknown to the planning board, it would be impossible for it to tell whether or not plant managers are obeying the rules" (Lavoie 1985, 123). By assuming given costs, Lange neglects a valuable characteristic of market competition: the way in which it constantly stimulates producers to be alert to local, firm-specific changes in data. Because Lange supposes that knowledge of technology and resource availability is objective and accessible to all, there is no obstacle to this knowledge quickly finding its way into a factor valuation table. Hayek, however, believes that state ownership reduces the incentive to discover or reveal such knowledge. Without market competition, much of this knowledge will be lost.

Third, Hayek argues that if Lange's planning board were in place, individuals would have less incentive to create new economic knowledge. In the absence of private property in the means of production, new firms cannot freely enter an industry, even if they surmise that they can successfully produce a new type of commodity or an existing commodity at lower cost. A new firm would first have to persuade the planning board to allow it to establish operations. The need to perform this bureaucratic step would likely inhibit the formation of new firms, with the detrimental effects of less innovation and higher prices. Requiring the approval of a planning board would discourage free entry, an important mechanism facilitating the individual pursuit of creative, subjectively perceived opportunities for gain.[6]

Hayek concludes that a system of private property and an unregulated market process promotes the discovery, creation, and coordination of dispersed, subjectively held economic knowledge in ways that any form of national economic planning is simply unable to replicate. Central planning reduces the incentive individuals have to discover opportunities contingent on the unique circumstances of time and place, and individuals in a planned economy have a more difficult time exploring and implementing creative projects. Hayek's defense of economic liberalism against central planning is thus primarily epistemological, a fact that went unappreciated by most economists during the 1930s and 1940s. His subjectivism and notion of market process were not recognized by the bulk of the economics profession. As a result, general opinion held for some time that the market socialists, who couched their proposals in the language of neoclassical economics, had effectively refuted Hayek's contention that all forms of central planning were unworkable (Lavoie 1985, 1–27). Before the collapse of central planning in the former Soviet Union, many economists continued to pronounce Hayek's defeat at the hands of the market socialists. Today, most economists think that Hayek was right.

The Market and the Common Good

Does Hayek's postmodern individualism leave him, like so many postmodernists, with no normative grounds on which to develop a consequentialist evaluation of market processes; that is, does Hayek's subjectivism leave him with a purely deontological case for markets, one that ultimately borders on relativism or nihilism? Does a perspective that accepts an applied epistemological postmodernism lead inevitably to a libertarian or even anarchist political theory? These are important questions for postmodern Marxists to consider in determining whether the pursuit of a socialist project that is concerned with outcomes as well as processes makes sense in a post-Hayekian world.

James Buchanan and Viktor Vanberg's evaluation of the market process suggests that the answer to these questions might be yes (Buchanan and Vanberg 1991). They adopt a radically subjectivist perspective to describe the market as a creative process, a description similar to Hayek's vision of a market economy. For radical subjectivists, market economies are open-ended, evolving processes that are always being constituted by creative individual choices. Picturing the market as a creative process means that an omniscient observer, if one might be conceived to exist, would be unable to see all the economic opportunities that are possible, because those opportunities only exist after individual producers and consumers each decide on a course of action. If we think that the market economy is a creative process, then Buchanan and Vanberg assert that we must recognize that the market, in the aggregate, "neither maximizes nor minimizes anything." They further explain:

It simply allows participants to pursue that which they value, subject to the preferences and endowments of others, and within the constraints of general "rules of the game" that allow, and provide incentives for, individuals to try out new ways of doing things. There simply is no "external," independently defined objective against which the results of market processes can be evaluated. (Buchanan and Vanberg 1991, 181)

In effect, Buchanan and Vanberg claim that a radically subjectivist perspective precludes any consequentialist notion of the "common good" or any other way to determine whether the market process serves the public interest in any sense other than that it enables those successful at earning an income the opportunity to explore consumption possibilities.

Buchanan and Vanberg argue that radical subjectivism rules out theories of distributive justice that have long been the centerpieces of many socialist visions. Hayek's postmodern individualist views do as well. Buchanan, Vanberg, and Hayek each advocate procedural justice, that is, justice in the fairness of the rules regulating market interactions. Hayek gives us a thin theory of the common good that, to many free market advocates, appears to shut the door on a thicker, socialist theory of social welfare that strives for more equitable outcomes in addition to fair processes. To see whether this appearance is necessarily correct and whether one can simultaneously be a postmodernist and a socialist, chapter 3 of this book will consider how Hayek links his theories of social evolution and procedural justice to his postmodern individualism. Chapters 4 and 5 exploit weaknesses in this theory to argue for a consequentialist, socialist theory of justice against the backdrop of epistemological postmodernism.

CHAPTER 3

Hayek's Theory of the Common Good
Social Evolution, Law, and Justice

★

In *The Road to Serfdom*, Hayek defines the common good to be "limited to the fields where people agree on common ends," and he maintains that "people are most likely to agree on common action where the common end is not an ultimate end to them but a means capable of serving a great variety of purposes" (Hayek [1944] 1976, 60). One of these multipurpose means—and arguably the centerpiece of Hayek's vision of limited government—is the enforcement of agreed-on rules, that is, rules discovered and codified through systems of common law. Hayek understands the common law process to produce an evolved, legal order that articulates rules that people already implicitly accept. He also sees the common law as generally consistent with the rule of law.

The Road to Serfdom celebrates the rule of law as a shield against government tyranny. Hayek equates the rule of law with the enforcement of formal rules that "do not aim at the wants and needs of particular people," in contrast to socialism and other forms of central planning in which governments enact substantive rules to direct "the means of production to particular ends" (ibid., 73). In other words, Hayek distinguishes end-independent (formal) rules that apply equally to all people from goal-oriented (substantive) rules that involve government "picking winners" or that direct certain people and businesses to do specific things. By not favoring some people or firms over others, the rule of law establishes a fair, impartial process—a procedurally just framework—for the conduct of economic activity. The alternative to the rule of law, Hayek believes, is arbitrary government.

After reading *The Road to Serfdom* in 1944, John Maynard Keynes, the father of modern macroeconomic thought and advocate of government regulation of market economies, wrote a notable letter to Hayek (Keynes [1944] 1971). He applauded Hayek's critique of central planning but asserted that Hayek's free market conclusions were overdrawn. Keynes pointed out that Hayek's critique of central planning did not provide a framework to determine other, limited ways in which government policymakers might be able to contribute to social betterment. Hayek raises this issue indirectly in *The Road to Serfdom*, remarking that the distinction "between formal law or justice and substantive rules is . . . most difficult to draw precisely in practice" ([1944] 1976, 74). For example, he suggests that a wealthy society can assure to everyone "some minimum of food, shelter, and clothing, sufficient to preserve health and the capacity to work" (ibid., 120).

Keynes highlighted this ambiguity and noted that The Road to Serfdom offered no principles or criteria to help economists decide where to draw the line between the proper domains of government and the market. Keynes wrote in his letter: "You [Hayek] admit here and there that it is a question of knowing where to draw the line. You agree that the line has to be drawn somewhere, and that the logical extreme is not possible. But you give no guidance whatever as to where to draw it" (Keynes [1944] 1971, 386–87). Keynes went on to criticize Hayek, as many others have since, for implying that any movement toward government planning or regulation leads society over a precipice to totalitarianism.

In response to Keynes and other critics, Hayek endeavored in subsequent works (Hayek 1960, 1973, 1976, 1979b) to carefully specify the line of demarcation between arbitrary government and a competitive market economy governed by the rule of law. He describes common law rules as generally reflecting an evolved, social agreement about the boundary between legitimate and illegitimate government action. He also sees the rule of law as the outcome of a spontaneous, common law process. Hayek's later work thus elevates the rule of law itself as the proper arbiter of the boundary between appropriate and arbitrary government action. As long as public policy is consistent with the rule of law, property rights and market exchanges will be insulated from politics and discretionary public policy.

For Hayek, evolved common laws place a crucial barrier between public and private law. Public law is concerned with the organization, jurisdiction, and responsibilities of government. The legitimacy of public law, according to such liberal political theoreticians as Hayek, lies in an elected legislature or in a constitution adopted by a sovereign people. Private law, in contrast, concerns relations among and between private individuals, most notably in their exchanges of property. While Hayek recognizes that public law stems in part from the will of the people, he looks elsewhere for the foundation of private law. For unless the private domain is insulated from public authority, what he calls "totalitarian democracy" (Hayek 1979b, 4) will constantly threaten to usurp private property rights and erode the freedom of contract. Hayek grounds private law in a theory of evolved common law rules, and he limits public policy by its need to respect the wisdom of those rules, insofar as they are consistent with the rule of law.

The task of this chapter is to analyze Hayek's defense of the rule of law as the only practical and just framework to regulate economic activity. First, I will describe Hayek's evolutionary concept of spontaneous order and its connection to his postmodern individualism (outlined in chap. 2). Second, I will explain how the notion of spontaneous order underpins Hayek's claim that a competitive market economy governed by the rule of law is a procedurally just system. I will discuss how the rule of law promotes economic freedom (defined by Hayek as "a state in which each can use his knowledge for his purposes" [Hayek 1973, 55–56]), as well as Hayek's understanding of the rule of law as a spontaneously evolved, rather than rationally designed, principle. Finally, I will consider Hayek's radical claim that his legal theory, in conjunction with what I have called his epistemological postmodernism, forecloses all theories of distributive justice. Understanding the strengths and weaknesses of Hayek's legal theory is necessary in order to fashion a practical and persuasive vision of post-Hayekian socialism in which democratic governments would be authorized to alter the rules of the economic game based on socialist notions of justice. Developing that vision will be the principal task of the subsequent chapters.

Spontaneous Order and Social Evolution

Hayek uses the term *spontaneous order* to describe social institutions that are the product not of human design but, rather, of an evolutionary process that is not guided by human reason and not reducible to universal regularities in human behavior. Examples of spontaneous orders include markets, money, language, and the common law. Spontaneous orders exist because people stumble on certain rules and institutional forms that help to produce social cohesion: "the formation of spontaneous orders is the result of their elements following certain rules in their responses to their immediate environment" (Hayek 1973, 43). There is no need for these rules to be known by people (the "elements" of society), since they can follow rules without knowing that their actions will produce a particular outcome—for instance, that they will remain afloat in water if they breathe more deeply or that they will increase aggregate wealth if they respect individual property titles. Spontaneous orders crystallize out of the evolved regularities of human action and interaction, even if these actions are not motivated by a desire to produce any kind of social order.

The evolutionary nature of a Hayekian spontaneous order is further revealed in Hayek's distinction between what he calls "cosmos" and "taxis," two concepts of order derived from ancient Greek thought. A taxis is a constructed order, rationally designed to serve a particular purpose. A family, a corporation, or a military unit would qualify as a taxis. A cosmos, in contrast, is an evolved or "grown" order. A cosmos forms spontaneously, not as a result of human intention, but "from regularities of the behavior of the elements which it comprises" (Hayek 1978b, 74). Because a cosmos is not a product of human will, it cannot be said to have a goal or purpose. A market economy, for example, is not a constructed organization but, rather, an evolved institution that has emerged out of certain regularities of human behavior that have developed in dialectical interaction with the human environment. As such, a market economy aims toward no single end and has no single purpose. It does not maximize anything. It may, however, be highly conducive for "the pursuit of many purposes," insofar as it allows people the freedom to undertake creative ventures and to satisfy personal goals (ibid.). In this way, the market promotes individual liberty and social welfare.

According to Hayek, one of the fatal conceits of modern social thought is the tendency to treat a cosmos as if it were a taxis. Hayek argues that when people believe they can direct society toward some predefined goal or when they are willing to accept social outcomes only if these outcomes adhere to some rational criterion, they have overestimated the power of human reason and underestimated the tacit, unarticulated knowledge that is embodied in evolved institutions. Hayek consistently maintains that to regard a cosmos as if it can conform to a rational standard or be engineered to serve a social purpose is the source of much discontent and discoordination.

The intellectual roots of Hayek's notion of cosmos lie in Adam Smith's conception of natural order. Smith reacted to the rationalist tradition as exemplified by the Physiocrats, who understood human society as a natural order that arises from the natural ability of human reason to deduce natural laws. In the rationalist view, natural laws discoverable by reason were the glue binding society together. Smith was skeptical of the power of humans to correctly select these so-called natural laws. Instead, he proposed that social order was the outgrowth of "the normal operations of the instincts and feelings of men, supplemented by their intelligence as that may work in the sphere in which it is effective" (O. Taylor 1955, 88). In other words, for Smith, social order was the evolved product of people's natural propensity to truck, barter, and trade. Human nature led people to engage in systematic behavior—trucking and bartering—whose unintended consequence was extensive division of labor, economic growth, and social cohesion. Hayek accepts Smith's antirationalism and adopts his evolutionary view of economic and social development.

But in one important respect, Hayek's conception of order differs from Smith's: Hayek does not root the essence of spontaneous order in human nature.[1] For Smith, human nature is the source of the regularity in human behavior that engenders social order. Social order is reducible to human actions, actions grounded in natural instinct. But Hayek goes further than Smith, to insist that spontaneous orders are not reducible to human nature.

> The existence of such ordered structures as galaxies, solar systems, organisms, and social orders . . . [display] as wholes regularities which cannot be wholly reduced to the regularities of the parts, because they also depend on the interaction of the whole with the environment which placed and keeps the parts in the order necessary for the specific behavior of the whole. (Hayek 1967d, 74)

According to Hayek, the regularity of human action cannot be the source of a spontaneous order on the scale of a society, because human action is constituted by a plurality of spontaneous orders—articulate and inarticulate rules of conduct—that must themselves fit together to produce a coherent whole. This fitting together of rules and institutions is dependent on an evolutionary process that is not predetermined. The institutional complex of any society is path dependent. The existence of and interaction among existing institutions is contingent on the social structures from which they evolved. Regularities in human action are similarly evolved products.

Hayek's theory of spontaneous social order is closely connected to his evolutionary notion of group selection. He views the survival of a culture, for example, as the result of its adoption of rules that have proven to be successful (even if unconscious) guides to coordination. "The cultural heritage into which man is born consists of a complex of practices or rules of conduct which have prevailed," he maintains, "because they made a group of men successful but which were not adopted because it was known that they would bring about desired effects" (Hayek 1973, 17). He adds, "These rules of conduct have thus not developed as the recognized conditions for the achievement of a known purpose, but have evolved because the groups who practiced them were more successful and displaced others" (ibid., 18). Here Hayek employs a functional argument to explain the emergence and survival of rules and institutions in terms of their ability to yield socially beneficial results. The social environment constitutes human behavior insofar as the environment limits the range of human behavior to those actions that will not destroy the society. He remarks that social order exists "because the elements [i.e., people] do what is necessary to secure the persistence of that order" (Hayek 1967d, 77).

If we interpret Hayek's methodological individualism as a reductionist, rational choice individualism, his theory of group selection would clearly seem to violate his methodological views. Viktor Vanberg calls attention to this supposed inconsistency in Hayek's thought. For Vanberg, a theory of spontaneous order consistent with rational choice individualism shows how an institution "can be explained as an unintended, but systematic outcome of a process of interaction among individuals who are separately pursuing their own ends" (Vanberg 1986, 81). Hayek, however, relies on a theory that explains the survival of institutions in terms of their ability to promote group survival. The weakness of this sort of explanation, Vanberg believes, lies in its inability to illustrate how the free rider problem is overcome. A theory of institutional evolution that appeals to a process of group selection rather than individual selection cannot explain why individuals should follow rules or preserve institutions that benefit the group but provide no direct benefit to the individuals themselves.

Vanberg's critique does not seem to be consonant with Hayek's actual view of methodological individualism. The individual's epistemic circumstances and the constituted nature of perception are fundamental considerations in Hayek's version of methodological individualism. Hayek stresses the limits to individual reason and emphasizes the often inarticulate, practical knowledge that guides human action and that constitutes human perception. He understands rule following and the constitution of the individual by the cultural environment largely as a response to ignorance. Individuals follow rules and conventions because they do not know the consequences of alternative actions. Vanberg's free rider critique is firmly rooted in the rational choice tradition that assumes all human action to be motivated by a rational quest to achieve maximum individual gain. In this framework, isolated individuals know their private interests, and they know how to achieve their respective interests. Individuals obey and preserve rules, conventions, and institutions only when such behavior is demonstrably optimal. This free rider critique loses its force when Hayek's methodological individualism is understood to imply a rule-following individual with constituted perceptions and purposes, rather than a totally rational individual. In Hayek's view, because people lack the epistemic capacity to conduct all behavior rationally, they might very well follow rules that an omniscient observer could see are not in their individual self-interests. In this light, Hayek's seemingly functionalist or holistic evolutionary theory can be interpreted as pointing to (or at least consistent with) the social constituents of human action.

Hayek's discussion of spontaneous orders helps to clarify the difference between his form of methodological individualism and the forms prevalent among many social theorists. Spontaneous orders, for Hayek, are responses to a social problem: how can individual behaviors motivated by potentially unique subjective perceptions and expectations result in social cohesion? Hayek explains that his concept of order "describe[s] a state of affairs in which a multiplicity of elements of various kinds are so related to each other that we may learn from our acquaintance with some spatial or temporal part of the whole to form correct expectations concerning the rest, or at least expectations which have a good chance of proving correct" (Hayek 1973, 36). Within this concept, spontaneously emergent institutions are evolved adaptations to the myriad coordination problems posed by dispersed individuals with partial knowledge, in that they help individuals to determine which course of action will most likely succeed. Hayek highlights the autonomy of institutions in ways that rational choice methodological individualists cannot. His socially constituted individuals cannot possess the knowledge necessary to design efficient coordinating institutions, as tends to be assumed by the more conventional methodological individualism associated with neoclassical economics and other forms of social theory based on rational choice individualism.

Don Lavoie contends that modernist understandings of science are largely responsible for the failure of much social theory to grasp Hayek's concept of cosmos. Modernist science, according to Lavoie, is characterized by a mechanistic understanding of nature that pictures it as "the outgrowth of predictable laws that are not the design of any conscious entity, but in principle are subject to human mastery" (Lavoie 1989, 616). Knowing these predictable laws provides a way to bend the forces of nature to human purposes. Because social scientists often adopt the dominant conception of physical science, "the economy" in modernist political economy is also "rendered as a systematic mechanism that can be mastered if we only learn its principles of operation" (ibid.). Lavoie claims that new conceptions of science emphasize the nondeterministic and nonmechanistic nature of the world. These new approaches to science (some would call them postmodern) draw attention to the creative and self-organizing aspect of physical systems in a manner similar to Hayek's presentation of the spontaneous emergence of a cosmos. Whereas modernist physical and social sciences stress control of natural and social phenomena as one of their primary goals, the purpose of theoretical inquiry from the perspective of the new science is to learn how to cultivate self-organizing processes.

Hayek uses an agricultural metaphor to describe the proper conduct of government in the cultivation of a self-organizing economic process. Good government, he says, is more like farming than building bridges: the formulation of public policy is similar to "the sense in which the farmer or gardener cultivates his plants, where he knows and can control only some of the determining circumstances" (Hayek 1967a, 19). The goal of effective government is "to cultivate rather than to control the forces of the social process" (ibid.). An attitude of cultivation respects the limits people face in manipulating social outcomes. Hayek does not deny that purposive human actions partly constitute history. His protests against the illiberal and impractical conceit of social engineering notwithstanding, Hayek holds tightly to the notion that intentional human action can influence the course of events. But he maintains that the best way for public policy to be effective is to create the conditions for spontaneous social orders to emerge, much as scientists can induce the formation of crystals by creating the proper environment (Hayek 1973, 39–40).

The Rule of Law, Social Order, and Justice

Hayek recognizes that we cannot speak of markets and market coordination without also speaking of law, since the spontaneous order that arises from markets is constituted in part by the spontaneously evolved legal system in which market exchanges occur. It is impossible to separate market processes from the rules that shape their boundaries.

> The decision to rely on voluntary contracts as the main instrument for organizing the relations between individuals does not determine what the specific content of the law of contract ought to be; and the recognition of the right of private property does not determine what exactly should be the content of this right in order that the market mechanism will work as effectively and beneficially as possible. (Hayek 1960, 229)

For Hayek, it is the legal system, particularly common law courts, that offers the appropriate arena in which to settle questions about which rules would best contribute to the effective functioning of a market-based economy. Hayek therefore distinguishes between appropriate and inappropriate legal rules. Some rules will guide individual action to produce social coordination and cohesion, while other rules will quickly produce social disintegration. For instance, if people followed the rule "Run the other way when another person comes into view," a social order would likely be impossible (Hayek 1973, 44). Appropriate rules set the conditions for a spontaneous order to form, while inappropriate rules undermine social cooperation by fostering distrust, conflict, and other kinds of social discord or disorder. The legitimate role of government in a private property, market economy is to enforce those rules that, by their survival through a long evolutionary process, have proven their ability to enhance social coordination.

Hayek is equally attentive to the justice or injustice of legal rules. He defines just rules as those consistent with the rule of law, that is, the restriction of government action to the legislation and enforcement of laws that are general, universally applicable, and well-announced (Hayek 1960, 205–10). "General" laws, for Hayek, are long-term rules that will apply to unknown future cases. "Universally applicable" laws apply equally to all persons, not just to particular types or classes of people. Finally, laws must be well announced, known, and certain, so that individuals can reasonably predict the decisions of courts and the government's use of its coercive powers. This is an important practical attribute of the rule of law for Hayek, because the predictability of law enables individuals to have a good sense of the range of acceptable behavior. Legal clarity and stability allow people to form reliable expectations about how others will be permitted to act, and these expectations are essential to guide individual action in a manner consistent with social coordination.

Hayek develops these ideas most fully in his book *The Constitution of Liberty* (1960). He conceives the rule of law as a metalegal doctrine that should constrain the content of particular laws and hence the government's authority to enforce rules of conduct in a free society. Whether the government's use of coercion to enforce a particular law is warranted, legitimate, and compatible with individual freedom or arbitrary, illegitimate, and a violation of individual freedom depends on the law's consistency with the rule of law. "[T]he rule of law," Hayek argues, "provides the criterion which enables us to distinguish between those measures which are and those which are not compatible with a free system" (Hayek 1960, 222). This holds true for economic policy as well: "The classical argument for freedom in economic affairs rests on the tacit postulate that the rule of law should govern policy in this as in all other spheres" (ibid., 220).

The rule of law thus provides a framework for human conduct that yields a twofold benefit: commutative justice and the material prosperity that flows from an extensive division of labor and social cooperation. Hayek reaches this conclusion through a series of steps. First, he argues for the importance of minimizing coercion based on a particular conception of individual freedom. Second, he links the minimization of coercion to the development of individual spheres of responsibility, or private property. Finally, he defends the uncoerced exchange of private property on the basis of its beneficent (albeit unintended) consequences for the economy and society at large.

According to Hayek, an individual is coerced when "somebody else has power so to manipulate the conditions as to make him act according to that person's will rather than his own" (ibid., 13). The absence of coercion allows an individual to be free in the sense that "he can expect to shape his course of actions in accordance with his present intentions," given the set of resource constraints he faces (ibid.). Thus " 'freedom' refers solely to a relation of men to other men" (ibid., 12) and does "not depend on the range of choice" that the possession of a given amount of resources might allow or disallow (ibid., 13). For Hayek, the state of freedom has nothing to do with the amount of resources a person possesses; it refers only to the ability to act with independence from another person's will. Thus, whether an economic process is just does not depend on a person's real opportunities or achieved standard of living but only on whether the rules regulating individual conduct are enforced impartially, so that government officials do not arbitrarily interfere with an individual's ability to explore a perceived economic opportunity.

An important role for government in a free society is to prevent some individuals from coercing others. In order to accomplish this goal, governments need to use coercion, as in the case of imprisoning murderers, extorters, and thieves. But Hayek is careful to note that the coercive power of government must be constrained. The coercive power of government must itself be governed by general, universal rules in order to prevent the discretionary exercise of force.

> While we want to allow coercion by government only in situations where it is necessary to prevent coercion (or violence, etc.) by others, we do not want to allow it in all instances where it could be pretended that it was necessary for that purpose. We need therefore another test to make the use of coercion independent of individual will. It is the distinguishing mark of the Western political tradition that for this purpose coercion has been confined to instances where it is required by general abstract rules, known beforehand and equally applicable to all. (Hayek 1961, 29–30)

Hayek's argument is that government coercion should not be guided by an estimate of the net social benefits that are imagined to result from the enforcement of a rule or regulation aiming for a specific end, because such estimates are likely to reflect the subjective opinion of those in power rather than an objective assessment of the common interest.

Consequence-independent rules are therefore a prerequisite for freedom. Hayek claims that rules implemented to achieve a specific goal cease to be laws and become authoritarian commands. When the achievement of presumably "social" goals takes precedence over the enforcement of the rule of law, nothing restrains government coercion to serve the interests of whoever happens to control the state apparatus. Any attempt to justify government interference in the affairs of individuals or government coordination of the economy in the name of social improvement is both a misunderstanding of the spontaneous nature of the market process and a hubristic overestimation of the powers of human reason. State direction of economic affairs to achieve larger social goals is a chimera, as no government could obtain the information necessary to pursue a truly communal project. Since a government cannot act according to everyone's preferences, any action that it takes that departs from the rule of law will arbitrarily favor some people over others.

For Hayek, the rules of law carve out domains in which individuals bear the costs and reap the benefits of their actions. Inside these domains, individuals are responsible for their actions: "Rules frame individual action by maintaining 'spheres of responsibility,' identifying 'certain attributes which any such action ought to possess'" (McCann 2002, 11, quoting Hayek 1976, 14). By creating spheres of responsibility and defining acceptable characteristics of action within that sphere (i.e., no lying, cheating, or use of violence), the rules of law create what we more usually identify as private property.

Hayek understands private property as a social relation that has emerged from a rule-generating, evolutionary process. Private property and its constituent laws of contract, tort, and acceptable use survive because the uncoerced exchanges of property titles allows society to utilize individual knowledge and initiative to a degree unprecedented in human history. The pursuit and maintenance of private property gives self-interested people the incentive to act in the collective interest, as if directed by an invisible hand. Hayek maintains that no better type of social relation has yet emerged that helps to coordinate individual action and generate wealth as effectively as the creation, protection, free exchange, and competitive market valuation of private property titles.

The linchpin of Hayek's argument is human ignorance, the ignorance of each individual about most dimensions of day-to-day provisioning. To take a simple example, most people do not know how to use a plot of land to grow grain or how to build a stove to bake grain into bread. We are all dependent on an unfathomably vast network of specialized production and exchange in order to obtain our daily bread. Our ignorance necessitates reliance on others. The rules of law and the establishment of individual spheres of responsibility give guidelines and incentives for ignorant people to assist others voluntarily—and usually unintentionally—in the achievement of their goals. Hayek expresses this state of affairs as follows: "it is largely because civilization" and its attendant rules of law and property forms enable "us constantly to profit from knowledge which we individually do not possess and because each individual's use of his particular knowledge may serve to assist others unknown to him in achieving their ends that men as members of civilized society can pursue their own individual ends so much more successfully than they could alone" (Hayek 1960, 25). The rules of law regulating private property establish an institutional framework that provides "the maximum of opportunity for unknown individuals to learn of facts that we ourselves are yet unaware of and to make use of this knowledge in their actions" (ibid., 30). Here we encounter Hayek's consequentialist argument for a system of impartially enforced, abstract, and well-announced rules that minimize coercion: "Coercion thus is bad because it prevents a person from using his mental powers to the full and consequently from making the greatest contribution that he is capable of to the community" (ibid., 134). Hayek is not a natural rights libertarian who seeks to protect individuals' natural or God-given rights and freedoms. He defends economic freedom because it yields beneficial social consequences.[2]

In this regard, Leland Yeager emphasizes, Hayek is best understood as a rule utilitarian. A rule utilitarian believes that laws consistent with the rule of law (i.e., well-announced, abstract, universally applicable rules) help to promote social cooperation and coordination. When individuals can form reliable expectations about how other people, including government officials, will be permitted to act, this increases the security of their possessions and the ability to exchange them with others. They are thus encouraged to specialize in production and to engage in mutually beneficial trade to satisfy their respective needs and desires. Hence Hayek advocates a free market economy on the grounds that it "best facilitates the success of individuals seeking to make good lives for themselves in their own diverse ways" (Yeager 1985, 72). Voluntary exchanges that are enabled by a set of abstract, universally applicable rules create a form of social cooperation that helps individuals to attain well-being, as they subjectively experience it.

In addition, rule utilitarians are reluctant to judge institutions and individuals' actions according to their ability to promote individual or aggregate well-being in particular cases. The pervasiveness of human ignorance renders impossible the full accounting of costs and benefits that would be necessary to decide whether (or how much) a particular activity contributes to happiness. The rule utilitarian favors actions and policies based on well-announced principles rather than on case-by-case cost-benefit calculations, because rule-guided action helps to overcome the paralysis or arbitrary decisions that can result from our ignorance of the true costs and benefits of a particular course of action. A rule utilitarian, such as Hayek, "perceives the rationality of acting, in certain cases and aspects of life, on generally applicable abstract principles instead of on the fragmentary and probably accidentally biased bits of concrete information that one may happen to possess" (Yeager 1985, 73). Hayek's rule utilitarianism is thus consistent with his postmodern emphasis on the fragmented and socially constituted nature of human knowledge.

In sum, Hayek asserts that two benefits will accrue to all members of a society when market processes are regulated by rules consistent with the rule of law. First, the predictability of these rules will help to create a common set of expectations that will in turn contribute to the spontaneous emergence of a wealth-generating, goods-providing market order. Second, since these rules are end independent, the economic order that emerges will be procedurally just, operating in the interest of no particular individual or group.

EVOLUTION AND THE LAW

The principle of the rule of law does not specify the content of any particular law, and Hayek's postmodern subjectivism leads him to avoid locating the source of law in human reason. Thus Hayek needs a theory to explain the determination of the content of specific laws that does not rely on rational construction. He accomplishes this by further developing his basic notion of the common law as a set of evolved rules that ordinarily satisfy the requirements of generality, universality, and certainty.

According to Hayek, the common law rules that define and regulate the private sphere are "the result of an evolutionary process and [have] never been invented or designed as a whole by anybody" (Hayek 1978b, 78). In his jurisprudence, social evolution performs the same function for rule formation as the market does for price formation: a society's common law rules emerge through a long process of trial and error in which rules that are conducive to social order survive precisely because they help coordinate the actions and expectations of dispersed individuals. Hayek argues, "Society can . . . exist only if by a process of selection rules have evolved which lead individuals to behave in a manner which makes social life possible" (Hayek 1973, 44). Such rules are selected not by anyone's volition but ultimately because of the material advantages they bestow on a community.

Hayek maintains that in systems of case law, such as the British common law, legal "development proceeded through a process of law-finding in which judges and jurists endeavored to articulate the rules which had already for long periods governed action and the 'sense of justice'" (Hayek 1978b, 78–79). By "sense of justice," Hayek refers to the "capacity to act in accordance with non-articulated rules" that are commonly accepted because they have proved useful in avoiding and adjudicating conflict (ibid., 81). When common law judges produce a legal decision, they generally are just verbalizing certain customary, previously inarticulate rules that govern people's expectations of others' actions. For Hayek, the common law is at root an articulation of custom, that is, of a preexisting, evolved sense of justice. The judicial process is thus primarily a discovery process in which judges bring to light a previously inarticulate rule or a previous legal decision that should have guided the conduct of the disputing parties. Common law judges discover precedents—either in past legal decisions or in commonly accepted behavior—that they apply to the case at hand. In this way, Hayek contends that social order is not a product of law as much as law is derived from evolved, order-generating interactions among individuals.

To reinforce the centrality of evolved rules and to diminish the role of reason in the formation of social order, Hayek calls on the distinction between "knowing how" and "knowing that." "Knowing how" is embodied in all of the articulated and unarticulated rules people obey. It is "the habit of following rules of conduct" that are not the product of human design (Hayek 1988, 74). "Knowing that" is the "knowledge that one's actions will have certain kinds of effects" (ibid.). Hayek attacks consequential arguments that a particular policy or law will have specific socially beneficial effects, because, he contends, people are constitutionally unable to acquire and make use of all the information necessary to know that a particular rule will lead to a particular outcome. Similarly, he insists that many social institutions are not and cannot be the product of human reason. Hayek argues that the rules of common law generally exhibit not "knowledge that" but "knowledge how," customary and habitual knowledge that has contributed to society's continued survival. He thus sees the common law as the most visible manifestation of articulated rules of "knowing how."

Hayek's common law judges are discoverers, but not creators, of law. They merely find rules that are compatible with the existing common laws, laws that have survived due to their superiority at coordinating human action. When judges follow precedent, Hayek believes that their decisions are based on past cases and conventional behaviors that people already accept as guides to action. Adherence to common law precedent therefore enables judges to be neutral, objective referees. Hayek locates the impartiality of common law in the "fact" that common law is a spontaneous order rather than a designed order. In Hayek's view, spontaneous orders, like the weather, do not act in the interests of any particular group or person, so it is nonsensical to consider the outcome of a spontaneous order, like a rainy day, to be either just or unjust. Moreover, because he supposes that following precedent limits the creative power of judges, he expects that individuals are able to make rough predictions about what kinds of action judges will find to be acceptable and unacceptable. Finally, Hayek maintains that because common law judges are constrained by precedent, common law rules are generally consistent with the rule of law.

Most forms of liberal jurisprudence defend the rule of law as a rational and universal principle. For example, Kant treats the rule of law as the general foundation of an impartial legal system that can be recognized and implemented by rational people. Likewise, John Rawls and Robert Nozick attempt to found their jurisprudence on the universal truths of pure reason (Thomson 1991, 93). Thomson notes: "As a first approximation [modern] jurisprudence could be defined as the project of reason in pursuit of universal truths about law and justice" (ibid., 69). This rationalist project is incompatible with Hayek's postmodernism, because the former embodies the presumption that human reason is able to identify universal truths and to design from scratch a spontaneous order, such as a legal system. Though Hayek acknowledges that isolated rules can be created in a manner approximating the Kantian liberal ideal, he maintains that the entire legal framework governing a market order could never be the product of rational design, because human reason does not have the capacity to foresee the unintended consequences of the imposition of a particular legal structure. "Hayek's view of the limitations of reason," explains Chandran Kukathas (1989, 61), leads "him to argue against those political theories which seek to organize society or to bring it under the control of rational conceptions of the good." Hayek is notable among major legal thinkers in that he understands the law, particularly the common law, as the sediment of an evolutionary process and because he sees the rule of law as an evolved principle that has emerged as an unintended consequence of a common law procedure based on precedent.[3]

Hayek describes the rule of law as an evolved principle that emerged spontaneously in the attempt of common law judges to frame their legal opinions to be consistent with existing rules. In order for their decisions to be accepted by the disputing parties, judges followed precedent and adhered to the inarticulate sense of justice prevailing in society. To give judicial decisions credibility, the common law doctrine of precedent emerged to require that new decisions be compatible with past decisions, so that judges did not have the discretion to decide cases according to their personal prejudices or values. The doctrine of precedent then leads to the idea of the rule of law: "it is part of the technique of the common law judge that from the precedents which guide him he must be able to derive rules of universal significance which can be applied to new cases" (Hayek 1973, 86). Hayek believes that "as a necessary consequence of case law procedure, law based on precedent must consist exclusively of end-independent abstract rules of conduct of universal intent which the judge and jurists attempt to distil from earlier decisions" (Hayek 1978b, 79). The doctrine of precedent ensures that the common law will display characteristics associated with the rule of law.

Hayek's legal philosophy challenges theories that place the origin of law in a sovereign individual, legislative body, or politically articulated "will of the people." To propose that the source of just law is the decision of a sovereign individual or group is, for Hayek, to suppose that people possess the knowledge and ability to design an entire system of socially acceptable rules consistent with social coordination. The tendency for modern legal theory to locate the authority of just law in a sovereign subject results from a confusion between a taxis and a cosmos, a rationally engineered system or organization versus a spontaneous order. Hayek argues that much modern social and legal theory fails to appreciate the undesigned, pluralistic nature of society and many of its supporting institutions, misunderstanding them as organizations designed for a particular purpose. While he accepts that some institutions, such as firms, are organizations that are formed and controlled to achieve particular goals, he contends that the treatment of legal institutions as organizations is inappropriate, because it overestimates the capacity of reason to design and direct social life.

Hayek's differentiation between organizations and spontaneous orders is part of a more extensive argument for the common law and against democratic government as the preferred institutional structure to regulate a market economy. He does concede that the common law is fallible and will occasionally develop in "very undesirable directions" (Hayek 1973, 88). In such exceptional cases, democratic legislation may be necessary. He offers two general examples that might call for such legislation. First, he points out that economic transformation may occur more rapidly than the gradual evolution of the common law can accommodate. Hayek supposes that case law is by nature slow to change, since it must always maintain consistency with precedent. Advanced market economies can develop much more rapidly. So economic and social change may often outpace legal change and thereby create the need for corrective legislation. Second, Hayek acknowledges that at times "the law has lain in the hands of members of a particular class whose traditional vision made them regard as just what could not meet the more general requirements of justice" (ibid., 89). For example, he mentions the laws regulating interactions between masters and servants and between organized business and consumers as cases in which the law served the interests of a particular group rather than the more general interests of society.

To avoid deleterious consequences, corrective legislation must, however, be consistent with the rule of law and must be constrained by the customs and prevailing sense of justice that are embedded in the common law. Democratic legislation should be so restricted, Hayek maintains, because it is often written in the attempt to achieve a particular outcome, such as distributive justice. It will then be arbitrary, reduce individual freedom, and result in the failure of all possible entrepreneurial activities to be undertaken. In Hayek's view, economic freedom requires the rule of law (i.e., a legal system in which laws rather than authorities rule over people), and the rule of law requires an enduring appreciation of the evolutionary and customary nature of law itself. Just as a gardener is constrained by the climate and soil, democratic legislators need to acknowledge constraint by the customs and prevailing sense of justice embodied in the common law. Whether or not government action respects the rule of law and the wisdom of evolved common laws is how Hayek finally answers Keynes's question about where to draw the line between the market and government policy.

Because Hayek understands economic freedom to be a state in which people can use their subjective knowledge for their individual purposes and because he believes that competitive markets are uniquely able to elicit and coordinate the tacit, subjective knowledge of individuals, he claims that any goal-oriented policy, or government command that arbitrarily obstructs individual action (i.e., any policy inconsistent with the rule of law) is likely to be an impediment to social coordination. This understanding of the benefits of the rule of law leads him to argue against such policies as progressive taxation, a minimum wage, affirmative action, industrial policy, and other economic programs aimed to adjust the outcomes of the market process. He rejects these policies because he regards them as inconsistent with the rule of law as well as potentially discoordinating and wealth reducing.

This line of argument leads Hayek to oppose all forms of government action intended to promote distributive or social justice, that is, an end-state, or thick, notion of the common good. A law that is implemented to produce a patterned distributive outcome must usually treat people differently. For example, to produce a more equitable distribution of income, the government might tax people with different incomes at different rates or take income from some and transfer it to others. Hayek's subjectivism leads him to conclude that it is impossible to define what a fair or good outcome of such a policy would be. Since the judgment of what counts as a good result is subjective, policy aiming at particular purposes can express only the values of the specific people who make this policy, rather than a genuinely common interest. In Hayek's mind, this would constitute an arbitrary policy, since it would direct the actions of some people according to the interests of others, rather than according to a general and impartial rule.

The context for Hayek's conclusion was his alarm over the rising tide of socialist thinking among intellectual and political leaders—especially his fellow economists—following the Great Depression and the Second World War. The Road to Serfdom forcefully expressed the dangers that Hayek perceived in what he understood as arbitrary, goal-directed uses of government power. His central theme is that "unless we mend the principles of our policy, some very unpleasant consequences will follow which most of those who advocate these policies do not want" (Hayek [1944] 1976, xxi). Acceptance of government power that is not constrained by the rule of law opens the door to government coercion that has no principled limit. For instance, if we believe that either equality of opportunity or equality of outcome is a prerequisite for economic justice, Hayek fears that we soon could have government officials regulating all aspects of our lives. He concludes that the concept of justice must be restricted to an evaluation of human conduct in our relations with each other and not to an evaluation of outcomes or the material opportunities available to individuals.

Hayek thus attacks all theories of economic or social justice that aim for a patterned or result-oriented distribution of resources and opportunity. For him, all notions of social justice can be exposed as theoretically and practically bankrupt, as is apparent from the title of his volume *The Mirage of Social Justice*. He rejects the notion of distributive justice because he sees the distribution of income in a market economy as a perfect example of a state of affairs that is not subject to any authority's control: "Since only situations which have been created by human will can be called just or unjust, the particulars of a spontaneous order [e.g., a market economy] cannot be just or unjust: if it is not the intended or foreseen result of somebody's action that A should have much and B little, this cannot be called just or unjust" (Hayek 1976, 33). In his conceptual structure, the starvation of Soviet peasants during government-sponsored collectivization would thus be a horrible injustice, while famines induced by market-generated income shifts would be an unfortunate—but not unjust—consequence of a change in the data underlying the spontaneous market order. Hayek considers the notion of social justice a mirage because society is merely a collection of individuals who each possess their own subjective interests, bound together only by an evolved set of articulate and inarticulate rules. Only an omniscient observer could obtain sufficient knowledge to direct an improvement in their individual and collective well-being.

Hayek takes this strong position because he thinks that two sorts of "knowledge problem" undercut notions of social justice. The first knowledge problem faced by a patterned, distributive conception of social justice is an ethical one. Hayek accepts the view, common to most strands of liberal thought, that there is no objective account of the good life to which people can be forced to assent. Individuals have their own private assessments of what is valuable, and they do not agree about the nature of the good. In the liberal perspective, individuals' values and associated notions of the good life are potentially incommensurable with one another, which is why Milton Friedman asserts that in conflicts between people holding different values, people "can ultimately only fight" (M. Friedman 1953, 5). Thus, for many liberals, there is no objective theory of distributive justice that can be used to justify or criticize any particular distribution of resources among people, provided that the distribution has emerged from a process regulated by impartial rules.

The second knowledge problem that Hayek claims undercuts the notion of social justice confronts the practical implementation of any substantive distribution of social resources that people believe to be just. It is what we might call a "factual knowledge problem" and is Hayek's unique contribution to ethical theory. As I previously discussed, Hayek believes that much of the knowledge guiding individual action is tacit and inarticulate, representing the individual's subjective and perhaps unique knowledge of the changing circumstances of time and place, knowledge that can only be obtained through practice. The knowledge of economic opportunity is subjectively held, contingent on its holder's practical experience and spatiotemporal location. Rivalrous market competition is uniquely qualified to make use of this knowledge, according to Hayek. Government officials, like all individuals, can have only a limited grasp of the economic opportunities that a competitive market process can create and realize. The factual knowledge problem means that even if an objective or intersubjective account of distributive justice could be established, government officials may have difficulty implementing it, both because the knowledge necessary to achieve this distribution may be unavailable to government officials and because any government attempt to alter the distribution of resources will likely alter the incentives of individuals and thus diminish the market's ability to elicit subjective knowledge. In other words, Hayek sees an unavoidable and perhaps fatal trade-off between distributive equity and the effectiveness of the market process.

The preceding discussion provides a more sophisticated understanding of Hayek's vision of the "common good" than is provided by my initial sketch in chapter 2. Hayek relies heavily on the evolutionary notion of spontaneous order to defend his vision of a market order guided by the rule of law. His embrace of this notion of the "common good" derives from its supposed ability to overcome the knowledge problems entailed by the social dispersion of knowledge. Hayek believes that the ethical knowledge problem can be addressed through the discovery of fair rules—typically in a common law process—that permit all individuals the maximum flexibility to pursue their own subjective ends. The factual knowledge problem can by overcome through the uncoerced exchange of private property, that is, by a rivalrous market process that generates social coordination as its unintended by-product. These two points combine in Hayek's thinking to produce the conclusion that the rule of law is the only notion of the common good to which all individuals will (or should) agree.

In addition, we have seen that Hayek's political economy rests on the normative ideal of impartiality (legal, political, and economic neutrality). He argues that "we should regard as the most desirable order of society one which we would choose if we knew that our initial position in it would be decided purely by chance" (Hayek 1976, 132). Such a society would be one in which we might choose to live if the choice were made behind a Rawlsian veil of ignorance. Hayek sees this "good society" as a reflection of the impartiality embodied in the rule of law. Hayek believes that in a market process guided by the rule of law, government regulation favors no one individual over others and thus enables markets to reward individuals according to their ability to satisfy the needs and desires of others, rather than on the basis of their personal characteristics, imagined merits, or material endowments.

Hayek is not unaware of real-world inequity and deprivation. He does acknowledge the potential for the common law to favor particular class interests. He also recognizes that market processes, even when perfectly just by his standards, are capable of generating regrettable outcomes from a humanitarian point of view, in terms of the misfortune and misery experienced by some individuals: he states that "the preservation of a spontaneous order often requires changes which would be unjust if they were determined by human will" (Hayek 1976, 39). Nonetheless, Hayek insists on a tight line of demarcation between appropriate and inappropriate government action. In his eagerness to counter socialist thinking among intellectual and political leaders, he makes a strong case for free exchange guided by the rule of law as a necessary and sufficient prerequisite for the realization of his good society. For Hayek, this strong free market position offered a philosophically satisfying, antisocialist response to Keynes's challenge. However, as chapter 4 of this book demonstrates, there are several hidden costs to Hayek's position: (1) an intellectual inconsistency, in his recourse to modernist assumptions about the objective knowledge and rational faculties of common law jurists; (2) a related blindness to the possibility that legal rules purportedly regulated by the rule of law may not be impartial; and (3) a failure to take seriously the possibility that market outcomes are systematically biased in favor of the asset rich over the asset poor.

Recasting Hayek's Good Society
The Non-Neutrality of the Law and the Market

★

This chapter opens the door to a post-Hayekian socialism by critically examining Hayek's vision of the good society. Hayek claims that a market economy guided by the rule of law is an impartial, procedurally just system that improves the life chances of anyone chosen at random and thus that such an economy serves the common good more effectively than any other method of large-scale social cooperation. This chapter challenges this conclusion by exploring two objections to Hayek's line of argument.

The first objection concerns Hayek's assumption that common law systems are able to discover latent agreements about the common good, that is, agreements concerning the legal rules governing the market. The American legal realist tradition casts doubt on this assumption through an emphasis on the subjective knowledge and agency of jurists. Legal realists argue that agreements concerning the common good are not waiting "out there" for judges to find them. From this perspective, it is not clear that a common law system could ever produce a neutral (impartial, unbiased) agreement about how to make a market order work beneficially and effectively. The radical subjectivism of the legal realist tradition suggests that Hayek's theory of legal evolution and his related defense of the rule of law are not consistent with the subjectivist understanding of human knowledge that underpins his postmodern economics.

The second objection concerns the impartiality of markets themselves, based on the long-standing contention that markets tend to serve the interests of the wealthy more so than the poor. Hayek, of course, does not see it this way. As long as the rule of law is in place, he maintains that "each individual [will] be able to act on his particular knowledge, always unique, at least so far as it refers to some particular circumstances, and that he [will] be able to use his individual skills and opportunities within the limits known to him and for his own individual purpose" (Hayek 1960, 29). In this way, the market does not discriminate in favor of the poor or rich. However, the modern credit rationing literature, whose emphasis on asymmetric information parallels Hayek's arguments about the dispersion of knowledge, demonstrates that market processes can indeed be biased systematically against the poor. Absent significant real and financial wealth, it may simply be impossible for a poor individual to "be able to use his individual skills and opportunities . . . for his own individual purpose." The inability to obtain credit will prevent some individuals from being able to pursue opportunities that they uniquely and subjectively perceive. This possibility seriously undermines Hayek's contention that market economies improve the life chances of anyone chosen at random, and it further reinforces the claim that the agreement about the constitution of the common good that Hayek sees in the common law is illusory.

Together, these criticisms indicate the possibility that a different institutional structure might better contribute to the common good than would Hayek's market process regulated primarily by the common law. Hayek's insights offer us much fruitful guidance as to how this alternative order might be constructed so as to avoid the knowledge problems that he has shown to be prevalent in a complex society. Yet his image of the good society stands to be revised, particularly to allow for an expanded role for democratic processes within a post-Hayekian political economic order.

THE NON-NEUTRALITY OF THE COMMON LAW

The starting point of my critique of Hayek's normative conclusions is to show that his theory of legal evolution and his related defense of the rule of law are not consistent with the subjectivist understanding of human knowledge that underpins his economics. A considerable body of legal theory written from a broadly conceived subjectivist perspective—in particular, American legal realism—challenges the notion of legal neutrality that Hayek makes so central to his liberalism. This challenge is significant for two reasons. First, as we have seen, Hayek suggests that markets cannot be defined independently of legal institutions, because the law determines what contracts are enforceable and how property may be used. The legal system plays an important role in determining whether the market works beneficially and effectively, and Hayek concludes that a common law process produces a neutral and apolitical method to determine the rules that constitute the common good. However, a thoroughgoing subjectivist perspective in legal theory contests this conclusion.

Second, based on the claim that a common law process, guided by the rule of law, can determine beneficial and effective rules for a market order, Hayek restricts the role of democratic policymaking. He fears that democratic majorities may threaten to usurp private property rights and erode the freedom of contract, thereby opening the door to totalitarian government. Hayek thus limits the legitimate role of democratic public policy in determining the rules and shaping the outcomes of the economic process, by insisting that policies adhere to the rule of law and respect the wisdom of evolved, apolitical common law rules. But perhaps a subjectivist approach to social theory should give a larger role to democracy than Hayek is willing to grant.

It is instructive to remind ourselves at this point that in Hayek's subjectivist perspective, there is no necessary isomorphism between the objective world and human perception and knowledge of that world. His work in psychology attests that perception and knowledge are socially constituted (Hayek 1952, 1967e, 1978d). Perception depends on the mental patterns that create and order meaningful experience. These patterns are constructed through experience, the acquisition of language, and the adoption of particular theories. Hayek's understanding of subjective knowledge is compatible with the postmodern assertion that all knowledge is "discursive"; knowledge and meaning are irreducibly dependent on the languages, theories, and practices—all of which constitute discourse—adopted by diverse individuals. The test of this individual and discursively constituted, or subjective, knowledge is not whether it somehow "mirrors" reality but whether a community agrees that this knowledge is useful.[1] A subjectivism that accepts the irreducibly discursive nature of knowledge is connected to a psychology that recognizes the creative and socially constituted nature of the human mind.[2]

One of the tenets of Hayek's legal theory is that common law judges can discover impartial, universally applicable rules to adjudicate economic conflicts. To reach his conclusion about the possibility of obtaining neutral law through an evolved, common law process, he casts judges as decidedly uncreative beings. He describes judges as "unwitting tools" whose decisions are limited and determined by the set of already existing rules (Hayek 1973, 66). This conclusion seems odd considering his work in psychology, where he notes that a limited set of rules may be combined to produce an almost infinite array of actions (Hayek 1978d, 49). Nevertheless, he supposes judges to be limited to making mechanical choices, and he regards this to be the essence of legal objectivity and neutrality: "it is because the judge who applies [rules] has no choice in drawing the conclusions that follow from the existing body of rules and the particular facts of the case, that it can be said that laws and not men rule" (Hayek 1960, 153). Hayek's judges cannot decide cases based on their sympathies and prejudices or on the potential consequences of a particular decision, insofar as such consequence-oriented decisions might not cohere with past cases.

At first glance, it might appear that judges must have either rational or empirical access to objective truth—legal facts and rules—in order to reach the neutral decisions Hayek believes that judges are able to pronounce. But rather than viewing judges as rational fact and rule finders who are able to deduce the correct decisions based on knowledge of these facts and rules, he describes judges as endowed with a special intuitive capacity, acquired through years on the bench, which enables them to reach the correct decisions: "That the judge can, or ought to, arrive at his decisions exclusively by a process of logical inference from explicit premises always has been and must be a fiction. For in fact the judge never proceeds in this way" (Hayek 1973, 116–17). Here Hayek approvingly quotes Roscoe Pound to describe his understanding of judicial reasoning: "the trained intuition of the judge continuously leads him to right results for which he is puzzled to give unimpeachable legal reasons" (ibid., 117). For Hayek, in order to arrive at a judgment, a judge tests hypotheses "at which he has arrived by processes only in part conscious" (ibid., 120). Hayek assures his readers that despite this intuitive reasoning process, judges are not usually swayed by their emotions and prejudices and generally discover the objectively correct, neutral result.

In contrast to Hayek, the legal realists challenge traditional claims about the neutrality and predictability of law and of the ability of judges to pronounce objective, apolitical decisions. The work of Jerome Frank (1970, 1973) and Karl Llewellyn (1960) is especially corrosive of Hayek's account of the judicial process. Frank emphasizes that judges do not have access to the objective facts of a case and thus have to rely on subjective hunches to determine the circumstances of a case. Llewellyn highlights the indeterminacy of rules. He argues that the common view of precedent that describes judges as bound by previous decisions does not accurately convey the nature of judicial reasoning. Judges, according to Llewellyn, can easily discard previous rulings if they can show that the circumstances of a case before them are somehow different from past cases.

Frank (using his analysis of the subjectivity of legal facts) and Llewellyn (using his discussion of the subjectivity of rules) argue separately that the judicial process is creative and not merely a matter of discovery. As a consequence, both maintain that legal decisions are less predictable than Hayek thinks is possible, and their analyses of the legal process indicate that the law is far less a neutral set of general, universal rules of just conduct than an instrument of public policy. Another implication of legal realism is that what Hayek views as exceptional—the development of law in directions beneficial to the interests of a particular group rather than to the interests of all—may be an ineradicable feature of the legal system. Legal realism suggests that the evolution of law is not as disinterested and idyllic as Hayek describes.

Frank draws attention to the inability of judges to obtain objective knowledge of the facts relevant to cases on which they have to pass judgment. He points out two reasons why objective facts are inaccessible. First, courts have to rely on the often-competing testimonies of antagonistic witnesses, and these testimonies are grounded in the witnesses' irreducibly subjective perceptions. Second, courts must make subjective judgments about what portions of whose testimony will count as legally recognized facts. Frank writes:

> The facts as they actually happened are therefore twice refracted—first by the witnesses, and second by those who must "find" the facts. The reactions of trial judges or juries to the testimony are shot through with subjectivity. Thus we have subjectivity piled on subjectivity. It is surely proper, then, to say that the facts as "found" by a trial court are subjective. (Frank 1973, 22)

The subjectivity of facts implies that a "trial court's facts are not 'data,' not something that is 'given'; they are not waiting somewhere, ready made, for the court to discover, to 'find'" (ibid., 23). Faced with the subjectivity of facts, Frank, like Hayek, believes that judges often rely on intuition and hunches to reach their decisions. Frank differs from Hayek, however, in that he makes no presumption that judge's hunches are correct. Frank does not treat hunching as somehow reflective of an objective truth: hunching is a creative activity rather than revelatory of an underlying reality. Rather than viewing legal facts as discovered, Frank considers it to be more appropriate to regard them as created through the legal process.

The most important conclusion that Frank draws from the subjectivity of legal facts is that law is indeterminate and unpredictable. Since no one can know what the court will find as the facts of the case, there is no way to tell what or how existing rules will apply to the case. The law relevant to a particular case cannot be known until the court actually reaches a decision. As a result, it is a "myth or illusion . . . that law can be entirely predictable" (Frank 1970, 37). However, Frank does not share Hayek's view that the unpredictability of judicial decisions will impede human action. Frank argues that the unpredictability of law did not present a serious obstacle to human action "since most men act without regard to the legal consequences of their conduct, and, therefore, do not act in reliance upon any given pre-existing law" (Frank 1973, 38–39). Unlike Hayek, Frank holds that there is a gap between custom and law, which makes it possible for people to act according to customary behavior and then to find this behavior deemed illegitimate by a law court. His main point is that habits and customs, not law, guide human behavior, so that the unpredictability of judicial decisions does not prevent people from planning a course of action.

Whereas Frank illustrates the indeterminacy and unpredictability of law by emphasizing the subjectivity of legal facts, Llewellyn demonstrates the indeterminacy and unpredictability of law by emphasizing the subjectivity of legal rules. Llewellyn challenges the common understanding that the doctrine of precedent binds judicial rulings to the decisions of past courts. He points out that precedent is Janus-faced. By describing precedent this way, Llewellyn brings to light the two, opposite approaches judges can adopt toward previous judicial opinions. Because judges have a choice about how to handle past cases, precedent becomes an instrument in the hands of skillful judges, not a bridle leading them toward a preordained result.

Llewellyn labels the two approaches to precedent the "strict view" and the "loose view." The loose view of precedent is the one most commonly understood when judges say precedent determined their decision: "That is the view that a court has decided, and decided authoritatively, any point or all points on which it chose to rest a case" (Llewellyn 1960, 67–68). Having decided authoritatively, the court's decision becomes the standard for all future cases. To make use of the loose view of precedent is to use past decisions as the guide by which present decisions are reached. In the loose view of precedent, judges take the facts of the case before them to be similar to the facts of previous cases: if a similar case has been decided in a certain way in the past, it should be decided similarly in the present.

When judges exercise a strict view of precedent, they argue that previous judicial decisions do not apply to the case before them because the facts of the present case are different in some significant way, which invalidates the application of rules that were established earlier in ostensibly similar cases. Previous decisions do not automatically apply to the current case, because judges might deem those decisions as relevant only to the unique constellation of facts surrounding those past cases. Thus the strict view of precedent is "in practice the dogma which is applied to *unwelcome* precedents"; it is "the recognized, legitimate, honorable technique for whittling precedents away, for making the lawyer, in his argument, and the court, in its decision, free of them" (Llewellyn 1960, 67). The notion that precedent binds the decisions of judges is not, in Llewellyn's view, a realistic description of the judicial process, since judges have a choice whether to accept precedents as guides or to reject them as irrelevant. As a result, Llewellyn concludes, like Frank, that it is difficult to predict the decisions of courts based on knowledge of rules alone, because it is indeterminate how judges will interpret the applicability of those rules.

Despite the creative potential of the judicial process and despite the inability to predict a court's decision based on knowledge of rules, Llewellyn does not think it is impossible to form reliable guesses about the outcomes of a case. Lawyers who are familiar with the personalities of particular judges and with the kind of arguments these judges generally find persuasive will stand a better chance of winning a trial than lawyers who have little basis on which to develop this knowledge. Llewellyn's lawyers are thus like Hayek's economic actors: they have subjective knowledge of time and place—specifically, the knowledge of judicial temperaments—that enables them to present cases more likely to prove persuasive to particular judges and, hence, ultimately to be successful. Nevertheless, Llewellyn makes it clear that those "who think that precedent produces or ever did produce a certainty that did not involve matters of judgment and of persuasion . . . simply do not know our system of precedent in which we live" (ibid., 69). The subjectivity of rules further undermines Hayek's position that a common law system guided by precedent constitutes a method through which judges simply administer law rather than actively create it.[3]

Both Frank and Llewellyn agree that the law relevant to a case does not precede the judge's decision. Judges continually create law. A legal system governed by the rule of law that promises that laws, rather than authorities, rule over people is inoperable in a world in which human actors—lawyers, judges, and juries—apply rules and determine facts based on their subjective interpretations of events and of the applicability of rules. There is no reason to believe that judicial decisions must reflect the customs regulating behavior or an inarticulate sense of justice, as Hayek proposes. A common law system thus may not necessarily fulfill the requirements of objectivity and neutrality that Hayek believes the rule of law ensures. Law may always be the instrument of particular interests. The facts and rules that judges find to be relevant are filtered and shaped by their values, theories, and preconceptions, so that their decisions will, in part, be expressions of those values, theories, and preconceptions. For legal realists, common law decisions cannot be disinterested pronouncements of some objective interest made by judges who cloak their subjectivity behind the robes of justice.

Legal realism rejects the atheoretical, evolutionary claims Hayek makes about the common law. Hayek understands the common law to have progressed through a process of trial and error, so that the laws establishing the assignment of contested property rights and the enforceability of contracts are those that have survived a long evolutionary process directed by no one. Significantly, he depicts the common law as operating independently from theoretical influence to reach a neutral, apolitical resolution of what rules determine whether the market works beneficially and effectively. It is also possible to question Hayek's claims about the neutral evolution of the common law by considering that judicial decisions are constituted, in part, by the theories of justice that judges implicitly hold. Since judges are not bound by precedent and can generally choose whether or not past cases are relevant to the case before them, the theoretical perspectives that judges adopt will play a critical role in shaping their decisions. Legal judgment is always theory laden, which implies that the common law is partly the creation of particular philosophic assumptions and notions of justice.[4]

Morton Horwitz's (1977) description of how American common law judges used their creative ability to recast the common law in the interests of industry and commerce during the first several decades of the nineteenth century gives us one example of how the law can serve particular interests. During this period, the U.S. economy shifted from being primarily based on agriculture to become increasingly industrial and commercial. Up until the turn of the nineteenth century, however, the common law generally reflected agrarian interests. Horwitz demonstrates how judges came to identify with the industrial and merchant classes and began to decide cases in order to promote industrialization and economic growth. According to Horwitz, judges consciously manipulated the common law to be more supportive of the emerging commercial order rather than the old agricultural order. He writes: "The basic system of tort and property law . . . was judicially created. And, by and large, it was strongly geared to the aspirations of those who benefited most from low cost economic development" (M. Horwitz 1977, 255). While it is not necessary to endorse all the details of Horwitz's legal theory to recognize that the legal system can serve particular interests, his main conclusion reinforces the injustice (discussed in chap. 6) of the wage-for-labor-time contract as it has evolved in industrial societies.

The realist account of the legal process raises an important question, a question Hayek would likely ask of it: if it is the case that law is as unpredictable as Frank and Llewellyn describe and if law is often used as an instrument of social change that may be difficult to portray as in the common interest, why do so many people, judges and citizens alike, accept law as a stable, authoritative system of rules? Why, for instance, do judges insist on describing their task as the discovery of consistent rules, as a task bound by precedent? Hayek doubts that accounts of legal change as instrumental are accurate, because he thinks that people will not tolerate the aggressive and interested uses of law to promote social change. For Hayek, the legitimacy of law flows from its internal consistency and its consistency with custom, requirements that he believes the common law generally fulfills. He claims that people's allegiance to law depends on the law satisfying certain expectations concerning the general, consistent, purpose-independent character of rules and that this allegiance will vanish when these expectations are disappointed (Hayek 1973, 92). From his perspective, it would be difficult to reconcile the widely perceived consistency of law with judicial creativity, particularly creativity expressed on behalf of specific interests.

Edward Levi answers the question of why law is generally perceived as stable and consistent by observing that the law is a "moving classification system" (Levi 1964, 266). By describing law as a moving classification system, Levi draws attention to the possibility that the legal system is able to retain the appearance of consistency even while new laws are continually being created. This is because legal texts are filled with ambiguous rules and malleable language that can be mined and interpreted in support of a variety of judicial decisions. Judges are able to describe themselves as merely discovering and applying already existing law, rather than actively creating policy, since legal texts are open to multiple and creative interpretations. Levi writes:

> [M]ovement in the [legal] system frequently will not be apparent. When it is apparent, it is often justified obliquely on the basis that this policy step was taken some time ago and is reflected in prior decisions. The system permits a foreshadowing of results and therefore has built into it the likelihood of a period of preparation so that future decisions appear as a belated finding and not a making of law. The joint exploration through competing examples to fill the ambiguities of one or many propositions has the advantage of permitting the use in the system of propositions or concepts saved from being contradictory because they are ambiguous, and on this account more acceptable as ideals or commonplace truths. (ibid., 272)

In Levi's view, the perceived consistency of law is partly a function of the persuasive efforts of judges, who exploit the polysemy of legal texts to underpin the decisions they reach, and partly a function of the theoretical perspective adopted by observers of the legal system. Levi's characterization of law as a moving classification system implies that the legal system could as easily be perceived as inconsistent or consistent.

CREDIT RATIONING AND INEQUALITY OF OPPORTUNITY

Hayek does accept the possibility that a common law system occasionally violates the objective, universalist aspirations of the rule of law to serve particular interests. He believes that such circumstances are exceptional and self-correcting, insofar as the doctrine of precedent forces judges' decisions to conform impartially to the set of previously articulated rules. However, the legal realist critique of legal neutrality shows that Hayek overstates the case for neutrality in a common law process. Hence the law may always be a servant of particular interests, or be biased against a particular group or certain types of people, thereby skewing the results of market processes. This possibility undermines Hayek's contention that a market process constrained by a common law system generally improves the life chances of any person chosen at random. Hayek's belief that the market serves the interests of the poor as well as the rich and the interests of people who perform wage labor as well as people who hire labor may not be correct if the law favors certain class interests.

The socialist tradition has consistently doubted beliefs like Hayek's, instead claiming that the market is systematically biased against the interests of the poor. I will examine this possibility by bringing a radical interpretation of the economics literature on credit rationing to bear on Israel Kirzner's defense of the justice of a free market distribution of income. Kirzner is a long-standing champion of Ludwig von Mises's and Hayek's theories of the market as a discovery process. Kirzner insists that if the theory of the market as a discovery process were more widely accepted, the popular idea that it is possible and desirable to challenge the justice of free market outcomes would be discredited. As he puts it, understanding the market as a discovery process makes end-state notions of distributive justice "highly problematic" (Kirzner 1995, 46). He reinforces Hayek's conclusion that in a market economy, conceptions of social justice are a "mirage" (Hayek 1976).

But Kirzner also makes an explicit argument for what is only implicit in Hayek's work: that the results of the market process are just because they are the product of individual initiative, which markets enable all people the opportunity to exercise. While Hayek tends to say that the outcomes of a fair process are neither just nor unjust (they are like the weather), Kirzner takes the stronger position that a proper conception of the functioning of the market process, combined with the widely held acceptance of a finders-keepers ethic, should also lead people to accept the justice of free market outcomes, especially entrepreneurial profit. An evaluation of Kirzner's theory of justice will serve as the second element in my critique of Hayek's normative conclusions. More precisely, I will criticize Kirzner's thesis that in a market economy, everyone has in principle an equal opportunity to be an entrepreneur who is able to initiate a productive or speculative endeavor. I have already challenged Hayek's case for legal neutrality, but if I can also show flaws in Kirzner's strong case for equality of opportunity in markets and in his resulting strong case for free market distributive justice, I will in a different way be calling into question Hayek's position that markets are impartial processes allowing people to exploit their skills and opportunities for their own purposes.

According to Kirzner, in a market economy that places no statutory limits on the economic activities in which an individual may participate (as long as those activities do not infringe on the property rights of others), every person has in principle the same opportunity of acting on an entrepreneurial insight as any other. Specifically, ownership of wealth provides no entrepreneurial advantage: a poor person who notices an opportunity for entrepreneurial gain is in principle no less able to seize this opportunity than is a wealthy person. Kirzner's conclusion reinforces Hayek's notion that a market economy improves the life chances of any person chosen at random. Kirzner reaches his conclusion because he believes that credit markets in a free economy do not systematically discriminate among types of borrowers. Thus a poor entrepreneur who notices a speculative or productive opportunity has the same access as a wealthy entrepreneur to the money necessary to seize the opportunity (through credit), after transaction costs are taken into consideration.

This belief has been called into question by credit rationing models demonstrating that asset-poor individuals who are not able to provide collateral to lenders will be unable to obtain credit, no matter the interest rate they are willing to pay. The credit rationing literature erodes the underpinnings of Kirzner's application of the finders-keepers ethic to the evaluation of entrepreneurial profit, because it implies that all individuals do not in principle have an equal opportunity to be an entrepreneur. To extend an old adage, "it takes money to make money" entrepreneurially, and this possibility challenges Kirzner's belief that a finders-keepers ethic can undergird the normative conclusion that entrepreneurs should necessarily be able to keep the profits that they find. The credit-rationing literature also suggests that the life chances of the asset poor may be considerably worse compared to those who possess significant real and financial wealth.

Kirzner's theory of the market process, like Hayek's, rests on subjectivist foundations. Knowledge of economic opportunity, technology, potential market demand, and resource availability is subjective, in the sense that each individual has his or her own perception of cost conditions, market demand, and resource availability. These perceptions may be unique to each individual, and thus they may turn out to be wrong. The principal actor in Kirzner's conception of the market process is the entrepreneur, a person who is alert to the possibility of economic gains, or profits, that arise from disequilibrium price discrepancies. Kirzner praises entrepreneurship because it leads to the coordination of individual action sparked by subjective perceptions and imaginings.

Kirzner describes three types of entrepreneurship. First, an entrepreneur may profit from arbitrage: buying a commodity from a low-priced producer and immediately reselling it at a greater price to a consumer who the entrepreneur alertly notices values the commodity more highly. Prior to the intervention of the entrepreneur, the producer and consumer are ignorant of each other's existence. The consumer was unaware that the producer offered the commodity for sale, and the producer did not notice the potential customer willing to pay more than he was asking. Second, entrepreneurship can be speculative: the entrepreneur speculates that a commodity currently selling for a low price will sell for a higher price in the future, after taking into consideration the interest expense of carrying the commodity. Finally, entrepreneurship can take the form of what Kirzner calls "productive creativity": buying low-priced inputs and combining them to produce a commodity with a higher price. For instance, an entrepreneur might buy oranges and rent capital and labor time to manufacture orange juice that consumers value more highly than the inputs taken separately. The lure of profit is to find and act on these price discrepancies in order to try to get something for nothing. In Kirzner's words, "[w]hat the market process does is to systematically translate unnoticed opportunities for mutually profitable exchange among individuals into forms that tend to excite the interest and alertness of those most likely to notice what can be spontaneously learned" (Kirzner 1979b, 150).[5]

Central to Kirzner's conception of entrepreneurship is that it is an activity entailing no opportunity cost. To see this most clearly, it is instructive to contrast entrepreneurship with deliberate search behavior. Searching involves looking for opportunities that are known to exist, and we can understand the search process to involve the comparison of costs and benefits. For instance, when we search for a library book, we have good reason to believe it exists, and it is sensible to ask whether the benefit we expect to receive upon locating the volume is worth the additional time we expect that it will take to find it. Entrepreneurial behavior is different than search. We act entrepreneurially when we notice a potentially valuable resource that, prior to its discovery, we had no idea existed. For instance, if when searching for a library book, we happen to perceive a different book, previously unknown to us, that stimulates a startling insight, this alert noticing is entrepreneurial in nature. The flash of inspiration that caused us to perceive this book did not involve the deliberate forfeit of any other opportunity. We did not weigh the expected additional costs with the expected additional benefits.

Given that there are no opportunity costs associated with entrepreneurship, Kirzner also advances the potentially questionable claim that entrepreneurial activity does not require the prior ownership of any resources. Take the case of arbitrage, in which an individual notices a resource that he or she can purchase, with a check drawn on an account with a zero balance, and immediately resell at a higher price, enabling that individual to deposit the proceeds in his or her checking account before the initial check clears. In the case of speculation or productive creativity, an individual may have to borrow the funds to finance the purchase of the low-priced resources, since the higher-priced output will not be available for sale until the future. But again, as long as individuals are able to obtain the credit needed to initiate speculative or productive endeavors, they do not need to possess any assets to be entrepreneurs.

From Kirzner's subjectivist perspective, the profit that the entrepreneur earns by acting on perceived price discrepancies is a discovered gain, a gain that did not exist for human purposes until its discovery: "it is plausible to treat the discoverer of a hitherto unperceived opportunity as its *creator*, its originator. That which is grasped by the discoverer did not, in a relevant sense, exist at all prior to its discovery" (Kirzner 1992, 221). Entrepreneurial discovery creates an opportunity whose existence others did not recognize. Understanding market exchange as motivated by the discovery of previously unnoticed and unconceived gain allows us, in Kirzner's view, to apply the widely held ethical belief in the finders-keepers rule to evaluate the justice of entrepreneurial profit. Kirzner observes that many of us accept the finders-keepers rule—or that of first come, first served—when we need to decide how to reward property rights to a scarce resource with no previously existing property title that is in principle available to any particular person to appropriate. If this observation is correct and if we understand profit to be the reward for alertly grasping previously unnoticed economic gain, then we should, from Kirzner's perspective, accept the justice of entrepreneurial profit. This is the essence of what Kirzner characterizes as an arbitrage theory of profit, which he uses to advocate a finders-keepers ethic to support the justice of profit income.

Kirzner's analysis of enterpreneurship allows him to draw broader conclusions about the justice of wage and property incomes earned in a market economy. He argues that all exchanges exhibit an element of entrepreneurship. Sellers of factor services must always decide whether a particular offer should be accepted or whether they should hold out for a higher price. In an economy that is out of equilibrium and permeated by true ignorance of possible opportunities, every decision to sell or to buy is contingent on an entrepreneurial judgment. Kirzner thus believes that all incomes contain an element of entrepreneurial profit and that the legitimacy of these incomes can therefore also be evaluated with a finders-keepers ethic. In effect, he asserts that the finders-keepers rule supports the justice of all income receipts resulting from uncoerced exchanges in a market economy. Thus it is unnecessary (and perhaps even inappropriate) to apply other criteria to evaluate the justice of the market determination of income.

In *Discovery, Capitalism, and Distributive Justice* (1989), Kirzner fleshes out his portrayal of the actors on both sides of the labor market as entrepreneurial. He does this to reinforce the applicability of the finders-keepers rule to an ethical evaluation of all income receipts in a capitalist economy, including wage incomes and not just pure profits. Because real-world labor markets are never in equilibrium, self-owners of labor time must act, in part, as entrepreneurs, since wage incomes are never guaranteed prior to their receipt. Kirzner describes the entrepreneurial nature of the labor supply decision as follows:

> Inevitably the laborer must determine for himself—in an open-ended world fraught with inescapable uncertainty, pervaded by the sheerest of utter ignorance—which job to apply for, which job to accept, and what wages and working conditions to hold out for. This means that the more successfully "entrepreneurial" laborer will in fact enjoy a job offering wages, working conditions, prestige and prospects for advancement, which may substantially exceed those won by a fellow laborer with equal talents qua laborer, but with less potential as entrepreneur. (Kirzner 1989, 116)

The decision of a worker to sell his labor time is entrepreneurial because the worker has to judge which producer in what industry offers the greatest chance for his labor to be most productive and hence to be rewarded with the highest possible wage.

Yet one wonders whether this kind of analysis undermines Kirzner's intentions. After all, if workers are entrepreneurs when they evaluate different employers in search of the most "profit" (or the highest wage), what prevents workers from using these same entrepreneurial insights to initiate their own productive enterprise? Is there, in Kirzner's view, any difference between an entrepreneurial employee and an entrepreneurial employer?

Kirzner seems to suggest that workers who do not employ their entrepreneurial facilities to direct a productive enterprise prefer to take fewer risks than those who do. He asks us to imagine two men, Jones and Smith, who each own no resources but who both believe that cab driving is a rewarding economic activity. Kirzner contrasts the case of Jones, who borrows money to rent a taxicab to become an independent cab driver, with the case of Smith, who rents his labor time to an owner of a fleet of taxicabs. Both the independent contractor Jones and the wage-laborer Smith act entrepreneurially when deciding to work in the taxi-driving industry. For Jones, there is no guarantee that the cab-driving business will generate enough revenue to cover all of his opportunity costs. Kirzner also notes: "Smith never was assured of anything at all. . . . In selling his driving services to Brown, the fleet owner, Smith is not simply transforming these services into their fully known cash value, he is taking a step into the dark, uncertain entrepreneurial future, guided entirely by his entrepreneurial hunches" (Kirzner 1989, 118). The only difference between Jones and Smith appears to be that Jones is willing to take the risk of running his own firm to exploit the perceived opportunity in the taxi business, while Jones is not willing to incur this risk.

There are two problems with Kirzner's analysis and conclusion. First, in this example, the amount of risk incurred by Smith and Jones is not very different, contrary to Kirzner's claim. Since Jones borrowed the money to finance the purchase of his cab, if the cab business is not profitable, all he runs the risk of losing is the labor time he devoted to the enterprise. The lending bank or capitalist bears all the risk if Jones does not generate enough revenue to pay back his loan. This is the same exact loss to which Smith is exposed. If the fleet owner Brown goes out of business and is unable to pay Smith his wage, Smith will have lost perhaps the same amount of labor time as Jones. However, if the cab business proves to be extremely successful, Jones will gain entrepreneurial profit, while Smith will receive no more than his contracted wage. What, then, prohibits Smith from starting his own cab-driving business? For that matter, if Kirzner is right that factor owners are all making the same kinds of entrepreneurial judgments, why would anyone ever choose to work for someone else if credit were easily accessible to all?

Kirzner's discussion of the cab drivers Smith and Jones reveals that he sees the entrepreneurial profit that accrues to the independent contractor Jones as readily available to Smith. Nothing stands in Smith's way of himself receiving this profit except either his choice not to pursue it or his inability to notice that being an independent contractor has more potential rewards, without incurring any more risk, than does being an employee in a firm offering taxi services. It is apparent that Kirzner thinks that perceptible opportunities for gain are "in principle available to others," not just to the entrepreneurs who happen to notice and grasp them (Kirzner 1995, 40, emphasis added). For Kirzner, lack of fungible assets poses no barrier to acting on entrepreneurial insights. Thus he can write: "Entrepreneurial profits . . . are not captured by owners, in their capacity as owners, at all. They are captured, instead, by men who exercise pure entrepreneurship, for which ownership is never a condition" (Kirzner 1979a, 94). He draws this conclusion because he believes the asset poor cannot be systematically denied credit in an unregulated market economy.

If Kirzner is right that anyone can borrow to finance a speculative or productive investment project, whether or not they can demonstrate any collateral, then he is correct that any perceptible opportunity for gain is in principle available to others. The possibility that anyone can be an entrepreneur gives Kirzner's defense of the finders-keepers rule its ethical force. As Sen (1992) notes, all theories of justice call for the equal (or impartial) treatment of people in some conceptual realm. The claim that people are equal in some way is used to defend the justice of circumstances. For instance, in his defense of a market economy, Hayek appeals to the formal equality of all people under a legal regime that adheres to the rule of law. Kirzner points to the equal opportunity for all people to be entrepreneurs in his argument for the finders-keepers rule as a theory of distributive justice.[6]

Contemporary theories of the interest rate mechanism suggest that Kirzner's presumption that credit is available to anyone willing to pay market rates of interest is not an accurate description of a real-world financial system. Interestingly, Hayek seems to take the same position in the socialist calculation debate with Lange. He notes that one lamentable feature of market socialist models is that they would replace the competitive banking system with one large, government-run superbank that can only use the interest rate to allocate credit. Because the government bank would have to "lend to persons who have no property of their own," it would "bear all the risk and would have no claim for a definite amount of money as a bank has" (Hayek 1948g, 200–201). Hayek implies that one virtue of a competitive bank is that it can force borrowers to bear some of the risk involved in a loan agreement by requiring collateral. If so, since everyone does not have collateral, everyone is not in principle able to negotiate a bank loan. If everyone does not in principle have equal access to credit, then in the context of both production in a capitalist firm and speculation, everyone does not in principle have the opportunity to be an entrepreneur.

Bowles and Gintis call Kirzner's belief that the possession and distribution of wealth do not affect the outcomes of economic processes the "asset neutrality proposition" (Bowles and Gintis 1986, 68–71). They contend that the widespread acceptance of this proposition is due to the fact that the economics discipline has not shed itself from general equilibrium, perfect competition models that practitioners have used to show that the distribution of income would be the same irrespective of whether capital hired labor or labor hired capital (see, e.g., Samuelson 1957). The asset neutrality proposition supports the classical liberal belief that wealth holders have the same power in the determination of economic outcomes as do households with few assets. Although the foundations for this conclusion—based on perfect competition and equilibrium—are not compatible with Kirzner's own thinking, the asset neutrality proposition parallels his contention that the possession of wealth does not determine whether or not an entrepreneurial opportunity will be realized. Bowles and Gintis maintain that the asset neutrality proposition is false because credit markets are inherently plagued by imperfections that may prevent the asset poor from obtaining any credit no matter how high an interest rate they are willing to pay, while those possessing assets suitable as collateral to lending capitalists will be able to obtain loans at market rates of interest.

To make their case, Bowles and Gintis follow the model of Joseph Stiglitz and Andrew Weiss (1981), whose work shows that asymmetric information may prevent the interest rate from being an equilibrating variable in the loan market. While demanders of credit may react in traditional fashion to interest rate movements, credit suppliers, such as banks, are not necessarily eager to increase their lending when the demand price of loans rises. Banks care about the expected returns on loans, not simply about the interest borrowers are willing to pay. The two classic problems of markets with asymmetric information—moral hazard and adverse selection—prevent there being an isomorphic relationship between interest rates and expected returns. Since the willingness to lend is determined by the expected return on loans, the interest rate consistent with the optimal expected return for lenders may not be the interest rate that demanders are willing to pay.

The problem here is that lenders can surmise the types of risk borrowers might take, but they cannot know the decisions that borrowers will actually make after the loan contract is signed. Because lenders cannot know the risks borrowers will incur once a loan has been initiated, they attempt, when calculating their expected returns, to infer this information from the interest rate borrowers are willing to pay. In particular, lenders understand that as interest rates rise, borrowers have greater incentive to increase the risks they take and are thus more likely to default. The increased likelihood of moral hazard at higher interest rates means that high interest rates may not be correlated with increased returns for the lender. In addition, banks know that as interest rates rise, the pool of willing borrowers is more likely to include risk-loving borrowers who will take actions incompatible with the interests of the bank. Since banks have difficulty identifying these borrowers, if they do not attempt to infer who are risk-loving individuals from the interest rates potential borrowers are willing to pay, the probability of bad lending decisions increases with a rising interest rate, thereby lowering bankers' returns. In sum, the problem of adverse selection and the possibility of moral hazard mean that raising the interest rate in response to an excess demand for credit may influence the pool and behavior of borrowers in such a way that the expected returns of lenders declines. Because "the interest rate directly affects the quality of the loan in a manner which matters to the bank," credit markets may consequently experience persistent excess demand (Stiglitz and Weiss 1981, 409).[7] Bankers may hold interest rates below market equilibrium and use nonprice means to allocate (or ration) credit.

Although Stiglitz and Weiss do not draw any critical conclusions from the possible existence of credit rationing in an unregulated banking industry, Bowles and Gintis insist that credit rationing vitiates the asset neutrality proposition. One strategy banks employ in response to ignorance of the risks borrowers will take is to demand that loans be partly collateralized. As a result, the potential borrowers who are ultimately approved for loans are more likely to be those who possess assets that can be easily liquidated.[8] This means that wealth holders possess a decided advantage when they seek loans to finance entrepreneurial endeavors, and it helps to explain the correspondence Kirzner notices—and dismisses as insignificant for his theory—between individuals who undertake entrepreneurial activity and individuals who fill the capitalist role (Kirzner 1979a, 97). Contrary to Kirzner's belief, entrepreneurs usually are capitalists, because the asset poor are unable to obtain credit, no matter the interest rate they are willing to pay, while owners of significant assets face no such restriction.

Kirzner recognizes that arguments for the existence of credit market imperfections damage his position that entrepreneurial opportunities are in principle available to everyone. He maintains, however, that most theories of financial market imperfection ignore the existence of transaction costs. He argues that if a potential entrepreneur is willing to pay the market rate of interest but is unable to obtain financing, this is not an indication that credit is being rationed but a sign that there are transaction costs requiring the entrepreneur to offer higher interest rates to make the loan worthwhile to the bank. For instance, Kirzner remarks that the reputation of a potential entrepreneur may be unknown to a bank, and thus he will be asked to pay above-market interest rates. Although such a requirement could render the entrepreneurial endeavor unprofitable, we must face the fact that there are social "costs of securing recognition of one's competence and trustworthiness" that may result in some entrepreneurs facing higher borrowing costs than others (Kirzner 1979a, 101). Kirzner thus echoes George Stigler's (1967) conclusion that it is inappropriate to label credit markets as imperfect simply because different would-be entrepreneurs with varying and unknown reputations are asked to pay higher rates than "the" market interest rate.[9]

While Stigler's dismissal of the existence of credit market imperfection is acceptable when the claim of market imperfection "rests ultimately upon the inability of borrowers to get cheap funds" (Stigler 1967, 289), the charge of credit market imperfection levied by Stiglitz and Weiss and by Bowles and Gintis is linked to the apparent inability of some borrowers, particularly asset-poor individuals, to obtain funds at any price. "[I]t is a mistake," Bowles and Gintis assert, "to treat the [the existence of credit rationing] simply as a reflection of the existence of *frictions* in exchange relations"; they contend that "[f]riction will produce out of equilibrium alternations between excess demand and excess supply but not consistent . . . quantity constraints" that prevent access to credit to some potential entrepreneurs (Bowles and Gintis 1990b, 306). A critical interpretation of the credit rationing literature calls into question Kirzner's employment of the Chicago-school notion of transaction costs to buttress his claim that entrepreneurial opportunities are in principle available to all.

Kirzner also pursues another line of defense against the claim that credit markets are imperfect. "If a new idea holds forth promise, even after all trad- ` ing costs have been taken into account, of a yield to capitalists higher than they can obtain elsewhere," he argues, "their failure to exploit it constitutes an entrepreneurial error on their part" (Kirzner 1979a, 102). Thus he might explain the purported existence of credit rationing as another example of the pervasiveness of entrepreneurial error in an economy out of equilibrium. However, if the inability to obtain credit from a lending capitalist by an asset-poor, would-be entrepreneur constitutes an entrepreneurial error on the part of the capitalist, one wonders exactly where this error lies? Is the capitalist making an entrepreneurial error when declining to lend to the asset-poor entrepreneur? Or is the capitalist making the entrepreneurial error by failing to notice the opportunity seen by the asset-poor and frustrated entrepreneur? If the theory of credit rationing is correct in its conclusion that it is some-times impossible for lenders to acquire the necessary information about the credit risks a borrower will take, it is difficult to see how we might interpret that impossibility and the credit rationing to which it leads as an entrepre-neurial error, an error that a competitive market could potentially correct. If the second reading (that the lending capitalist does not notice the actual opportunity seen by our frustrated entrepreneur) captures Kirzner's mean-ing, it would not challenge the conclusion that capitalists do have an advan-tage in acting on entrepreneurial possibilities. Both interpretations of the existence of credit rationing as an instance of entrepreneurial error under-mine Kirzner's belief that entrepreneurial opportunities in the cases of spec-ulation and productive creativity are in principle available to everyone.[10]

Kirzner asserts, "What the entrepreneur sees is a prospective increment of value which others, although in no way handicapped as compared with our entrepreneur, have somehow failed to see" (Kirzner 1995, 38–39). If the asset poor are systematically denied access to credit, then only in the case of pure arbitrage can we be confident that all potential entrepreneurs face no handi-cap in seizing upon profit opportunities. The possibility of credit rationing means that when an opportunity involves production or speculation, an alert, asset-poor, would-be entrepreneur—as opposed to a wealthy entrepre-neur—will face possibly insurmountable obstacles when attempting to grasp that profit. Thus what Kirzner calls entrepreneurial profit would seem to be partly enabled by the prior ownership of assets and not solely a reward for entrepreneurial alertness. If a "profit" opportunity requires the prior ownership of capital, perhaps it can and should be justified by what Kirzner calls "the fruit-of-the-tree" ethic. According to Kirzner, people generally believe that an individual may legitimately appropriate output that emerges from a justly held asset. In cases where we might use the fruit-of-the-tree ethic to justify an income receipt, there would be no need to apply a finders-keepers ethic. This ethic would be applicable only in the evaluation of pure arbitrage opportunities.[11]

Denying the applicability of the finders-keepers ethic in cases involving production and speculation appears, however, to put Kirzner's positive theory of entrepreneurship in grave jeopardy. Real-world instances of pure arbitrage that require no interest expense because they do not involve the passage of time are likely to be rare, if not nonexistent. Most, if not all, profit opportunities have a speculative or productive element. In order to say that the fruit-of-the-tree ethic alone justifies income receipts from speculative and productive activities, one would have to accept that all the relevant factors of production were paid according to the value of their marginal products. Yet this could be so only in a world where all gains from speculative trade and production were exhausted. In such a world, there would be little, if any, room for entrepreneurship. This line of reasoning undermines the insights of Hayek and other Austrian economics concerning time, ignorance, and knowledge.

As an alternative, we might argue that pure profit opportunities are abundant in productive and speculative ventures but that they are not in principle available to everyone, because of the existence of credit rationing. Insofar as the finders-keepers ethic requires that any person may be a potential finder, this ethic cannot justify the receipt of pure profit. We might thus search for another ethic that is consistent with a world of ceaseless change and widespread ignorance and with a defense of free market outcomes. This alternative interpretation indicates that there are constraints on individual choice and impediments to entrepreneurial action. We might therefore legitimately conclude that these constraints and impediments call for a theory of distributive justice in order to understand the nature and possible ethical shortcomings of an unregulated capitalist market process. Perhaps the applicability of a finders-keepers ethic could be reestablished in an institutional environment where the possession of wealth did not confer any entrepreneurial advantage. Such an institutional environment might characterize a society that achieved Hayek's normative objective that the life chances of any person chosen at random would be maximized.

The preceding discussion shows, first, that we may not with confidence accept that a common law system produces a neutral set of rules and, second, that the market process may be systematically biased against the interests of the asset poor. These two conclusions lead us to search for an institutional structure—and the normative foundations to support that structure—that more fully promotes human well-being and the common good than does the market in a capitalist setting. This search will involve a greater role for democratic processes than Hayek is willing to grant. This chapter concludes with a brief argument for an elevated role for democratic processes in a subjectivist, post-Hayekian political economy. The rest of the book investigates the characteristics of an institutional structure that promotes universal human well-being in a way consistent with the socialist tradition, while remaining mindful of the knowledge problems Hayek has shown to be prevalent in a postrationalist, postmodern age.

The crux of Hayek's argument against democratic policy is that it often attempts to obtain interested (and hence unprincipled) goals—for instance, distributive justice. To accept goal-oriented policymaking as legitimate, he insists, poses a grave threat to individual freedom, because it opens the door to the use of government power to direct or limit the actions of specific individuals in order to achieve particular goals. Hayek maintains that individual freedom is protected if government power is restricted to ensuring that all people obey the same set of abstract, universal rules. He thinks that the common law achieves this objective, because he believes that it generally evolves into a system of mutually consistent, universal rules that aim at no particular result and are equally applicable to all. A legal system with these attributes ensures that people are ruled equally under the law, rather than being subject to the arbitrary commands of a group of people.

But Hayek's legal thought is not consistently subjectivist. While he acknowledges that the people controlling the government may well use government power in the effort to achieve their subjective goals, he does not recognize that common law judges may also act according to their subjective, theory-laden perceptions of just outcomes. Hayek does not recognize this because he imagines judges are somehow able to discover correct, commonly accepted rules appropriate to the objective facts of a case. A subjectivist account of the judicial process inspired by legal realism emphasizes the subjectivity of rules, facts, and even the perception of consistency in the law itself and pictures the judicial process as irreducibly creative. To understand the judicial process as creative erodes—partly, if not completely—the barrier

Hayek places between democratic, sometimes interested policymaking and the supposedly disinterested, evolved common law. From a subjectivist perspective, common law rules may well be as interested as Hayek thinks democratic policymaking is prone to be.

Others reach a similar conclusion. Hasnas (1995b) calls the rule of law a potentially dangerous myth. He accepts the realist critique of legal neutrality and worries that widespread belief in the rule of law leads to the public's acceptance of illegitimate uses of state power. Christainsen agrees that judges in government courts cannot know all the circumstances of time and place that would be necessary to pronounce objective decisions. He asserts that because "common law judges are decision-makers of enterprises—government courts—for which rights are not transferable, and sometimes not even defined, they are in the position of central economic planners" (Christainsen 1990, 503). Thus there is no discovery process in a common law court system to ensure what Christiansen calls "efficient" judicial decisions (ibid.). Both Hasnas and Christainsen believe that the solution to the potentially inefficient and biased nature of a common law system can be solved if we end the state monopoly over the provision of legal decisions and allow the development of a private court system with competing providers of adjudication services.

While private adjudication may have merits in particular cases, it is not obvious that private courts provide the best forum to determine the constitution of the common good. It is readily apparent that wealth can influence the outcomes of government court trials, even when some minimal efforts are made to provide legal representation for the poor. In a setting where adjudication is exclusively marketed, it would not be surprising to see an even greater correlation between wealth and the interests served by the decisions of private courts. Arthur Okun calls the threats that wealth and income pose to substantive equality before the law the "transgression of dollars on rights" (Okun 1975, 22), a transgression that Okun believes might be checked by limiting the domain of the market, rather than expanding it, and by invigorating the democratic sphere of social life.

The main point of the discussion in this chapter is that if law courts are as political as legal realism suggests, Hayek's defense of a common law system as a neutral method to discover the sense of justice and the rules that constitute the common good is called into question. Perhaps the chief difficulty with Hayek's legal theory is that, like economic opportunity and true knowledge, a singular sense of justice—or the common good—is not "out there" waiting to be found. Perhaps the common good needs to be created. As several critics of Hayek have argued, democratic government provides a framework where the nature of the common good might be debated and forged.

Unfortunately, finding a compelling defense of democracy in Hayek's thought is difficult. As Juliet Williams points out, "the real problem for Hayek is not that his commitment to liberalism conflicts with his desire to limit democracy, but rather that his version of central liberal principles does not entail democracy in the first place" (Williams 1997, 108). Hayek tends to emphasize the problems with democracy rather than recognizing that perhaps democratic institutions have evolved to help negotiate an agreement about the nature of the common good in a world in which knowledge is limited and subjective.

Gus diZerega's work on democracy as a spontaneous order is instructive in this regard. DiZerega follows Hayek in claiming that spontaneous orders "are rooted in the principle of voluntary consent," but diZerega argues, in contrast to Hayek, that democratic institutions aim to create "consent over community values and practices" (diZerega 1989, 206). Democracy involves a set of noninstrumental procedures—one person, one vote; freedom of speech, press, and assembly; and other rights of citizenship, separation of powers, and so on—that establish a framework permitting a collective conversation about the nature of the common good. DiZerega sees this as an ideal type that would exist "if citizens were to come to a free and uncoerced agreement about public policy" (ibid., 225).[12]

DiZerega defines the common good as "includ[ing] policies and practices which cannot be provided by markets alone, or which cannot be provided in adequate supply" (ibid., 228). These include the standard public goods identified by conventional economic analysis, protection against the harmful effects of the negative externalities generated by others, and those "measures and values [individuals] think will benefit [themselves] and others in [their] capacity as equal members of society" (ibid., 231). DiZerega argues that democracy performs an important function in allowing people, in their roles as citizens, to determine what is in the collective interest. What this collective interest, or common good, is and how citizens might discuss its nature are matters that diZerega does not address. One can tease out of his discussion, however, the possibility that social justice is, contrary to Hayek, part of the constitution of the common good. Chapter 5 of this book explores this possibility.

Before proceeding to the next chapter, I should acknowledge the argument that the real-world outcomes of democratic politics are dramatic departures from any ideal-type notion of the common good.[13] For instance, in The Political Order of a Free People, Hayek argues that the "so-called approval by the majority of a conglomerate of measures serving particular interests" that he believes is characteristic of modern democracy is a "farce" (Hayek 1979b, 134). Yet earlier in the same book, he explains that it is legitimate for government to use coercion to supply collective goods, even if those goods are not demanded by a "considerable majority." He contends:

> it will clearly be in the interest of the different individuals to agree that the compulsory levying of means to be used also for purposes for which they do not care so long as others are similarly made to contribute to ends which they desire but the others do not. Though this looks as if the individuals were made to serve purposes for which they do not care, a truer way of looking at it is to regard it as a sort of exchange: each agreeing to contribute to a common pool according to the same uniform principles on the understanding that his wishes with regard to the services to be financed from that pool will be satisfied in proportion to his contributions. (ibid., 45)

Yet since there is no way for Hayek to know how others value collective goods provided by democratic political action, it is not clear why a subjectivist or postmodernist should accept his portrayal of modern democracy as a farce.

Admittedly, real-world democracy may be imperfect and messy, but given the contestable nature of questions concerning justice, democracy has an attribute that the common law lacks: democratic politics institutes a forum for multiple, competing views of justice to be heard and debated.[14] In his critique of Hayek, Brian Crowley argues, democratic "politics relies on procedures to make possible and to encourage critical analysis in the constant search for agreement on the meaning of the good life and how it is to be pursued" (Crowley 1987, 291). If we accept the subjectivist and postmodern view that all facts, interpretations, and judgments are theory dependent and socially constituted, then the evaluation of what is an effective and beneficial economic order, or what is the common good, is open for discussion. The articulation of the common good needs to be created. Hayek, though, wishes to silence debate over the natures of justice and the common good by asserting that justice involves little more than the establishment of universal rules through a neutral case law procedure. Rather than following Hayek's failed path (if the legal realists are right), we might better conceive justice to be a goal—not a given—of an ongoing and collective conversation about the meaning of social welfare. In such a world, democratic policymaking is attractive because it often allows the possibility of a plurality of visions of distributive and procedural justice to be inspected. It permits the definition of a beneficial and effective economic order to be created in an open, dialogical process.

Social Justice and Hayekian Knowledge Problems

★

If there is reason to think that the common law process might not yield a disinterested evolution of property rights that serve the collective interest, then democratic processes and institutions should have a more prominent role than Hayek is willing to grant to deliberate about the nature of the common good and about the scope and limits of the property rights that promote it. But appealing to a democratic deliberation of the common good to replace Hayek's common law determination of the collective interest is not enough to develop an alternative conception of justice to compete with Hayek's. As Hayek notes, democracy, "being a method, indicates nothing about the aims of government," and "[i]n order to know what it is that we want others to accept [as the collective interest], we need other criterion than the current opinion of the majority" (Hayek 1960, 104). Several questions then arise: How should we understand the rough outline of the common good when we engage in democratic discussion of its specific features? In other words, what principle of justice does it make sense to use to help determine a welfare-enhancing distribution of property rights? Is there a socialist principle with some sort of objective basis that might successfully contend with Hayek's free market position? Can such a principle effectively address Hayekian knowledge problems? These are the questions that this chapter addresses.

To avoid the arbitrary exercise of power unleashed by temporary majorities, Hayek maintains that the legislation democratic government enacts to rectify the occasional injustices identified in the common law must be consistent with the requirements of the rule of law. In particular, democratic legislation should be universally applicable and impartially enforced. We have seen that Hayek thinks that the notion of impartiality embodied in the rule of law prohibits the use of government power to redistribute wealth and income. But the possibility of credit rationing and the inequality of opportunity that it engenders (which I pointed to in chap. 4) is a compelling instance of a bias or impartiality in the process of a capitalist market economy. This bias would seem to call for the redistribution of wealth and income in the interest of establishing an impartial market process that promotes the life chances of any person chosen at random. The well-being promoted by Hayek's rule-of-law utilitarianism will likely be seriously circumscribed to those already in the possession of substantial material wealth. This likelihood motivates a search for a different principle of justice that might guide a more universally applicable approach to advancing well-being.

In addition, the subjectivist account of well-being present in Hayek's thinking privileges individual preferences and self-knowledge in ways that can lead to perverse judgments about the collective interest. For example, impoverished and illiterate people might express complete happiness with their position in life. If so, it is difficult for the subjectivist utilitarian to challenge the self-evaluation of these people and to advocate public policy to address the apparent problems of poverty and illiteracy. Yet Hayek himself approvingly notes that modern governments "have made provision for the indigent, unfortunate, and disabled and have concerned themselves with questions of health and the dissemination of knowledge" (Hayek 1960, 257). Though Hayek here expresses support for a safety net, one searches his work in vain for any discussion of how adherence to the rule of law might encourage or oblige a government to establish such social welfare measures.

In light of the substantive inequality of opportunity in a market economy with an unequal distribution of wealth and in light of Hayek's inability to ground his support for welfare policies that might objectively improve the quality of life, this chapter argues that the principle that should focus a democratic and socialist discussion of the common good is the goal of developing in all people the capabilities to achieve an intersubjective account of human well-being. I will employ the capability perspective developed by Martha Nussbaum (1990, 1992a, 1992b, 1995) and Amartya Sen (1992, 1999), both following the work of Aristotle (1998). I will argue that many, if not all, of Hayek's criticisms of theories of social justice can be met by using the method of Nussbaum and Sen's capability theory to produce a principled account of the distribution of resources and opportunities. In chapter 6 and 7, I will use this capability perspective to provide normative foundations for an institutional arrangement—a variant of market socialism—that might achieve classical socialist objectives, while at the same time remaining mindful of the knowledge problems Hayek identified as endemic to centrally planned socialism.

A SKETCH OF THE CAPABILITY THEORY
OF SOCIAL JUSTICE

The main conclusion of Nussbaum and Sen's Aristotelian theory of social justice is that one of the primary goals of good government is to ensure that all people have the means or resources to develop their capabilities to lead choiceworthy lives. A choiceworthy life is one that a person has reason to value, because the available options allow him or her to achieve vital, or essential, human functions. Government should ensure, to the extent that natural, technical, and social constraints permit, that all individuals have the means so that they can choose to lead a complete, flourishing human life. A flourishing life is defined in terms of the attainment of essential functionings. For example, in order to lead a flourishing life, a person must be well nourished and educated, have access to adequate health care and shelter, have property that allows exploration of one's subjective appraisal of beneficial opportunities, and possess the ability to participate in social institutions and interactions with dignity. For the capability theorist, these are just some of the essential human functionings that public policy historically has attempted to support.[1]

How are these essential functionings to be specified? This is a rather controversial point, since theorists as diverse as Marx and Hayek have questioned whether there is any objectively definable, transcendent human nature that might be used to locate such functions. Nussbaum proposes that the capability approach does not require a transcendent or outside perspective on the nature of human being. Instead, human nature can be specified intersubjectively, through cross-cultural conversation that is oriented toward answering the question, what makes us recognize others as human; that is, when we notice other beings, how do we determine whether or not these beings qualify as human, rather than, say, as gods or monkeys? Nussbaum asserts that we make these distinctions by identifying certain essential qualities that we believe all human beings possess. We can discover these essential qualities through written, oral, and artistic records of diverse human societies scattered through time and geographic region, rather than through the isolated reflection of pure reason. Nussbaum characterizes the discoveries that we make in this cross-cultural search for the identifying characteristics of human being to be an "internalist essentialist" list (Nussbaum 1992a, 208), a list we can use to identify critical human functionings. Nussbaum's notion of internalist essentialism is compatible with what McCloskey calls the "conjective": our shared social and scientific discourse and language (Klamer and McCloskey 1989, 144). The hermeneutic tradition identifies this as the intersubjective: "the result of agreement reached through conversation and dialogue on the part of a community of historically formed and culturally embedded subjects" (Madison 1990a, 38).

Since the list of essential human functions is a social product, it cannot be fixed in stone; it is always subject to revision through ongoing conversation. Nevertheless, once we have constructed this provisional list, we have a tool that permits us to ask the extent to which social institutions allow individuals the opportunity to lead lives that enable them to achieve characteristic human functions. The list provides a benchmark to judge whether the prevailing set of social structures and distribution of resources enable all people to lead flourishing lives, if they should choose. If all people are not so enabled, then from the Aristotelian perspective, government has an obligation, in the name of justice, to design and implement policies that enhance the capability of people to achieve the essential human functions, or the opportunity to lead flourishing lives.

CAPABILITIES EQUALITY AND THE ETHICAL KNOWLEDGE PROBLEM

Five critical issues divide the Aristotelian conception of social justice from the elements of Hayek's critique that are based on what I have called the "ethical knowledge problem." First, Hayek's subjectivism leads him to be skeptical that people can agree on a substantive, outcome-oriented definition of justice that is characteristic of the Aristotelian capability theory. Second, the capability approach does not extol the virtues of individual choice in the same way as Hayek's utilitarianism. Third, the capability theory believes that people should be treated equally in a different conceptual space than under the law, as in Hayek's defense of the rule of law. Fourth, the two contending theories of justice have different notions of the claims individuals can make on society. Fifth, Hayek has a more extensive view of individual responsibility than does the capability perspective. I will consider each of these issues in turn and ask whether the capability theory can answer Hayek's likely criticisms.

Among the attributes of Hayek's thought, the first and in many ways most significant that is common to most varieties of liberalism is his skepticism regarding the possibility that individuals in a modern society can reach any principled agreement about the substantive characteristics of a good life. Liberal theorists, such as Hayek, reject the belief that diverse and differentially constituted individuals can share any common, outcome-oriented ends. What individuals can agree on, Hayek and other liberals believe, is a fair set of rules that increases the range and domain of activities that individuals can pursue without interfering in the affairs of others. The supposed agreement about a set of fair, neutral rules is the defining characteristic of what Hayek, following Adam Smith, calls the "Great Society," or free market capitalism (Hayek 1973, 2).

Nussbaum maintains that the liberal skepticism is overstated. Diverse individuals and societies have agreed and continue to agree about the attributes that are necessary for a being to be considered as human, rather than as god or monkey. The possession of practical reason, mortality, the need for nourishment, and dignity are some of these characteristics. Nussbaum believes this factual agreement can be employed to forge another agreement about the means a human being must possess in order to be capable of choosing to live a human life. If a being that we recognize as human lacks the means (say, adequate food) necessary to choose to function in a manner consistent with his or her nature (he or she is malnourished), then we can reasonably conclude that he or she does not have the capability to function as a good or flourishing human.

The notion of human nature functions here in an evaluative, rather than a descriptive, role. For example, the judgment that a malnourished woman without adequate food is not flourishing is similar to the judgment that a young child just learning the violin plays Vivaldi poorly. If we can create a working list of essential human functionings, we can also evaluate whether or not an individual is capable of choosing to function well. In the capability perspective, good human functioning can serve as a focal point around which diverse and differentially constituted individuals might conceivably forge an ethical consensus. If so, then perhaps it is not as difficult as the liberal holds to generate an agreement about the means necessary to be capable of choosing to live a flourishing human life. The liberal complaint that it is impossible to establish unanimity about any sort of substantive account of the requirements necessary for a good life would seem to be exaggerated. Nussbaum's assessment of the theory of John Rawls is instructive on this point.

In his famous theory of justice, Rawls proposes what he calls a "thin theory of the good," to ground his claim that a theory of economic justice should focus on the distribution of primary goods—such instruments as political and economic freedoms—that all people can use to pursue their separate conceptions of a good life (Rawls 1971, 396). Rawls's thin theory of the good accepts the classic liberal assumption that people have plural conceptions of the good life. However, Rawls also presupposes that the beings who pursue these plural conceptions are defined by the employment of two essential powers of moral responsibility: the capacity to honor fair terms of cooperation (sociality) and the capacity to pursue a conception of the good (the exercise of autonomous choice). The thin theory of the good presumes that social institutions should be created to nurture these two moral powers. Consequently, Rawls believes that liberal communities can rule out some subjectively conceived conceptions of the good life, for example, banditry and slavery. In this regard, Rawls is similar to Hayek, who also is not completely agnostic about the nature of the good life.[2]

Nussbaum argues that "Rawls's use of primary goods already commits him to a moral theory or conception of the good that intends to be comprehensive but is significantly incomplete" (Crocker 1992, 599). She admires Rawls's willingness to identify characteristics of a good life, and the characteristics that Rawls identifies—sociality and the exercise of autonomous choice—are shared by the Aristotelian capability approach. Nussbaum contends that if Rawls did not perform this exercise, there would be no way for him to support his theory of justice in the distribution of primary goods; that is, "Rawls cannot evaluate his primary goods as having worth without himself presupposing a thicker theory of good living, without taking 'some stand about what functions are constitutive of good human living' " (Crocker 1992, 599, quoting Nussbaum 1992b, 180). If the success of Rawls's liberal project and others like it requires some account of good living that is thought to be shared by the wider community, there is no easy way to foreclose a collective discussion of a broader, Aristotelian description of the good life by appealing to the subjective nature of individual happiness. A Rawlsian thin theory of the good and the Aristotelian thick theory of the good share a concern with the requirements for making choices that enhance well-being. If one accepts that the possession of the "procedural" capabilities to exercise choice and to obey fair rules are necessary to lead a good life, there is no principled reason to reject (perhaps in the name of a supposed antiperfectionism) that the possession of other "material" capabilities may be necessary as well.

Some cultural relativists might accept that members of a particular community could be able to agree on the attributes of a good life, but these relativists would point to the diversity of human communities and reject the Aristotelian presumption that a universal, cross-cultural agreement can be forged. This position has an affinity with certain strains of postmodernism that criticize the totalizing nature of Western thought and culture. From this perspective, the notion of human flourishing varies from culture to culture, thereby making the universality of any proposed list of human functions the product of invalid essentialist presumptions. Nussbaum (1992a) and Sen (1999) both argue against the vision of autonomous human communities that undergirds this sort of cultural relativism, for two different reasons. First, throughout history, communities have engaged in trade of merchandise and ideas, making it difficult to locate the origin of many supposedly culturally specific concepts in a singular, uncontaminated cultural past. Human cultures are historically intertwined. Second, every cultural tradition contains dissenters from the views that are presently dominant, making it suspect for, say, someone like former Singapore prime minister Lee Kuan Yew to claim that democracy is a Western idea that is foreign to East Asian societies. Sen points out that Asian cultural traditions contain their fair share of thinkers who have advocated democratic ideals and other notions of human flourishing that also exist in the Western tradition. The creation of a list of essential, universally applicable human functions is an empirical project that Nussbaum and Sen believe is supported by a careful and thoroughgoing empirical study of human communities, past and present. Its creation cannot be foreclosed by a rationalist, relativist presumption (often wearing postmodern garb) that such a list is impossible to produce.

In her advocacy of postmodernism, McCloskey remarks: "to admit that our only standard is our interpretive community is not to surrender to *arbitrary* standards, but to standards. There are no timeless standards outside those of an interpretive community" (McCloskey 1992, 108). When we pursue questions of justice, the relevant question is whether the "interpretive community" is the historical, worldwide human community or a particular society bound by the strictures of a particular time and geographic location. The Aristotelian capabilities approach supposes the relevant definition of "interpretive community" to be the historical, worldwide human community. DeMartino's critique of cultural relativism reinforces this conclusion. DeMartino argues that the belief that there are cultural insiders and outsiders depends on a narrow essentialism of culture that is vitiated by a thoroughgoing antiessentialism. DeMartino thinks that postmodernists should understand human cultures to be engaged in mutual constitution that blurs the boundaries between societies of a particular time and place (DeMartino 2000, 133–43).

This discussion about the possibility of agreement on the nature of the good life is closely linked to the second critical issue that merits attention in this discussion: the inviolability of individual choice. Liberal thinkers might resist the conclusion of the previous discussion because they would not wish to second-guess individuals' self-evaluations. Perhaps the previously mentioned malnourished woman reports that she is happy with her life. Perhaps she freely chooses to eat less food because only if she does can she feed her children so that they might be attentive students. If so, on what ground can the Aristotelian stand to claim that the woman's life is not a flourishing one? Perhaps she is simply choosing to maximize her utility subject to the material and social constraints that all individuals necessarily face. If individuals are the best judges of their well-being, then there is no place for the Aristotelian to claim that this or that freely choosing individual is not leading a flourishing life. Thus the normative work that the notion of human flourishing performs for the Aristotelian turns out to be no work at all. For the liberal, flourishing, like utility, is subjectively defined.

Both Nussbaum and Sen reject the belief in the sanctity of individual choice on which this liberal argument rests. They point out that it is a common attribute of human behavior for people in deprived situations to report satisfaction with their position. It seems that people often put a positive face on their negative circumstances. Thus the Aristotelian accepts the possibility that individuals can make deformed choices when in an environment deprived of the means enabling them to choose a flourishing life. Unless we accept the inviolability of individual choice as axiomatic, coterminous with a particular set of pregiven rights (see, e.g., Nozick 1974, ix), contemporary experience suggests that many people often find the pure liberal position difficult to sustain. For instance, it appears to be widely believed that the purchase of narcotic drugs and the sale of sexual services by children are often manifestations of deformed choices. This belief lies behind the prohibition of market exchanges for certain drugs and sexual acts in the United States and other countries throughout the world. Such widespread agreement to prohibit detrimental choices lends support to the Aristotelian belief that there can be a difference between the actions of individuals who have the resources to make choiceworthy decisions and the actions of individuals who possess the formal freedom to choose but lack the material, educational, and cultural advantages widely enjoyed by others.[3] A choiceworthy decision, once again, is one taken in an environment in which people have the means to choose a life that the collective human community regards as flourishing.

The third question for debate between the rule-utilitarian and capability perspectives is the dimension of social life in which people should be equal. Sen argues that every theory of justice that has gained acceptance in the modern world appeals to equal treatment of people in some conceptual space important to that theory. This appeal to equality serves as a marker that justice must be impartial, that a just society is one in which all people face similar circumstances (again, in some appropriate space). Given that all theories of justice stake a claim to equality, Sen astutely notes that what separates rival theories is the realm or space in which equality is supposed to apply, not whether or not the theories advocate some notion of equality. For example, procedural theories of justice, such as Hayek's, appeal to equality under the law: the rules specifying the acceptable use of government coercion should not discriminate among (types of) persons. Kirzner's finders-keepers theory of justice appeals to the possibility that everyone has an equal opportunity to be an entrepreneur. Contemporary liberals, such as Rawls, claim that justice requires people to have equal access to primary goods. Some socialists argue that the distribution of income is the critical space in which societies should strive for equality. Nussbaum and Sen explain that the capability approach to justice asks that society (through government policy) works to provide people with the resources allowing the equal capability to achieve essential human functionings.

In his review of Sen's Inequality Reexamined (1992), Robert Sugden challenges Sen's claim that all theories of justice are egalitarian. He points to Nozick's libertarianism as one notable exception to this claim. Because Nozickian libertarianism begins with the supposition that people have rights that limit the actions others may take with regard to them (and their rights) and their property, Sugden claims: "There is no space in which Nozick's theory *seeks* equality. Indeed, the theory does not seek anything at all: it has no goals, only constraints" (Sugden 1993, 1961). Sugden reinforces the long-standing belief, expressed also by Hayek in *The Constitution of Liberty* (1960), that there is a fundamental categorical distinction between the pursuit of material equality and that of freedom—or, to use different language, between positive liberty and negative liberty.[4] Sen is not so sure of this distinction. He anticipates Sugden's criticism: "Libertarians must think it important that people should have liberty. Given this, questions would immediately arise regarding: *who, how much, how distributed, how equal?* . . . In fact, the libertarian demands for liberty typically include important features of 'equal liberty,' e.g. the insistence on equal immunity from interference by others" (Sen 1992, 22, quoted in Sugden 1993, 1960). Sugden mistakenly focuses on Sen's appeal to the distribution of liberty in this passage and concludes that since there is no distributing agent in Nozick's utopia, Sen's characterization of libertarianism is misguided. However, what Sugden misses is that even in Nozick's utopia, rights are to be impartially (i.e., equally) enforced. In respect to rights enforcement, libertarians are indeed egalitarian. Thus from Sen's perspective there is not a categorical distinction between equality and liberty. There are only different ways in which modern theorists of justice answer the question, in what realm should people be treated impartially, that is, equally?

Hayek advocates the rule of law and its promise of equality under the law, because this form of equal treatment minimizes government interference with each individual's pursuit of his or her subjectively perceived opportunity. Hayek believes that this (negative) freedom from the coercive apparatus of government allows the market to work as beneficially and effectively as possible, not because freedom from coercion is necessary to secure a set of libertarian natural rights. In this context, "benefit" and "effectiveness" mean that individuals are free from community intervention in their pursuit of mutually beneficial opportunities for exchange and cooperation, as judged by each individual. The rule of law, in Hayek's mind, establishes a framework that "provide[s] the maximum of opportunity for unknown individuals to learn of facts that we ourselves are yet unaware of and to make use of this knowledge in their actions" (Hayek 1960, 30). In his defense of equality under the law, Hayek minimizes the degree to which material constraints can prevent individuals from seizing opportunities yielded by their unique insights and focuses his concern on the ways in which arbitrary government can restrict individuals. Despite observing that "the benefits we derive from the freedom of others become greater as the number of those who *can exercise* freedom increases" (ibid., 32, emphasis added), Hayek believes that we must confine the notion of justice to how people's actions affect others—in this case, government officials who interpret and enforce rules—and that we must exclude from it any concern for the material possessions and substantive opportunities individuals possess.

Sen maintains that consequentialist, rule-utilitarian liberals, such as Hayek, poorly identify the appropriate realm of equality. In order to achieve Hayek's goal of increasing the "number of those who can exercise freedom," more will often be required than following the rule of law. Negative freedom and the presence of equality under the law can be compatible, for example, with the starvation of peasants, who lack food not because a coercive power has denied them their nutrition but because they possess no property acceptable in a market exchange for food. Sen notes that if, at the heart of the matter, theorists, such as Hayek, are concerned with actual freedom of individuals and not merely their formal freedom, "there is no escape from looking for a characterization of freedom in the form of alternative sets of accomplishments that we have the power to achieve" (Sen 1992, 34). In other words, we only have reason to value a particular state of freedom if individuals can make choices that can lead to intersubjectively identifiable good consequences. Hayek's rule utilitarianism cannot elude this point by focusing on the way in which coercion limits choice and defining away concern for the way in which material deprivation limits choice.

For Sen, freedom is valuable to the extent that individuals have the capability or opportunity to choose a life that is characterized by good human functioning. People are then free only if they are able (whether or not they so choose) to achieve a state of well-being. In this regard, a starving peasant lacks what Sen calls "well-being freedom," even though he might enjoy Hayek's negative freedom. Sen's position is that justice requires not equality under the law but the equal capability for all people to lead choiceworthy lives, lives that are consistent with human flourishing.

The fact that Hayek's equality is consistent with starvation and other forms of deprivation while Sen's is not would seem to make Sen's well-being freedom more attractive as a normative goal than Hayek's freedom under the law. The appeal of an approach like Sen's would seem to be implicitly attractive even to Hayek. Throughout his writing, from The Road to Serfdom ([1944] 1976) to The Mirage of Social Justice (1976), Hayek maintained that a modern government should ensure a minimum income to those who are not able to participate in market exchange. While this position is laudable, it is unprincipled and groundless in a framework that elevates equality under the law as the guiding normative principle for modern society.[5] As Nussbaum remarks, without an account of the constituents of a good life, "however vague, that we take to be shared, we have no adequate basis for saying what is missing from the lives of the poor or marginalized or excluded" (Nussbaum 1992a, 229). In his framework, Hayek has no way to justify his concern for the poor as anything more than a personal preference. Libertarians, such as Block (1996), can thus reject Hayek's defense of a minimum income as unprincipled. A more appealing and just way to evaluate basic income and other welfare-enhancing proposals is to use Nussbaum and Sen's equality of capabilities standard and its advocacy of well-being freedom, rather than Hayek's equality under the law standard and its support for negative freedom.

In the fourth critical debate between the rule-utilitarian and capability perspectives, Nussbaum notes that the Aristotelian conception of social justice holds that individuals have a claim on the larger society, particularly government, to provide the resources necessary to develop the basic human capabilities (Nussbaum 1992a, 228–29), while Hayek rejects this view. Hayek argues that these Aristotelian claims on society are meaningless, "because 'society' cannot think, act, value, or 'treat' anybody in a particular way"; he contends that "[i]f such claims are to be met, the spontaneous order which we call society must be replaced by a deliberately directed organization" (Hayek 1976, 103). This argument is crucial in Hayek's emphasis on the distinction between the material constraints on choice and the coercive governmental constraints on choice.

Hayek's position here is rather precarious and, in the end, probably untenable. In effect, he is saying that because society is not a responsible individual—it is a spontaneous order, like the weather—it makes as much sense to insist that individual members of society can make a claim on it for any particular substantive benefits as it does to argue that these same individuals have a claim on the weather to be sunny on a particular day. Despite his conviction that it is nonsensical to think that individuals can make a claim on a spontaneous order, such as the weather or society, Hayek does believe that government rightly exists to protect individuals' separate property rights. Because it serves what Hayek sees to be the common interest, individuals do have the right to expect government to devote coercively collected resources (i.e., taxes) in the protection of their private domains. Government must appropriate resources to be able to prosecute thieves, swindlers, and trespassers in order to secure individual property. Individuals can legitimately expect that government will take positive action to enforce the rules of law. Hayek's comparison of society to the weather as equivalent, impersonal spontaneous orders in order to demonstrate the bankruptcy of concepts of social justice ignores the fact that protection of private property also involves government agencies providing individuals with substantive benefits. These benefits take the form of collectively appropriated resources supporting the legal and enforcement apparatus that is called into action when an individual's property right is violated. Individuals interested in protecting their property have a claim to substantive benefits from government agencies that is not categorically different from a claim to welfare rights.

In their book *The Cost of Rights*, Stephen Holmes and Cass Sunstein challenge the distinction between the so-called negative freedom from government coercion that is usually associated with the possession of property rights and the positive freedom that might require material support from the government and that is associated with welfare rights. This distinction underlies Hayek's criticism of social justice. Both property rights and welfare rights require the public authority to rectify violations of those rights. Governmental agencies must use tax revenues to fund the capture of thieves or the sanction of government officials who arbitrarily confiscate property, in a similar way that governmental agencies must deploy tax revenues to provide food to the hungry or education to the illiterate. Any legally enforceable right requires some form of active governmental response when that right is absent or violated. The fact that legal rights of any sort always require government performance leads Holmes and Sunstein to the conclusion that all rights are "positive": "The financing of basic rights through tax revenues helps us see clearly that rights are public goods: taxpayer-funded and government-managed social services designed to improve collective and individual well-being. All rights are positive rights" (Holmes and Sunstein 1999, 48). The real issue at hand in the defense of Nussbaum and Sen's capability approach against Hayek's rule utilitarianism is thus not the legitimacy of individuals' positive claims on government for substantive benefits but the underlying definitions of the common good and individual well-being that support the justice of any particular governmental use of coercive power to collect and deploy resources.

The fifth and final question to consider in this discussion bridges Hayek's ethical knowledge problem and his factual knowledge problem: to what extent are individuals responsible for their actions? In Hayek's view, in order to give people the incentive to act in a socially beneficial manner, they must be held to be responsible for both their material successes and their material failures. When individuals understand that the government will not compensate them for their lack of material success, even when their material shortcomings reduce the life chances of their children, they are more apt to engage in mutually beneficial market exchanges that contribute to the general interest.

Sen maintains that the capability perspective also values individual responsibility, but in a somewhat attenuated form when compared to Hayek's views (Sen 1992, 148–50). Sen accepts that it is generally desirable for people to be held responsible for both good and bad choices. But responsibility for the result of bad choices only pertains if the choice was made in a capability-rich environment. A young adult who lacks proper nutrition, adequate education, and appropriate shelter cannot be judged as wholly responsible for that plight if he or she was raised in an impoverished environment. Nevertheless, as Sen puts it, "[i]f the social arrangements are such that a responsible adult is given no less freedom (in terms of [capability] set comparisons) than others, but he still wastes the opportunities and ends up worse off than others, it is possible to argue that no unjust inequality may be involved" (ibid., 148). For Sen, this conclusion only reinforces the distinction between the formal freedom people enjoy under the rule of law and the substantive well-being freedom that the capability theorist advocates.

CAPABILITIES EQUALITY AND THE FACTUAL KNOWLEDGE PROBLEM

Hayek's factual knowledge problem refers to the dispersed, fragmented, and subjective nature of human knowledge. There are two dimensions of Hayek's factual knowledge problem that the capability theory of justice must confront. One concerns the incentive effects of social welfare policies. Hayek argues that the desire for social justice often translates into some central authority deciding the resources that particular people should appropriately receive. He believes that altering the rewards people receive for their efforts from the spontaneous outcomes generated by diverse market exchanges impairs the incentives individuals face, to the overall detriment of most people. A second concern is whether government officials have access to knowledge necessary to implement social welfare policies.

The focus on incentives leads Hayek to distinguish between compensation received "inside" the market, as a consequence of productive efforts valuable to others, and compensation received "outside" the market, through government provision for no productive efforts, say, a subsistence food grant. As he admits, his arguments about the disincentive effects of centrally allocated resources are relevant only to those redistributive efforts that apply "inside" the market (Hayek 1976, 136). If a theory of social justice insists that a person should receive x for his productive efforts (where x could be the minimum wage or the minimum price of a bushel of wheat), its practical implementation would impair the functioning of the market process, since it would misdirect the productive efforts of some individuals. For example, ensuring that farmers receive at least some specified minimum price for wheat might result in the production of more wheat than other people desire at that price. But if government assures people a minimum income if they are unable to participate in market exchange, Hayek believes that such action should not have undesirable social consequences in terms of the effectiveness or efficiency at which the market coordinates and utilizes dispersed knowledge.

The question here is whether the Aristotelian demand that a just society provide, to the extent that it is able, the resources for all individuals to develop their capabilities to achieve good human functioning would impede the beneficial effects of the market process. One issue is how to judge those beneficial effects. Since the Aristotelian judges well-being in terms of capability rather than preference or utility satisfaction, if a greater degree and distribution of capability is achieved in an Aristotelian social democracy rather than in a Hayekian free market, social democracy is preferable to a society dominated by markets, even if the market society generates more aggregate wealth. For the Aristotelian, if we decide that the appropriate evaluative space in which to strive for equality is the capability space, then that is also the appropriate space in which to consider the problem of efficiency. The achievement of "[e]fficiency in the capability space . . . would require that no one's capability can be further enhanced while maintaining the capability of everyone else at least at the same level" (Sen 1992, 143–44). This means that as long as a policy to enhance some people's capabilities does not impair the capabilities of others, the policy should be undertaken in the interests of justice.

Since the evaluative space of the Aristotelian differs from that of the liberal Hayekian, the manner in which economists judge whether a policy impairs the results generated by the market process is clearly affected by the choice of this space. But even if we grant for the moment the merits of judging the market in terms of the fairness of the process, it is not apparent that the Aristotelian concern for capability enhancement falls prey to Hayek's critique of policies that apply "inside" the market. The Aristotelian argument as developed by Nussbaum and Sen does not insist that people should receive x for their productive efforts. The Aristotelian concept of social justice requires that people have the capability to make choiceworthy decisions when they engage in market exchange. The Aristotelian approach is concerned with capabilities and the means available to individuals, not with the actual achievements those individuals obtain.

To this point, it appears that the capability approach to social justice can answer the Hayekian objections. However, the last subject of contention is not so easy to resolve in the favor of the capability theory. The question is this: can government officials obtain the knowledge that would enable them to implement policies to achieve equality of capability?

Hayek's and Sen's separate remarks about the notion of equality of opportunity reveal some of the practical difficulties facing the capability approach. Hayek contends that to achieve true equality of opportunity, "government would have to control the whole physical and human environment of all persons, and have to endeavor to provide at least equivalent chances for each" (Hayek 1976, 84–85). To accomplish equality of opportunity in practice, government would have to control "every circumstance which would affect any person's well-being" (ibid., 85). Not only would this destroy the market order, but the knowledge problem facing a government that strives to control the circumstances affecting well-being would, Hayek asserts, be "apt to produce a nightmare" (ibid.).

One way to dodge Hayek's complaint might be to define equality of opportunity in a Rawlsian manner, as the equal possession of a set of primary goods—such as a basic education, a food basket with a minimum caloric intake, or a subsistence income—that are universally and equally distributed without regard to the concrete circumstances individuals face. While Sen is clear that the aspiration for equality of capability is indeed a desire for a type of equality of opportunity, he seeks to distance himself from conceptions of equality of opportunity—such as Rawls's—that are "defined in terms of the equal availability of some *particular means*, or with reference to equal applicability (or equal *non-applicability*) of some *specific barriers or constraints*" (Sen 1992, 7). This is because diverse people have different abilities to turn equivalent means into the capabilities to achieve the essential human functionings. For instance, an active pregnant woman requires more calories to be able to achieve good health than does a sedentary old man. From an approach that seeks equality of capabilities, the pregnant woman would need to receive a larger caloric intake.

Unfortunately for the capability perspective, achieving the goal of equality of capability does seem to place a large epistemic burden, at least in some circumstances and in regard to the attainment of some functionings, on government officials to obtain the requisite knowledge. How, for instance, would government officials know whether all people have the equal capability to appear in public with dignity and without shame? Hayek's knowledge problem places limits on the extent to which government officials can implement policies to achieve capabilities equality. But those limits should not let us overlook the possible benefits a capability perspective might produce. For instance, the Americans with Disabilities Act promotes the equal capability of mobility when it requires that public places be accessible to the disabled.

A theory of justice that focuses on equality under the law or equality of a basic income is not able to guide public policy in such capability-enhancing directions. Thus, as one counter to Hayek's knowledge-based critique of equal opportunity, Nussbaum notes that the thick theory of the good offered by the capability approach is intended to be "vague" (Nussbaum 1992a, 215). By this she means that capability-enhancing policies might have many different concrete specifications that attend to local variations in culture, resource availability, and community wealth. As a vague guide to public policy that admits the impossibility of human perfectibility but nevertheless seeks to improve welfare-promoting institutions where feasible, it would appear possible to encourage capability development without necessarily destroying the market order.

A crucial aspect to consider in the evaluation of Hayek's claim that totalitarianism lurks in theories of justice that call for some sort of equality of opportunity is the recognition that an ethical defense of the market can be derived from the capabilities approach to justice. Nussbaum claims that "strong separateness" is one of the basic functional capabilities. Strong separateness means "being able to live one's own life in one's very own surroundings and context" (Nussbaum 1992a, 222). One could argue that the achievement of this capability requires the ownership of private property and the freedom to exchange it. Sen explains: "We have good reasons to buy and sell, to exchange, and to seek lives that can flourish on the basis of transactions. To deny that freedom in general would be in itself a major failing of a society" (Sen 1999, 112). This is especially true in the area of choice of occupation. There are what Sen calls "process aspects" of freedom and human flourishing that place value on the capability to participate in social institutions, such as government and economic exchange (ibid., 17). At its root level, there are aspects of the capability approach that can provide normative justification for a market economy.[6]

The process aspects of human flourishing, however, do not foreclose the opportunity aspects of human flourishing afforded by the possession of adequate means to make choiceworthy decisions. The defense of the market that can be gleaned from the capability approach is not a defense of laissez-faire capitalism but a defense of a market economy embedded in an institutional framework that nurtures the opportunity aspects of human flourishing. Nussbaum calls this "institutional welfarism" (Nussbaum 1990, 228). This foundational commitment to capability enhancement is in contrast to a residual welfare state that provides only for those who fall through the cracks of a predominantly market economy. In short, Nussbaum believes that the capability approach calls for a form of social democracy similar to that found in the Scandinavian welfare states. She cites Sweden and Finland as examples of countries that have effectively utilized a capabilities-like approach to develop a set of public policies that allow their citizens the possibility of choosing to function well. In contradiction to Hayek's warning first raised in *The Road to Serfdom* and repeated thirty years later in *The Mirage of Social Justice*, it is not apparent that a market economy embedded in a welfare-promoting state will disintegrate into a nightmare. Perhaps Hayek's pessimism is a result of a failure on the part of the classic liberal tradition that he reveres to adequately theorize the requirements for effective individual choice. Nussbaum remarks:

> It is frequently charged that there is, in the kind of social democracy imagined in the Aristotelian conception, a deep tension between the value of well-being (and of public care for well-being) and the value of choice. . . . The Aristotelian conception insists that this tension is, to a great extent, illusory. . . . Choice is not only not incompatible with, but actually requires, the kind of governmental reflection about the good, and the kind of intervention with laissez-faire, that we find in Aristotelian social democracy. (ibid., 238)

SOCIALISM AND CLASS JUSTICE

The postmodern Marxist rejection of the evolutionary teleology that made socialism appear to be inevitable to Marx and Engels demands a normative reading of Marx, and many people have read Marx through an Aristotelian lens (see, e.g., Gilbert 1992, McCarthy 1992, de Ste. Croix 1981). The Aristotelian concern to fashion a multidimensional account of well-being and human flourishing resonates more with a postmodern Marxian normativity than with natural rights philosophies, utilitarianism, or some version of social contract theory. A Marxian interpretation of Aristotelian flourishing can supplement Nussbaum and Sen's capability theory of social justice in a manner that allows the capability approach to be a normative rudder for a postcapitalist, socialist future and not simply a justification for a humanized capitalism, or social democracy.

What the Marxian tradition can add to the capability approach is a concern to eliminate class exploitation, where class refers to the process of producing, appropriating, and distributing surplus labor. Surplus labor is the "*extra* time of labor the direct producer performs beyond the necessary labor" essential "to produce the consumables customarily required by the direct producer to keep working" (Resnick and Wolff 1987, 115). In contrast to social democracy, socialism aims to abolish class exploitation, which occurs when the producers of surplus labor do not participate in appropriating the fruits of their efforts. At a minimum, a socialist future calls for worker participation in the appropriation of surplus labor and in decision making regarding the distribution of that surplus.

While Nussbaum and Sen do not include participating in the process of appropriating and distributing surplus labor as one of the capabilities that promote human flourishing, George DeMartino (2003) argues that there is nothing problematic about incorporating a consideration for realizing class justice into the capability approach. Following Resnick and Wolff's understanding of the class process to involve the production, appropriation, and distribution of surplus labor, DeMartino is led to the conclusion that there are three dimensions of class justice: realizing productive justice, appropriative justice, and distributive justice. For DeMartino, productive class justice involves fairness in the allocation of the work to produce surplus labor. The achievement of appropriative class justice requires the elimination of exploitative class processes. Distributive class justice concerns fairness in the division of the social surplus, particularly the distribution of profit and wealth. DeMartino contends that each dimension of class justice contributes to the development of human capabilities.

Chapters 6 and 7 of this book use such a Marxian-enhanced capability approach to explore socialist perspectives on appropriative and distributive justice and the alternative institutional forms that might achieve them. The capability perspective can provide normative foundations for a theory of socialism that can avoid Hayek's notion of the factual knowledge problem and his related critique of central planning. Chapter 6 proposes worker appropriation and self-management as an institutional form that would both eliminate exploitation and avoid Hayek's critique of central planning. Marx explicitly called for the abolition of the wages system, a goal that would be achieved in worker self-management. I will defend worker self-management and appropriation on Marxian, capability-enhancing grounds, as an essential institution in a form of socialism that might not fall victim to Hayekian knowledge problems.

Chapter 7 takes up the question of socialist distributive justice. What might Marx's admonition to distribute "to each according to need" mean in the context of a just distribution of the social surplus in a Hayekian world without central planning? Given a commitment to worker self-management, I will link the discussion of the just distribution of the social surplus to the important issue of the finance of worker self-managed firms. Specifically, what sort of distribution of income and/or wealth will best facilitate creation of new worker self-managed firms? The answer to this question will bear on the ability of self-managed firms to function effectively in a market process. Chapter 7 investigates several proposals, paying special attention to two of them: (1)

John Roemer's defense of a coupon stock market and quasi-socialized owner-ship of capital goods and (2) Bruce Ackerman and Anne Alstott's plan to insti-tute an ongoing redistribution of wealth, while preserving the private owner-ship of capital. Both ideas appeal to the potential for advancing effective equality of opportunity. Chapter 7 evaluates these two different proposals especially in terms of their capacities to facilitate worker self-management and to dodge Hayekian knowledge problems. Finally, it seems prudent to leave aside any consideration of DeMartino's notion of productive class jus-tice, since on the face of it, fairness in allocating work would seem to require a central authority responsible for assigning work roles. I will here take Hayek's critique of central planning to be definitive in rejecting this possibility.

CHAPTER 6

Socialist Appropriative Justice
and the Labor-Managed Firm

★

To make the case that a socialist future absent exploitation might be achieved by labor-managed enterprises operating in the context of private ownership and markets, a more thorough exploration of the nature of the injustice of capitalist exploitation is necessary. This is so because many of the traditional Marxian interpretations of the injustice of exploitation invariably concentrate on the ownership patterns of the means of production. Exploitation is interpreted as the result either of illegitimate private ownership itself (see, e.g., Husami 1980) or of the uneven—and hence unjust—distribution of privately owned means of production (see, e.g., Roemer 1994). Both interpretations call for heavy state involvement in production to rectify exploitation, thereby exposing them to Hayek's knowledge problem critique. Unlike Marxists—such as Cohen (1995), Husami, and Roemer—who believe that capitalist exploitation involves the unjust ownership and distribution of private property, I will argue that exploitation violates principles of appropriative and contractual justice. To make this case, I will show how David Ellerman's labor theory of property might be combined with Resnick and Wolff's theory of exploitation and enriched by Nussbaum and Sen's interpretation of Aristotelian moral theory to support a novel explanation of the injustice of capitalist exploitation.

The strength of Ellerman's labor theory of property in a debate with Hayek is that it directs our moral gaze away from the ownership of productive property to focus on the agent of appropriation in the firm. Ellerman's theory of justice leads to a rejection of the capitalist form of private property, rather than to a rejection of private property altogether. By the capitalist form of private property, I mean the ability of the owner of the means of production to appropriate the entire output of an enterprise that employs wage labor. To eliminate the capitalist form of private property does not require that productive property be publicly or socially owned. The elimination of the capitalist form of private property is consistent with a worker's cooperative renting land, machinery, and buildings from private individual and corporate owners. Ellerman's theory of just appropriation is consistent with a position that can be teased out of Marx's writings but that is not usually considered by contemporary Marxist theorists.

As Ellerman presents it, the labor theory of property is a deontological theory of justice that couples Locke's contention that people have a natural right to their labor with Kant's categorical imperative that people should treat each other "never simply as a means, but always at the same time as an end" (Ellerman 1988, 1110, quoting Kant 1964, 96). In Ellerman's view, the fundamental injustice of capitalism is that wage labor assumes the legal status of a thing in a capitalist firm. To rectify this injustice requires prohibiting the wage-for-labor-time exchange, an exchange that Ellerman sees as fraudulent, thereby abolishing the typical capitalist enterprise. A just economy, for Ellerman, is one in which joint production processes are carried out cooperatively by democratic, labor-managed firms in which all staff members collectively appropriate the entire product of the firm. These democratic, collectively appropriating firms may have to rent the means of production from private owners, but ownership of the means of production would give no right to appropriate the entire product of the firm, as is the case in capitalism. In other words, the labor theory of property requires that labor, rather than capital, be the residual claimant. It insists on the abolition of the wages system, a goal that Marx explicitly advocated (Marx 1965, 79).

When read in the context of the question concerning the relationship between capitalist exploitation and the Marxist theory of justice, Ellerman's labor theory of property is consonant with authors—such as Bloch (1986), Gilbert (1992), Kain (1992), Kamenka (1972), Nussbaum (1992b), and Peffer (1990)—who see in Marx's work an underlying moral commitment to the promotion of human dignity, human flourishing, and complete human being. The labor theory of property elucidates at least one dimension of the young Marx's belief that in capitalism, man is not "the highest being for man," since in a capitalist enterprise, wage laborers are treated instrumentally (Marx 1975, 187). Ellerman's use of the labor theory of property to advocate democratic, labor-managed workplaces in a market economy with widely distributed property ownership goes at least part way in satisfying the traditional Marxian aspiration that in postcapitalist society, producers will associate with each other cooperatively, while at the same time avoiding the knowledge problems Hayek identified to be endemic to central planning. But the labor theory of property does not offer a clear principle of distributive justice. This lack necessitates a separate discussion, in chapter 7.

Much of the following argument hangs on a precise definition of exploitation. Resnick and Wolff's definition of exploitation is the appropriation of surplus labor by those who do not participate in the production of that surplus (Wolff and Resnick 1987, 167–68). This definition may be helpfully contrasted with that of John Roemer, who understands exploitation to be "the unequal exchange of labor for goods" (Roemer 1986, 260). Resnick and Wolff's definition seems to be more compatible with Marx's observations that "the consumption of labor-power is completed . . . outside the market or the sphere of circulation" and that "the consumption of labor-power is at the same time the production process of commodities and of surplus-value"— value that, when appropriated by nonproducers, constitutes exploitation (Marx 1976, 279). Marx's view was that exploitation occurs in the appropriation of property titles created in production, not during exchange.[1] This distinction between production and exchange is lost if we accept Roemer's definition of exploitation as the unequal exchange of labor and goods. Roemer's definition does not reflect Marx's assumption that in the market, labor power is exchanged for a wage with equivalent value, and it ignores the issue of the appropriation of newly produced commodities.

The following discussion is concerned primarily with capitalist exploitation: the appropriation by capitalists of the surplus value (or the value of the commodities produced by surplus labor) created by the productive workers. According to this Marxian understanding, the appropriation of surplus value in the capitalist firm constitutes a type of "social theft" (Wolff and Resnick 1987, 125), or "the theft of alien labor time" (Marx 1973, 705). Many Marxists believe that the labor theory of value describes the conditions that enable this theft; but because it is a descriptive theory, it is difficult to use the labor theory of value by itself in order to identify the moral basis of this injustice. My goal here is to discover a normative principle that is violated by capitalist exploitation, so that we may legitimately consider it to be a type of theft, or unjust taking.

Resnick and Wolff's definition of exploitation as the appropriation of surplus labor by those who did not participate in the production of that surplus leads to a narrowly focused theory of justice. Since their definition of exploitation maintains that exploitation occurs in production, criticizing market relations, monetary exchange, and private ownership does not necessarily result from an inquiry into the potential unjust nature of capitalist exploitation. To see this, we might consider three possible reasons that exploitation is unjust.[2]

First, exploitation might be unjust because—and only because—producers cannot retain the surplus labor they independently produce and appropriate. This appears to be the position of those Marxists, such as Roemer, who believe that independent commodity producers can be exploited. Second, exploitation could be unjust because surplus labor—and only surplus labor—is appropriated by someone (e.g., capitalists) who did not participate in the production of that surplus. From this perspective, the question of who appropriates the commodities created by necessary labor poses no problem for a Marxian theory of justice. Both of these two reasons generally lead to an indictment of private property in all of its forms, rather than to a criticism of the specific capitalist form of private property that is associated with capitalist appropriation.

The third possibility is that exploitation might be unjust because workers do not appropriate any of the product of the enterprise, even if surplus labor is not produced at all. We can begin to find a clear and persuasive normative foundation for criticizing capitalist appropriation—that is, that capitalists, not workers, appropriate the entire product of the enterprise—in Ellerman's labor theory of property. For Ellerman, the right to appropriate is distinct from the ownership rights in productive property. It is thus possible to implement a change in the appropriating agent without socializing the means of production, or necessarily altering the distribution pattern of property rights. The specifically capitalist form of private property in which the owners of productive property are the appropriating agents would, however, be abolished. From an Ellermanian perspective, eliminating capitalist exploitation does not entail government planning and centralized ownership of the means of production. Instead, Ellerman's labor theory of property challenges the justice of the wage-for-labor-time exchange and advocates a system of labor cooperatives in a market context in which property ownership may (or may not) be widely dispersed. In doing so, it provides a normative justification for Marx's call to abolish the wage labor system.

Defining Appropriation

The first step to show how Ellerman's labor theory of property might illuminate the injustice of exploitation is to define the concept of "appropriation." The meaning of appropriation is not always well specified in the Marxian literature. Resnick and Wolff define appropriation to mean to receive "directly into his or her hands" (Wolff and Resnick 1987, 146). Their definition may be rearticulated as "to become the first title holder of an asset." By this definition, appropriation can never occur as the result of an exchange, because during exchange, already-defined property rights are transferred between two parties.

In his classic presentation of the labor theory of property, John Locke confined the issue of appropriation to the first ownership of previously unowned (or commonly owned) natural goods. But Ellerman points out that the question of appropriation can also refer to the assignment of property rights to newly manufactured commodities that are produced using inputs with clearly defined property titles. In the process of production, new goods are created that were not previously owned by any one, and thus they cannot be acquired through exchange. For example, an automobile that emerges at the end of an assembly line has no obvious, preexisting property right attached to it. This automobile must, therefore, be appropriated by someone; someone must become the first owner of this automobile.

Ellerman also uses the word *appropriation* in another sense. In the process of fabricating a commodity, such as an automobile, some property titles are extinguished. For example, the electric power that is used to manufacture a car in a capitalist enterprise no longer exists as a legal entity that can again be bought and sold after the car has been produced. The firm is the last owner of the electric power that is embodied in the newly minted car. Perhaps more significant, in a typical capitalist production process, the capitalist is the last owner of workers' labor time. As Marx noted, in a capitalist enterprise, "the worker works under the control of the capitalist to whom his labor belongs" (Marx 1976, 291). To be the last owner of a property right is sometimes referred to as expropriation. Ellerman asks us to think of this expropriation as the appropriation of the liabilities involved in producing the automobile. It is important to be alert to this additional dimension of appropriation in Ellerman's theory, because his version of the labor theory of property focuses our attention on the appropriation of the entire product of the firm. To speak of the appropriation of the entire product in Ellerman's sense refers to being the first owner of outputs or assets created in the production process, as well as to being the last owner of the input liabilities, especially labor time, con-sumed in the production process. While Marx apparently nowhere offers a clear definition of the concept of appropriation, Ellerman's notion does cap-ture two characteristics of the capitalist labor process that Marx noted to be particularly important: that workers do not own any of the product their labor jointly creates and that capitalists are the last owners of workers' labor time (ibid., 291–92).

Can Independent Commodity Producers Be Exploited?

To explore the question of why exploitation may be unjust, it will be instruc-tive to briefly examine the possibility of "self-exploitation," or whether independent commodity producers can be exploited. Although the ultimate goal here is to explore the injustice of capitalist exploitation, the investigation of self-exploitation is enlightening. Self-exploitation occurs when an independent commodity producer exclusively appropriates but is unable to retain the commodities produced by his or her surplus labor. Satya Gabriel calls simple commodity production the ancient class process (Gabriel 1990, 85). The notion of self-exploitation is contingent on the possibility of differentiating between the necessary labor and the surplus labor produced by an independent, or ancient, producer. Gabriel explains: "*Ancient necessary labor* is embodied in the portion of the total product of the ancient producer which goes to meet his/her subsistence needs. . . . Her labor in excess of this is defined as *ancient surplus labor*" (ibid., 87).

If the ancient class process, or independent commodity production, involves self-exploitation, it cannot be because someone appropriates the surplus labor of another, since the independent producer appropriates the whole product. The independent producer is the first owner of the commodities he or she produces, and he or she retains possession of his or her labor time in the process of production. Therefore, if it is possible to characterize the ancient class process as exploitative and if the characterization of the ancient class process as exploitative has any normative content, then perhaps the injustice of self-exploitation is due to the fact that individual commodity producers are not able to retain possession of the commodities created by their surplus labor.

In a private property, market economy populated by independent commodity producers, those producers must exchange part of their product with landowners, capital owners, and providers of credit in order to gain access to the means of production. Since we have ruled out misappropriation as the source of self-exploitation, those who believe that independent commodity producers can be exploited must think that the payments to owners of land, capital, and credit constitute this exploitation. If so and if we understand exploitation to be unjust, or a form of social theft, then perhaps we are judging private property in the means of production to be itself unjust and undeserving of payment. These payments must not be "necessary," which implies that private ownership in the means of production is an artificial and unfair social institution that should be eliminated.

Roemer is one Marxist who explicitly draws this conclusion. Using his definition of exploitation as the unequal exchange of labor for goods, Roemer shows that a model economy in which propertyless producers rent the means of production from their owners will yield the same pattern of income distribution as a model economy in which propertyless workers are employed by capitalists who own the factories (Roemer 1988, 90–107). His results reproduce Paul Samuelson's (1957) demonstration that it makes no difference from the perspective of economic distribution whether capital hires labor or labor hires capital. Roemer's analysis supports Gabriel's contention that exploitation can occur without the existence of a labor market, and Roemer explicitly endorses the view that the basis of a normative critique of capitalist exploitation lies in the unjust distribution of privately held titles to productive assets. However, if the Marxist phrase "appropriation of surplus labor" bears any relationship to Ellerman's notion of appropriation, it would seem that both Gabriel's notion of self-exploitation and Roemer's conclusion that independent commodity producers can be exploited ignore Marx's contention that exploitation occurs in the sphere of production, not in the sphere of market exchange. It is perhaps for this reason that Resnick and Wolff reject the possibility that independent commodity producers can be exploited (Wolff and Resnick 1987, 167–68).

PRIVATE PROPERTY OR MISAPPROPRIATION?

The second possibility to consider is that exploitation is unjust because the appropriation of the commodities produced by surplus labor—and only the appropriation of those commodities—by someone who did not share in the performance of surplus labor is morally wrong. In the capitalist class process, capitalists are the first owners of the commodities produced by surplus labor. Marxian value theory describes this appropriation as exploitative because the total value of the product that labor creates is greater than the wage. Bruce Roberts claims that the labor theory of value functions to provide the "categories with which to distinguish the total labor performed from the portion of that labor for which an equivalent is received" (Roberts 1988, 138). He goes on to add that "capitalist profit and other forms of non-labor income are predicated on the existence of surplus labor, *unpaid labor*" (ibid., 139).

In the process of capitalist production, workers are paid a wage to manufacture commodities that usually have an exchange value greater than the value of labor power, or the wage. When capitalists appropriate this surplus value, exploitation occurs. While many Marxists intend the labor theory of value merely to assist in the description of this exploitation, the language Marxists use to describe the existence of capitalist exploitation suggests certain normative conclusions. First, if capitalist exploitation is unjust, it is because there is an unjust appropriation of surplus labor. Second, there seems to be an implicit judgment that the capitalist appropriation of that portion of the produced commodities whose value is equal to the value of workers' wages constitutes a just and legitimate exchange of equivalents. For instance, in the preceding quote, Roberts speaks of labor power receiving an "equivalent" payment for the necessary labor it performs. The justice of this equivalency usually goes unquestioned in the Marxian literature. The implicit normative language of the labor theory of value ("unpaid" labor, "equivalent" payments) does not give us any reason to challenge the appropriation by the capitalist of the commodities created by necessary labor, since this value is equivalent to the wage. What the labor theory of value leads us to interrogate is the capitalist appropriation of the commodities whose value is equivalent to rent, interest, and profit.

If we focus on the appropriation of the commodities created by surplus labor only, however, it is easy to see how we might, once again, identify the injustice of capitalist exploitation with the injustice of the private ownership of productive property. Although Roberts does not speak to the question of justice, his essay could be read to support the normative conclusion that if we think capitalist exploitation is unjust, it might be because private property in the means of production is unjust. Roberts argues that the labor theory of value provides "a conceptual accounting system for understanding the redistributive nature of capitalist class relations" (Roberts 1988, 137), a method to explain how payments can be made to those who control the means of production but who themselves do not actually perform labor. In a market system where the means of production are privately owned, their owners will require some compensation for the use of their property. Capitalists have no choice but to extract surplus labor to make these payments. If, in trying to discover why capitalist exploitation is unjust, we focus only on the unjust appropriation of surplus labor, it is then a simple step to locate the injustice of surplus labor appropriation in the unequally distributed ownership of productive property.

There are many examples in the Marxist literature of authors who draw this conclusion. For instance, in his debate with Wood on the relationship between Marxism and justice, Husami (1980) identifies the unequal distribution of private property as the source of the injustice of capitalist exploitation. According to Husami, capitalists' ownership of the means of production enables them to extract surplus labor. The concentrated ownership of capital unjustly forces workers to produce commodities with a value exceeding the value of their labor power, because labor has no alternative other than employment by a capitalist. Husami cites Marx to gain some textual authority for this view: " 'Capital obtains this surplus labor without an equivalent, and in essence it always remains forced labor—no matter how much it may seem to result from free contractual agreement' " (Husami 1980, 62, quoting Marx 1967, 819). For Marxists, such as Husami, the injustice of capitalist exploitation lies in the injustice of unequally distributed private property.

This unjust distribution gives propertyless workers no choice, despite appearances, but to produce surplus labor for the appropriating capitalist.

The rhetoric of Marxian value theory and its focus on the appropriation of surplus labor does seem to lead to a normative indictment of private property, rather than to an indictment of its specifically capitalist form. Many political regimes guided by Marxian economic theory took action to socialize productive property with the goal of eliminating exploitation, and many Marxists concluded that this move successfully accomplished its goal. But Resnick and Wolff (1993, 1994) have pointed out some of the problems with this view. Their analysis of the Soviet Union makes clear that if exploitation is understood as the appropriation of the commodities created by surplus labor by those who did not participate in their production, in no way does eliminating private property in the means of production necessarily eliminate capitalist exploitation. Using their definition of exploitation to assess the Soviet experience, they conclude that inside Soviet state-owned enterprises, "laborers still produced surplus values for capitalists," but "now the latter were appointed state officials rather than private individuals" (Resnick and Wolff 1994, 11). A state-appointed board of directors—state capitalists—appropriated and distributed the output created by productive laborers. Even though property rights in the means of production were ostensibly socialized, workers in Soviet firms had no right to appropriate the product of their necessary or surplus labor. Resnick and Wolff's interpretation of Soviet firms as instances of state capitalism is consonant with Marx's assertions that during a capitalist labor process, workers do not own any of the product their labor jointly creates, while capitalists are the last owners of workers' labor time (Marx 1976, 291–92).[3]

If Resnick and Wolff's view of the typical Soviet firm as state capitalist has any merit, perhaps the traditional Marxian focus on the fact that workers do not own the means of production in a capitalist system is misguided, especially since socializing ownership of the means of production does not necessarily eliminate capitalist exploitation. If so, we ought to consider whether the injustice of capitalist exploitation has anything at all to do with the presence or absence of private property. Resnick and Wolff suggest that the source of the injustice of exploitation lies in the misappropriation of the whole product, not in the presence of private property per se. They argue that "laborers who produce goods and services *should* own them and decide what to do with them" (Wolff and Resnick 1987, 125, emphasis added). They note that direct labor "helps produce capitalist commodities" and that "[t]hese commodities are automatically and immediately the property of the capitalist, not the employed direct laborer" (ibid., 147).

Ellerman argues that most modern economic theorists, including Marx and his followers, accept what he calls "the fundamental myth of capitalist property rights" (Ellerman 1992, 11). According to this myth, the right to appropriate goes necessarily hand in hand with the ownership of capital goods. For instance, Marx wrote that in capitalist society, "property turns out to be the right, on the part of the capitalist, to appropriate the unpaid labor of others or its product, and the impossibility, on the part of the worker, of appropriating his own product" (Marx 1976, 730). So even if we agree with Resnick and Wolff or Ellerman that the source of the injustice of capitalism is that some party other than the workers appropriate the output of the firm, if we accept the "fundamental myth," then the object of Marxian moral inquiry becomes specifying either the just distribution pattern or the just form of social ownership in the means of production. We may, with Marx and Engels (1978), call for the elimination of private property rather than of the specifically capitalist form of private property.

There is some evidence, however, that Marx did not always accept the fundamental myth of capitalist property rights and that he recognized the difference between private property and capitalist private property. Marx wrote: "Private property which is personally earned, i.e. which is based, as it were, on the fusing together of the isolated, independent working individual with the conditions of his labor, is supplanted by capitalist private property, which rests on the exploitation of alien, but formally free labor" (Marx 1976, 928). If Marx did recognize a difference between private property and capitalist private property, perhaps it is not controversial to suggest that from a Marxist perspective, capitalist exploitation can be eliminated by prohibiting the wage-for-labor-time exchange, thereby abolishing the capitalist form of private property, rather than socializing or redistributing productive property.

Whether or not Marx accepted the fundamental myth of capitalist property rights, Ellerman demonstrates that the myth is clearly false. The right to appropriate is determined by the direction of the hiring contract, not the ownership of property per se. If a workers cooperative rents privately owned capital goods, the members of the co-op are the appropriators of the entire output of the firm. They are jointly the first owners of the manufactured output, as well as the last owners of the input liabilities, including their collectively exercised labor time. Owners of productive property are the appropriators in the typical capitalist firm only because capital hires labor. If we are interested in eliminating capitalist exploitation, then from a vantage point that rejects the fundamental myth, we should not allow owners of capital, whether they be private individuals or the state, to hire labor power and appropriate the whole product that labor produces. This conclusion implies that exploitation is unjust because the wage-for-labor-time contract allows the purchaser of labor time to appropriate wrongly the entire product that labor is responsible for creating.

If we reject the fundamental myth of capitalist property rights, what is it that makes capitalist appropriation unjust? To answer this question, Ellerman's version of the labor theory of property draws attention away from the ownership of existing property and the distribution of income and asks about the just appropriation of newly created goods. In his view, the important moral question is to specify the legitimate appropriator of the whole product, not just surplus labor; that is, who should appropriate all the new assets created in the production process, as well as the liability for the used-up productive factors? According to the labor theory of property, the injustice of what Marxists perceive to be the social theft that occurs in capitalist production is a result of the wrong party appropriating the entire product.

The meaning and significance of Ellerman's version of the labor theory of property are different from John Locke's more famous rendition of the theory. Locke argued that people have a natural right to their labor and a natural right to its fruits. But Locke also believed that it was legitimate for people to sell their labor time to others. In a significant passage, he wrote:

> Thus the Grass my Horse has bit; the Turfs my Servant has cut; and the Ore I have digg'd in any place where I have a right to them in common with others, become my Property, without the assignation or consent of any body. The labour that was mine, removing them out of that common state they were in, hath fixed my Property in them. (Locke quoted in Ellerman 1992, 51)

Locke accepted the legitimacy of people selling their labor time to others. When Locke referred to the "labour that was mine," he understood the labor of the servant to be owned by the master. In Locke's labor theory of property, it was the owner of labor time (i.e., the capitalist), not the performer of labor, who rightfully appropriated the entire product.

In rejecting Locke's argument, Ellerman first asks us to attend carefully to the facts of capitalist production. Although conventional economic theory treats workers as just another input, like capital goods, into the production process, human beings possess an attribute that buildings and machinery lack: human beings act intentionally or willfully. Since workers do act willfully, they are, at every moment, responsible for their actions. While capital equipment may be productive, in the sense that the use of capital enables more output to be manufactured, only human effort can be responsible for production.

For Ellerman, the error of Locke's version of the labor theory of property is its implicit assumption that workers can alienate their labor, that they can temporarily withdraw their will and responsibility from their work activity and in fact transfer this responsibility to another person, either to the owner of a firm's capital assets or to an entrepreneur, so that this other person becomes the owner of the workers' time and efforts. By validating the wage-for-labor-time exchange, capitalist practice, like Locke, does recognize the legality of labor transferring responsibility for its actions to the capitalist. In doing so, the capitalist legal system sustains the appropriation of the whole product by the capital owner. The legality of the wage-for-labor-time exchange, however, does not erase the factual reality that only human physical and mental effort can be the responsible agent of production. As Ellerman puts it, "[a]n individual cannot in fact vacate and transfer that responsible agency which makes one a person" (Ellerman 1992, 156). If people cannot in fact alienate their will and responsibility, all manual and intellectual workers must always share factual responsibility for the entire product their labor cooperates to produce.

The Juridical Principle of Imputation

Ellerman accepts Locke's claim that people have a natural right to their labor and its products. However, for Ellerman, it is unjust for people to sell their labor time: not only do people have a natural right to the product of their labor, they also have an inalienable right to their labor time, a right that should not be transferred even with consent. To sell labor time and the right to appropriate its product is to violate what Ellerman calls "the juridical principle of imputation," which states that "[p]eople should *always* be held legally responsible for the positive and negative results of their de facto responsible actions" (Ellerman 1992, 169). Not to be legally responsible for the results of one's actions is to assume the status of a thing and to lose one's dignity as a human being. Ellerman understands the labor theory of property to be an expression of the juridical principle of imputation in an economic context. According to his labor theory of property, people should appropriate (i.e., be legally responsible for) the entire product of their intentional acts of mental and manual labor, because workers are factually responsible for this output. Just as people should not be allowed voluntarily to sell their votes, thus alienating their responsibilities as citizens, workers should not be permitted to cede to a capitalist both the legal responsibility for the firm's output and the liability for their labor time. A typical wage-for-labor-time contract violates the juridical principle of imputation because it allows the employer to be the last owner of the worker's time, thereby transforming the worker into the legal instrument of the employer and giving the worker the legal status of a thing.

The argument that people should be held legally responsible for the results of their intentional actions is readily accepted in the case of a crime, no matter what kind of contract the criminals might have agreed on. A modern court system would not honor a contract signed by two bank robbers that gave one of the partners the sole legal responsibility for the robbery in exchange for a larger portion of the loot. If the two partners were factually responsible for the crime, a modern court would hold both partners legally liable for the robbery. Through a parallel argument, we can also conceive how hired labor is always jointly responsible for the product of the firm. Unless we believe that the wage-for-labor-time contract does actually transform human beings into nonwillful, inanimate things, then we must conclude that workers are always active and responsible agents in the production process. If we accept the moral principle that people should be legally responsible for the results of their intentional actions, then "the employment contract should *always* be considered null, void, and invalid" (Ellerman 1992, 169). This is so because the capitalist wage-for-labor-time contract denies the joint responsibility of wage labor by denying labor's right to participate in the appropriation of the entire product. Most notably, the wage-for-labor-time contract makes someone other than the worker the last owner, or appropriator, of the worker's time.

For Ellerman, the wage-for-labor-time exchange is not a coercive exchange, as it is portrayed in much Marxist literature, but a fraudulent exchange. When workers cede legal rights to their labor time and the output their labor creates in exchange for a wage, they do so because capitalist law and society do not recognize that the wage-for-labor-time exchange is inconsistent with the fundamental reality that people are not able to alienate their will and responsibility. The rectification of this fraud and of the injustice of capitalist appropriation does not require a change in the distribution of property. Instead, it requires the prohibition of fraudulent wage-for-labor-time exchanges.

We should also note that Ellerman's labor theory of property makes a different claim than traditional theories of value and the theories of distribution that they suggest. From a perspective informed by the labor theory of property, labor's right to appropriate the whole product is not tied to the productivity of labor. Many inputs are productive of a firm's output, and the labor theory of property does not challenge the payment for such inputs. The labor theory of property does not establish any link between productivity and the concept of just appropriation. The essential link is between appropriation and responsibility, and only human beings can be responsible agents. It is the characteristic of responsibility that singles out labor as the justly appropriating agent.

Ellerman's position is similar to that first expressed by Marx in his 1844 manuscripts and later repeated in *Capital*. A dominant theme Marx explores in the 1844 manuscripts is how capitalism estranges, or alienates, labor. Two of the alienating aspects of capitalism that Marx mentions are that workers do not own any of the commodities produced by their labor and that workers' activities in the labor process belong not to themselves but to another, the capitalist (Marx 1964, 111–12). Both of these characteristics of capitalism are indicted by Ellerman's labor theory of property. In the manuscripts, Marx seems to accept the fundamental myth of capitalist property rights. Accordingly, he links the alienation of labor to the existence of private property. As we have seen, however, a society that substitutes state-owned property for individually held property does not necessarily eliminate either of these problems. In the Soviet system, workers did not appropriate the entire product of the firm and thus were not the first owners of the output or the last owners of their labor time. Ellerman's labor theory of property shows that private property per se is not the culprit causing the alienation of labor. Instead, the direction of the hiring contract produces these two aspects of worker alienation. If labor hired capital—rather than capital hiring labor, as is the case in the conventional capitalist firm—workers would be the last owners of their labor time and the first owners of newly created goods and services.

WORKER SELF-MANAGEMENT
AND THE CAPABILITY THEORY

There is an important point to address in the present discussion: can we reconcile, on the one hand, Ellerman's attempt to challenge the justice of the wage-for-labor-time exchange by appealing to inalienable natural rights (i.e., to the idea that people have a natural right that should not be alienated to the entire product of their labor) with, on the other hand, the theories of Marx, who quipped, "To speak . . . of natural justice . . . is nonsense" (Marx 1967, 339), and who remarked, "Right can never be higher than the economic structure of society and its cultural development conditioned thereby" (Marx 1978, 531)? Other related comments by Marx on the question of justice have sparked a long debate by readers of Marx about whether or not the struggle against exploitation needs to be animated by a theory of justice. Allen Wood (1980a, 1980b, 1981) presents the well-known argument that Marx himself did not consider exploitation to be unjust.[4] Wood understands Marx to say that theories of justice are the epiphenomenal expressions of the mode of production: "justice is not a standard by which human reason in the abstract measures human actions, institutions, or other social facts. It is rather a standard by which each mode of production measures *itself*. It is a standard present to human thought only in the context of a specific mode of production" (Wood 1980a, 15–16). From Wood's perspective, there are no universal standards of justice that transcend those consistent with and determined by the existing mode of production. Rather, theories of justice function to legitimate the juridical requirements of the economic base. It is thus not possible to identify transhistorical, objective moral principles to criticize the practices of a particular society. In this account, capitalist exploitation is perfectly compatible with capitalist notions of justice.

Rather than making an argument against exploitation based on a theory of justice, Wood asserts that Marx believed "that the labor theory of value could be used to advance criticisms of capitalism which . . . derived simply from a correct understanding of the organic functioning of capitalism and the successive stages of development marked out for it by its nature as a mode of production" (Wood 1980a, 25–26).[5] There is no reason to criticize capitalist exploitation as an injustice, because the teleological progression of capitalism will generate the circumstances—the increasing tension between progressive forces of production and repressive relations of production; economic instability; and, ultimately, working-class revolution—that will inevitably lead to the demise of exploitation. In contrast to Wood, postmodern Marxists agree with authors, such as Cohen (1995), who maintain that it is misguided for radicals to continue to hope that capitalism will ultimately produce the conditions that will lead the working class to inaugurate a socialist society. Barring the inevitable collapse of capitalism, it behooves critics of capitalism to develop theories of justice and morality that might guide political action. While Ellerman's Kantian, rights-based language may not be perfectly consonant with Marx's political economy, the normative component of Ellerman's labor theory of property can be regrounded on an Aristotelian capability basis that does have clear affinities with Marx's thought.

According to Richard Miller, Marx inherited from Aristotle the view that rights are legitimate only to the extent to which they yield good consequences. Rival systems of rights always exist, and the judgment as to which system should be chosen depends on the results produced by each system; that is, systems of rights should be supported or criticized inasmuch as they promote the control over one's life and the "allied goods of dignity, self-expression, and mutual respect" (Miller 1992, 293). Thus Miller believes Marx held that the capitalist use of wage labor "should be overthrown because of its consequences, not because it violates rights" (ibid., 288), as is the case with Ellerman. Alan Gilbert (1992) draws on Miller's work to argue that Marx's consequentialist evaluation of institutions is related to Aristotle's eudaimonism, or his concern to foster the political and social environment conducive to good, flourishing human lives. If Marx did have an ethical position, it was Aristotelian and not rights based, and Marx's criticism of rights does not have to be, contrary to Wood, a wholesale rejection of the concept of justice.[6]

Nussbaum's development of the Aristotelian capability theory of justice is illuminating here, for it provides a method to evaluate the consequences of alternative institutional arrangements or policies in a manner that is compatible with postmodern interpretations of Marx on the question of justice (West 1991). Unlike utilitarians, who judge the merit of institutions insofar as they facilitate the maximization of a singular attribute of human life (pleasure or happiness), Aristotle (as well as Marx, according to Miller and Gilbert) has a multidimensional standard by which to measure consequences. For Nussbaum's Aristotle, a policy, a right, or any other institution generates good consequences if it promotes the capability for people to function in a mode that is consistent with a fully realized human nature that is defined in a conjective, intersubjective, or internalist essentialist manner. A fully realized human nature includes more than happiness; for instance, Nussbaum submits that the exercise of practical reason is essential. But to link Marx with Aristotle here would be extremely controversial, unless the meaning of the term *human nature* is specified very carefully, since Marx rejected absolutist conceptions of that nature.

Nussbaum is again helpful with this problem. She argues that for Aristotle, human nature is an internalist notion, not an externalist or a detached and impartial notion: "Human nature cannot, and need not, be validated from the outside, because human nature just *is* an inside perspective, not a *thing* at all, but rather the most fundamental and broadly shared experience of human beings living and reasoning together" (Nussbaum 1995, 121). Nussbaum argues that for Aristotle, beliefs about human nature "are matters for communal judgment and decision, not for independent investigation and discovery"—that "[t]hey are thoroughly internal to the community, and they serve to explain it to itself" (ibid., 101). Such a perspective on human nature coheres with postmodernist interpretations of Marx. For example, Cornel West makes a persuasive case that, as his thought matured, Marx developed a radical historicist or postmodern approach to questions of justice. West describes the radical historicist point of view as one in which "the only plausible candidates for the criteria, grounds, or foundations [of justice] in question would be the *contingent, community-specific* agreements people make in relation to particular norms, aims, goals, and objectives" (West 1991, 1). As long as we reject the essentialist notion of isolated and autonomous human communities, it is possible to see how Marx's writings reveal that capitalism does not produce the conditions necessary for good human functioning, as the historical world community might conceivably define it. On these grounds, capitalism is unjust.

How does this discussion relate to Ellerman's labor theory of property? Rather than appealing to the existence of natural rights, as does Ellerman in order to reach his normative conclusions, we can instead use his factual description of production in the capitalist firm to see how wage labor violates an Aristotelian conception of human flourishing and restricts the development of human capabilites. Sen argues that there are both opportunity aspects and process aspects to human flourishing, and Ellerman's analysis shows that the capitalist wage-labor relation establishes a work process inconsistent with human flourishing. A key element of Ellerman's argument is that certain essential human characteristics—in particular, responsibility and decision making—are factually inalienable (Ellerman 1992, 127). Yet in the capitalist firm, workers do not have legal responsibility for their actions, insofar as they do not appropriate the entire product for which their labor is factually responsible. Thus workers in a capitalist enterprise assume the legal status of things and are often treated similarly. Marx characterizes an employee of a capitalist this way: "in his human functions he no longer feels himself to be anything but an animal" (Marx 1964, 111). While participating in a capitalist work process, a worker loses his or her dignity.

Other writers have also noticed in Marx's work an implicit, but nevertheless consistent, appeal to the moral principle of human dignity (see Bloch 1986; Kain 1992; Kamenka 1972; Peffer 1990). For these interpreters of Marx, socialist politics should aim at a society in which universal human dignity is achieved, since without dignity, people cannot lead fully realized and flourishing human lives. All of these authors agree that a prerequisite for universal human dignity is that people cannot treat others as tools to achieve their ends. Ellerman's labor theory of property helps us to see that in a capitalist firm, wage-laborers assume the legal status of things and become the instruments of the capitalist's drive to maximize profits. Since workers do not appropriate the output their labor helps to create, they are not legally responsible for the results of their actions. Thus capitalist production is inconsistent with human dignity and flourishing, or good human functioning.

HAYEK AND WORKER SELF-MANAGEMENT

Is it possible to implement a system of labor-appropriating firms in a manner that escapes the knowledge problems that Hayek identified in the classical socialist prescription of state ownership of the means of production and central planning? Requiring that firms be labor appropriating does not entail central planning and state ownership of productive property. Labor-appropriating firms that eliminate the exploitation that Marx saw operating in capitalism could exist in an institutional context in which private property was widely held and in which labor-appropriating firms competed with each other in a rivalrous market process. Thus, at first glance, it seems that the labor-appropriating firm can hold up against the rule-utilitarian normative perspective developed by Hayek and other Austrian economists. Let us consider that conclusion more carefully.

First, a system of labor-appropriating firms is consistent with the rule of law. For example, Jaroslav Vanek suggests that labor appropriation could be instituted through a constitutional amendment. He proposes the following text:

> Whenever people work together in a common enterprise (whatever their number), it is they and they only who appropriate the results of their labors, whether positive (products) or negative (costs or liabilities), and who control and manage democratically on the basis of equality of vote or weight the activities of their enterprise. These workers may or may not be owners of the capital assets with which they work, but in any event such ownership does not impart any rights of control over the firm. Only possession of and income from such assets can be assigned to the owners, to be regulated by a free contract between the working community (i.e., the enterprise) and the owners. (Vanek 1996, 29)

To enforce such a proposed constitutional rule to require labor appropriation in jointly productive enterprises would not involve the arbitrary use of discretionary power, as Hayek understands it. The rule is universally applicable, well-announced, and abstract, in that it aims at no particular outcome. Such a rule would be similar to a constitutional provision against slavery. In this case, it is a constitutional provision against what some Marxists have called "wage slavery."

Second, Hayek, like Ellerman, highly regards the value of individual responsibility. However, for Hayek, unlike Ellerman, "the assigning of responsibility does not involve the assertion of a fact" but, rather, is "of the nature of a convention intended to make people observe certain rules" that promote social order and cooperation (Hayek 1960, 75). According to Hayek, the reason to accept the convention to hold people responsible for their decisions is to direct their "attention to those causes of events that depend on our actions," and "[t]he main function of the belief in individual responsibility is to make us use our own knowledge and capacities to the full in achieving our ends" (ibid., 79–80). Hayek does not accept the assignment of responsibility for its intrinsic value, as is the case with Ellerman's natural rights perspective and with the Aristotelian approach developed to this point in the present discussion. Hayek instead believes that we assign responsibility in order to obtain beneficial social consequences. The question that arises from a Hayekian perspective would be whether assigning the legal right of appropriation—and hence responsibility—to labor in a firm would contribute to the coordination of dispersed knowledge, the creation of wealth, and human flourishing to a greater degree than would the capitalist firm.

Bowles and Gintis (1993) contend that the typical capitalist firm is not necessarily the most efficient institution of production. They argue that it is quite conceivable that firms in which workers democratically appropriate the entire product may utilize resources more efficiently than firms in which capital owners appropriate. They reach this conclusion by pointing out that capitalist firms must expend tremendous resources monitoring the productive activities of workers. Firms can reap efficiency gains by transferring the right of appropriation to inputs that are hard to monitor: specifically, in this case, the collection of people working in the firm.[7] When workers appropriate the entire product, they have less incentive to shirk and act uncooperatively, since they, rather than capital owners, receive the benefits of their efforts. Bowles and Gintis also show that democratically appropriating firms are more likely to use wage incentives to elicit work effort, rather than employing resource-using and thus comparatively inefficient monitoring techniques. Their conclusions run counter to the typical views of neoclassical economists, who argue that capitalists need to monitor firms and act as residual claimants in order to promote economic efficiency (see, e.g., Alchian and Demsetz 1972).

Hayek's idea of the importance of tacit, local knowledge in the production process suggests there might be other efficiency-promoting benefits of a system of labor-appropriating firms. There is reason to think that the labor-appropriating firm will give more workers incentive to report their subjective perceptions of economic opportunity—such as more efficient technologies, since they share in the profits these technologies might allow. Insofar as capitalist firms often do not provide incentives to all employees to notice and report improvements in a firm's technology, the labor-appropriating firm may be more innovative than the capitalist firm. In addition, if workers participate in appropriation and act as the residual claimant, they might be more willing to invest in firm-specific forms of human capital. Margaret Blair (1995) argues that the importance of human capital in the production process strengthens the argument for worker ownership of the firm and for profit sharing as an incentive for individuals to undertake investment in their human capital.[8]

In a clear and penetrating analysis and rejection of the criticisms neoclassical economists level against the labor-appropriating firm, David Prychitko (1996) concludes that Austrian economic theory must remain at least neutral, if not favorably inclined, in an evaluation of the feasibility of a network of labor-appropriating firms operating in the context of widely held private property and market exchange. Using the tools of equilibrium theory, neoclassical economists sometimes fault labor-managed firms for reducing production and limiting employment in response to a price increase, thereby generating backward-bending product supply curves and perverse employment outcomes. This is in contrast to a typical capitalist enterprise that follows, in theory, the more socially rational strategy of increasing output and employment in response to a rise in price of the product it sells. Prychitko points out that the identification of these supposed faults of the labor-managed firm are the result of using a short-run, equilibrium methodology that is hostile to the market process perspective advocated by the Austrians. If we imagine the possibility of the free entry of new labor-managed firms in a rivalrous market process, Prychitko believes that labor-managed firms may act as socially rational as capitalist firms.

Prychitko's argument raises an important issue to consider in light of my discussion of credit rationing in chapter 4 of this book. Perhaps the inability to obtain credit would prevent a group of idle, asset-poor workers from starting up a labor-managed firm in response to noticed profit opportunities. Perhaps this possibility, if repeated often enough, vitiates entry as anything more than a formal freedom for many potential workers. If so, worker self-management in the context of a free market process may be as unstable as it is portrayed in neoclassical economics. How to establish an institutional structure that facilitates the entry of labor-managed firms is thus one of the pivotal issues to keep in mind during my examination of socialist distributive justice in chapter 7.

This synthesis of Ellerman, Nussbaum and Sen's Aristotle, and Resnick and Wolff's Marx has several advantages in debate with Hayek about the justice of capitalism. First, the reconceived labor theory of property carves out a space between, on the one hand, Marxists, such as Roemer, who dethrone the distinction Marx made between production and exchange and, on the other hand, Marxists, such as Cohen and Husami, who retain the conviction that exploitation occurs in production. Although these Marxists disagree about where exploitation takes place, they all conclude that this exploitation is the result of unequally distributed titles to productive property. Ellerman's labor theory of property, however, focuses our attention on the issue of appropriation and the legitimacy of the wage-for-labor-time contract, and it introduces an argument—rooted in widely held beliefs about human dignity and the inalienability of responsibility—for why the performers of labor should share collectively in the appropriation of the product that labor jointly produces. It shares the Marxian commitment to eliminating exploitation and to advancing cooperative production relations.

Second, in light of Resnick and Wolff's theory of exploitation, Ellerman's labor theory of property provides an answer to the question of the injustice of exploitation without challenging the legitimacy of private ownership of productive property. It shows that the existence of private property and markets per se are not the problems with capitalist exploitation. While critics of capitalism may believe that there are good reasons for questioning the justice of unequally distributed property, I hope the present discussion has shown that a concern with exploitation does not have to be one of them. Thus, advocating Ellerman's labor theory of property improves the chances of enlisting in the battle against capitalist exploitation those skeptical non-Marxists, such as Hayek, who until now were convinced that the Marxian political project must lead to centrally planned, state socialism.

Finally, regrounding the normative component of Ellerman's labor theory of property on an Aristotelian capability basis à la Nussbaum and Sen, rather than on a natural rights foundation, makes it easier to develop a socialist theory of distributive justice to go along with the socialist theory of appropriative justice. As I discussed in chapter 5, the Aristotelian focus on the requirements for good human functioning is largely (although not entirely) oriented toward distributive questions. Ellerman's appeal to natural rights to support his normative indictment of wage labor and advocacy of democratic firms raises difficulties if one also seeks to counter views, such as Nozick's (1974), that rule out redistribution of income and wealth using natural rights arguments. Since most critics of capitalism are not likely to be content only with prohibiting the wage-labor exchange, reconceiving Ellerman's theory on an Aristotelian capability basis facilitates a more encompassing critique of free market capitalism.

CHAPTER 7

Socialist Distributive Justice
and the Stakeholder Society

★

Suppose we imagine a future in which Jaroslav Vanek's proposed constitutional amendment to prohibit the capitalist employment relation (cited in chap. 6) obtained enough support to become the law of the land. His amendment requires that workers in a common enterprise democratically appropriate the results of their labor and democratically manage their collective efforts. Private ownership of capital is not prohibited, but capital ownership conveys no possibility—through right or contract—of control rights over workers. Vanek's amendment would thus result in the elimination of two markets: the market in which people rent control over their labor time, in exchange for a wage or salary, and the market for common stock, in which claims to the firm's capital stock entail control rights over workers. It would not bar other financial markets and intermediaries, however. Bond and preferred stock markets and various types of (labor-managed) banks, mutual funds, and finance companies could continue to exist.

Capital owners would be entitled to any income stream that they could obtain through contract and negotiation with the members of self-managed firms who might wish to employ capital goods at work. Workers might borrow or rent capital from nonworker owners. They also could themselves own the capital with which they produce, so that the worker self-managed firm would also be worker owned. Or some combination of worker ownership, capital leasing, and external borrowing would be permissible. If workers were to own the capital assets of the firm outright—financed through retained earnings, membership fees to join the firm, or loans—those ownership rights would entail only a right to an income stream from those assets and would not involve any control rights over the production process. Those rights would be reserved and shared exclusively—under the procedure of one person, one vote—for the worker-members of the firm, regardless of the amount of capital any particular worker owned.

The elimination of wage labor and common stock markets required by the Vanek amendment is compatible either with all remaining markets being free of any special regulation by government or with a capabilities-enhancing welfare state. Either way, the market process would likely generate substantial inequalities of income and wealth. The existence of credit rationing would also contribute to the persistence of these inequalities, since asset-poor labor-managed firms would face credit restrictions not encountered by their wealthier competitors. Hence asset-poor labor-managed firms would have more difficulty expanding. Systemic inequalities of income and wealth might also translate into the systemic influence of income and wealth in the political process, which likely would jeopardize the sustainability of a capability-enhancing welfare state, if one were to exist.

These distributive questions dovetail with financing constraints that many believe to plague labor-managed firms. Asset-poor workers face two difficulties when they attempt to form a labor-managed firm. First, in capital-intensive enterprises, poor workers would have to seek external funds to finance their activities, making the firm vulnerable to bankruptcy in the case of disruption to the firm's cash flow. Jacques Drèze (1993) illustrates this difficulty with the example of using a supertanker to transport oil. An oil supertanker requires only a few people to operate but costs millions of dollars to purchase. Most people could not collectively self-finance the purchase of the tanker. They would have to rent it or borrow money to purchase it. If anything interfered with the regular and timely delivery of oil, perhaps political turmoil in the Middle East, the self-managed collective of tanker workers would not be able to meet their rent or mortgage obligations, forcing it into bankruptcy. This problem makes worker self-management an unstable organizational form in capital-intensive industries. Second, a collective of risk-averse, asset-poor workers might be reluctant to sink any of their limited wealth into their worker-managed enterprise because both their labor and capital income would be hostage to the performance of the firm. For the risk averse, worker self-management would be an undesirable organizational form, if self-management entailed worker ownership of capital.

Both of these problems might be solved if all self-managed firms were required to use external finance to purchase capital equipment. Fleurbaey (1993) proposes a model with this characteristic. In his model, all finance of self-managed firms must take place through bank loans. This lets workers diversify their risk by allowing them to channel their savings into the banking system, rather than having to plow them back into their workplace. At the same time, bank loans can be structured to bring interest payments in line with anticipated future investment returns. Finally, Fleurbaey believes that his model can address Drèze's problem by encouraging workers and banks to negotiate insurance clauses and variable interest payments that would permit workers to receive a guaranteed income from the bank and to suspend interest payments in the case of a temporary economic downturn. Fleurbaey argues that because banks have a diverse loan portfolio, they would be in a better position than workers to absorb market risk, and regulations should encourage them to assume this role.

Fleurbaey's model of external finance with the possibility of variable interest loans would still, however, not address the fact that freely functioning financial markets routinely ration credit. Lenders might still deny credit to a collective of asset-poor workers. Or a collective of well-endowed workers might enjoy better terms than a collective of asset-poor workers. If so, then well-endowed labor-managed firms would have a tendency to outcompete asset-poor firms, further impoverishing the latter's members. In either event, income and wealth inequalities would be reinforced and reproduced through the normal operation of the market process.

The linkage between the inequality problem and the finance problem suggests the potential merit of socialist ideas to promote distributive justice. This chapter considers two of these ideas: (1) John Roemer's (1994) proposal to equalize profits through a coupon stock market and (2) Bruce Ackerman and Anne Alstott's (1999) proposal to institute what they call a "stakeholder society" to redistribute wealth, through wealth taxation and a substantial, once-in-a-lifetime cash grant to citizens at the age of majority. I will examine and assess each of these proposals in terms of their ability to address the financing problems faced by self-managed firms and to avoid Hayekian knowledge problems. My goal is to determine what type of socialist distributive class justice would be most sensibly coupled with the notion of socialist appropriative class justice developed in chapter 6, in order to complete a vision of post-Hayekian socialism.

THE ROEMER MODEL

The discussion in chapter 6 showed that Roemer believes a socialist theory of justice need not concern itself with worker self-management and should instead focus on the distribution of property. While I reject Roemer's criticisms of worker self-management and fault him for not distinguishing between issues of appropriative and distributive justice, his institutional proposal to achieve a just distribution of income flows resulting from the use of capital equipment is intriguing. He advocates eliminating the capitalist stock market and replacing it with a socialist, coupon stock market, in order to promote equality of opportunity and to disperse political-economic power. Since the coupon stock market would only allow the exchange of preferred, nonvoting stock, Roemer's idea is fully compatible with the Vanek amendment mentioned at the beginning of this chapter.

In Roemer's model of market socialism, all citizens would be given an equal endowment of coupons that could only be used to buy shares of preferred stock in conventional firms. Firms would issue the shares and exchange the coupon revenue for cash at the state treasury in order to raise funds to buy capital equipment. The government would tax citizens to fill this investment fund in the treasury. The amount of tax revenue in the fund, in conjunction with the volume of shares issued during any time period, would determine the cash price of a coupon. Citizens who purchased shares would receive a portion of the firm's profit resulting from the use of capital equipment, but they would have no right to determine the composition of firm management.

While citizens could not exchange coupons for cash, they would be permitted to sell their shares for coupons at any time, and they would do so if they thought they could turn around and purchase shares in other companies that promised a higher profit flow. In this way, the coupon price of shares would reflect citizen's expectations about the future profitability of firms. A citizen's stock holdings would be sold at death, and the coupon revenue would return to the state, preventing concentration of coupon and stock wealth through inheritance. By giving all citizens an equal share of coupons and by preventing stock and coupon inheritance, Roemer's proposal would result in a more or less egalitarian distribution of aggregate profits.

One advantage of a coupon stock market is that all people would receive an annual sum of money independent of their wage and salary income. Roemer estimates that annual dividend income would amount to between one and two thousand dollars per adult. Although this is not a large sum, it would represent a substantial increase in income for poor individuals and families. The primary benefit Roemer sees in this plan is that it would reduce the political power that a few wealthy elites enjoy under capitalism. Roemer reasons that the concentration of stockholding in capitalism means that a few shareholders have the incentive to influence the political process in order to increase their profit incomes. Such influence is used to minimize antipollution laws, labor regulations, and other legislation that threatens to reduce profits, as well as to increase the probability that governments will undertake profit-enhancing foreign aggression—perhaps, for instance, to ensure the flow of cheap oil. An equitable distribution of profit income would reduce the concentrated benefit of lobbying against policies that increase the public good at the expense of profits. Because it is costly to engage in political lobbying and because the benefits of lobbying would be diffused with the dispersed distribution of profit income, Roemer expects that his coupon stock market would lead to a government that was more interested in policies to enhance the common good. In light of my discussion of capability equality in chapter 5 of this book, Roemer might argue that something like a coupon stock market is necessary to achieve capability-enhancing goals.

While firms could raise funds for investment purposes via the sale of preferred stock, Roemer imagines that firms would mostly finance their activities through bank loans. He envisions a set of large public banks, modeled after banks in the Japanese *keiretsu* system, who compete for citizens' monetary savings and who arrange for loan consortia for firms' investment projects. Banks would actively monitor firm management, probably by having representation on the boards of directors of borrowing firms. At the same time, Roemer believes that the government should regulate bank lending policy, since he doubts that free markets achieve efficient investment outcomes. For instance, a government-managed financial system could allow politically favored sectors to receive below-market interest rates, while charging above-market rates to industries that produce undesirable commodities, such as tobacco or alcohol.

Since Roemer believes that banks must have some role on firms' boards of directors, his model, as proposed, is not consistent with worker self-management. However, we could modify his proposal to eliminate this feature. Banks would then have to rely on typical contractual methods to monitor and affect firm behavior. The use of collateral requirements and restrictive covenants, such as requiring borrowers to maintain insurance on purchased property or limiting the type of property that can be bought with borrowed funds, are alternative tactics lenders could use to increase the probability of repayment, without violating the principle of worker self-management. While these tactics do restrict the autonomy of borrowing firms, self-management is a principle that applies inside a productive enterprise, not to the types of exchanges firms are or are not permitted to make.

Roemer argues that a coupon stock market would retain the informational role that economists ascribe to conventional common stock markets. The coupon price of shares should be indicative of stockholders' collective assessments of expected profitability and the effectiveness of firm management. Banks would be able to use the coupon price of a firm's preferred stock as one piece of information to evaluate the quality of firm management. In a system of worker self-management, a poorly performing firm might face more stringent requirements to obtain credit or perhaps the termination of credit altogether. Thus workers would encounter a powerful incentive to ensure that their elected management was pursuing an efficient and profitable business strategy.

A coupon stock market grafted onto a system of worker self-management would produce another potentially attractive feature as well: a worker-managed firm that wished to use retained earnings to purchase capital equipment could issue nonvoting equity shares to its members in proportion to the funds it retained to finance investment. As long as workers remained members of the firm, they would not be permitted to sell their shares. On leaving the firm, they could sell the shares on the coupon stock market. While this institutional configuration would introduce an element of inequality into Roemer's coupon stock market—since members of successful, self-financing cooperatives might accumulate larger portfolios than members of unsuccessful co-ops—it would allow workers access to a relatively egalitarian form of nonvoting, equity finance that would facilitate a degree of internal finance and labor mobility in a self-managed system.

MARKET PROCESS CRITICISMS
OF THE ROEMER MODEL

To ascertain whether Roemer's coupon stock market could be an attractive feature of a post-Hayekian socialist model of worker self-management in a rivalrous market process, there are four substantive issues to consider. First, Roemer utilizes general equilibrium arguments to defend his model. Are those arguments central or peripheral to the implementation of his proposed institutional structure? Second, a coupon stock market eliminates the possibility that managers and directors of a company can become large stockholders in a particular company, thereby taking away the incentive for the firm managers and directors effectively to oversee the company. Does this impair the functioning of the market process, as at least one commentator influenced by Austrian economics has alleged (Arnold 1996)? Third, Roemer's model gives government a critical role to play in the formation of lending policy. Does this aspect of the model fall prey to Hayekian knowledge problems? Fourth, would Roemer's coupon stock market effectively restrict the power of concentrated financial wealth in credit markets and facilitate the entry of new labor-managed firms? In this chapter, I will also briefly address a political concern about the feasibility of Roemer's proposal vis-à-vis more conventional forms of income and wealth distribution. These last two concerns in particular will lead me to evaluate a suggestion to redistribute wealth as more conducive to the achievement of socialist distributive justice.

An indirect sign of Roemer's reliance on general equilibrium reasoning is his claim that redistributions of profit income are unlikely to affect economic efficiency. As he remarks, there is a "fundamental asymmetry between wages and profits as categories of national income"; that is, "while considerations of efficiency pretty much determine the distribution of wages among workers, they do not so determine the distribution of profits" (Roemer 1994, 120). In making this argument, Roemer misses the Hayekian point that profit serves as a lure for people to make entrepreneurial discoveries. Thus he takes the position that the "wealth of society is not due primarily to rugged individualists, as it were, but is reproducible according to blueprints that are quite well understood"; he further contends, "The market is necessary to implement competition and to economize on information, but not so much for cultivating the inspiration of rare geniuses" (ibid., 5). It is apparent that "rugged individualists" and "rare geniuses" are Roemer's terms for entrepreneurs. It is likely that the reason Roemer reaches his conclusion that market outcomes are reproducible according to blueprints is because he is captured by an equilibrium mind-set in which there is no room for entrepreneurship.[1]

It would be a mistake, though, to assume that Roemer's flawed equilibrium-based arguments invalidate his institutional proposal. After all, in my defense herein of worker self-management, I have already proposed to make workers the initial appropriators of profit income rather than capital owners. In chapter 6, I indicated that transferring residual claimancy from capital to labor might even improve economic efficiency. Grafting Roemer's coupon stock market onto a system of worker self-management does not challenge this reasoning, since a self-managed firm could raise money by issuing non-voting coupon stock certificates that distribute a share of firm profits to non-members, if the worker-managers thought it was in their interest to do so. This would not challenge the principle of worker appropriation.

The real issue is whether abolishing the capitalist common stock market, as both a system of worker self-management and Roemer's coupon stock market would do, would fatally impair the functioning of the market process by eliminating the possibility of managers-directors accumulating a large ownership share in a company and thus eliminating the possibility of ousting inefficient firm management through stock purchase by alternative manager-directors. These are the criticisms raised by Arnold's (1996) evaluation of Roemer. Arnold reacts to a specification of Roemer's (1994) model that does not include self-management. Arnold maintains that owner-managers must be substantial owners of common stock in order to have the incentive to monitor firms effectively. Only if they have substantial residual claims will they make decisions to maximize profit and efficiency.

Roemer responds to this criticism by pointing to the apparent success of the Japanese economy in its use of bank monitoring of firm management. He argues that there should be little reason why the success of bank monitoring in Japan could not be replicated in a socialist economy with a coupon stock market. Perhaps, though, market socialist managers who did not own capital would not view the threat of losing access to credit as compelling. After all, if banks deny credit due to ineffective management and then the firm is forced into bankruptcy, nonowner managers do not have a substantial ownership stake to lose. If, however, managers and directors were elected by the firm's workers (as would be the case in a system of worker self-management) and hence all workers were faced with the possibility of job loss and potential capital loss due to sloppy management and the inability to obtain external sources of credit, then perhaps managers would be effectively monitored by their worker-"employers." This is one argument made by advocates of worker self-management. In addition, there is nothing about worker self-management that precludes giving managers substantial salary bonuses that are tied to firm performance, if such incentives are necessary to elicit successful management.

Arnold delivers another, more consequential blow to Roemer's model. Roemer's proposed banking system consists of public banks subject to substantial governmental control. He gives banks the task of guiding investment plans through the use of interest rate incentives to politically favored industries. This attribute of Roemer's model is more evidence that he has not grasped the essentials of Hayek's economics. The upshot of Hayek's critique of Lange's market socialism is that government officials cannot have better knowledge of firms' economic opportunities than do the (worker-)managers on the spot. Arnold puts it nicely: "The general problem is that resources in profit-maximizing firms tend to flow to their highest valued uses as those uses are valued by the market, and by hypothesis, the political authorities have different values from those expressed in the market" (Arnold 1996, 52). Political influence over investment decisions would introduce potential inefficiencies that are not required in order to achieve worker self-management or a more equal distribution of profit income via a coupon stock market. In a system of self-managed, post-Hayekian socialism, the political control of investment advocated by Roemer would be rejected, and banks would follow the same organizational form as all other firms: they would be democratically controlled by their workers, with government establishing the universally applicable rules of market exchange.[2]

In considering Roemer's coupon stock market proposal, Frank Thompson (1996) has identified another flaw that probably makes it an unattractive fit with a system of worker self-management: Roemer's model does not address the unequal distribution of other forms of wealth—monetary savings and bonds. In addition, Roemer would allow wage and salary income to be entirely determined by the market. High-income earners perform the majority of saving, and most savings would flow to the banking system and bond markets, since cash cannot be used to purchase stocks. To the degree that firms finance investment by using debt, interest payments would flow disproportionately to those at the top of the income and wealth pyramid, who store their wealth in bonds and the banking system. If market socialist firms find debt finance more attractive than equity finance, then the distribution of income might become even more unequal under Roemer's coupon socialism than under capitalism. The political benefits Roemer sees in an egalitarian distribution of profit income would likely vanish as well.

The persistence of the inequalities in income, savings, and wealth under Roemer's model ultimately makes it unsuited for a system of worker self-management. Start-up self-managed enterprises whose members are asset poor would have to rely on external sources of finance. They would probably be unable to find buyers of preferred shares in the coupon stock market and would have to turn to the banks for loans. But here they would confront the same difficulties as cooperatives do in capitalist systems. Lacking collateral, they would be denied loans. Or they would face higher interest rates than their competitors, jeopardizing their chances for success. Roemer's egalitarian stock market would not increase the ease of entry of new labor-managed firms into new or existing markets. Given that it also might not alleviate the inequality of income and wealth, Roemer's market socialism is not the best place to turn to find an institutional structure that would promote the goals of socialist distributive and appropriative class justice.

In search of better paths to these objectives, Louis Putterman suggests that existing avenues of institutional reform may be more appealing, politically, than Roemer's coupon stock market. Putterman remarks, "it is hard . . . to believe that a Western citizenry that became further predisposed towards equality would be more likely to implement [Roemer's] radical institutional experiment than to bolster the redistributive tendencies in existing tax codes" (Putterman 1996, 144). Perhaps a more advantageous direction—to promote distributive justice and to increase the robustness of a system of worker self-management—would be to redistribute wealth via forms of taxation that already exist in industrial democracies. I will now turn to this possibility.

THE SOCIALIST, STAKEHOLDER SOCIETY

We all know that a person born in the United States today has more economic opportunities than a person with an equivalent genetic heritage born in the middle of, say, Mongolia. In part, these disparate opportunities are due to the more liberal form of government that exists in the United States. But even if Mongolia were to adopt the complete set of American political institutions, structural economic disparities would remain. This is so in large part because the capital stock in the United States is well developed, much more so than the capital stock in Mongolia. The existence of a rich productive infrastructure in the United States means that labor productivity and living standards are much higher, on average, for a person born in the United States than for one born in Mongolia. The person born in the United States inherits access to a large stock of social and privately held wealth, while the person born in Mongolia does not.

The disparate opportunities afforded by the existence of wealth, while obvious in the comparison between the United States and Mongolia, are also apparent within a well-developed country, such as the United States. While there is little doubt that poor American workers enjoy a higher material standard of living than the average Mongolian, it is also true that a person born into a wealthy American family has more opportunities than one born into the American standard of poverty. Personal wealth enables opportunities no differently than does social wealth. My earlier criticism of Kirzner's finders-keepers theory of justice (in chap. 4) makes this clear. The ability to capture an entrepreneurial opportunity will often depend on access to wealth, which can finance a speculative, productive enterprise directly or serve as collateral to obtain funds externally. Moreover, the development of the entrepreneurial capacity is itself contingent on quality of formal schooling and on networks of informal socialization, both of which are related to the possession of familial wealth. Arbitrary inheritance of personal and social wealth determines, to some extent, the opportunities that one is able to notice and to seize.[3]

To address the inequality of opportunity produced by disparate wealth holding, Bruce Ackerman and Anne Alstott (1999) propose the establishment of what they call a "stakeholder society." A stakeholder society is one in which all citizens have a claim to a social inheritance. Ackerman and Alstott suggest that this social inheritance should take the form of a large cash grant to all citizens when they reach the age of majority, a grant large enough to promote substantive equality of opportunity. As a benchmark for this, Ackerman and Alstott focus on the ability of each citizen to obtain a bachelor's degree at a private college. Their proposal sets the size of the stakeholder grant at the average cost of four years of private college tuition, which they calculate to be roughly eighty thousand dollars. Since a college degree is only an approximate indicator of equal opportunity, they would not limit the grant to educational purposes. Their proposal is in the classical liberal tradition insofar as they would allow each individual to determine the best use of his or her social inheritance.

Ackerman and Alstott also argue that stakeholding is in the individualist tradition of advancing freedom. To be effectively free requires more than equal treatment under the law; it requires the means to convert individual talents and potential into meaningful results. Redistributing wealth is imperative because "property is so important to the free development of individual personality that everybody ought to have some" (Ackerman and Alstott 1999, 191). Stakeholding is thus "based on the community's obligation to give each person equal respect by providing her with equal resources to develop her unique talents" (ibid., 194). The real possibility that the asset poor cannot obtain credit or can obtain it only at penalty interest rates supports and motivates an individualist case for wealth redistribution.

Ackerman and Alstott contend that a stakeholder society should be implemented gradually, since it obviously would be disruptive and inflationary to give grants of eighty thousand dollars simultaneously to all qualifying adults. They suggest that we select a first generation of stake recipients and thereafter grant a social inheritance to all qualified citizens who turn eighteen each year. To prevent a massive influx of immigrants seeking a stake and to limit the stake to those citizens living inside the country, Ackerman and Alstott believe the stake should be given only to citizens who have lived for at least eleven years inside the country. To gauge the approximate annual budget obligation for the U.S. government, they estimated the number of qualified eighteen-year-old American citizens in 1997: about 3.1 million. Providing each of these young men and women a stake would have cost about $250 billion, less than the annual U.S. military budget. This is certainly within the annual budget possibilities of the U.S. government.

To fund this annual outlay, Ackerman and Alstott argue for the implementation of a new wealth tax rather than relying on additional revenue from the income tax. In their view, the possession of wealth reflects an inequality of opportunity advantage, whereas unequal incomes partly reflect the disparate endowments people bring to the market. Since the goal of a stakeholder society is to promote equality of opportunity, taxing one source of unequal market outcomes to fund an equality-promoting social inheritance seems to Ackerman and Alstott to be the appropriate method to raise the necessary revenue. They calculate that an annual, 2 percent flat tax on net worth, after allowing a stakeholder exemption of eighty thousand dollars, would raise enough revenue to fund the program. Ultimately, however, they suggest that the system become self-financing, through the implementation of an estate tax on stakeholders. Stake recipients (or their estates) would be required to pay back their social inheritance, with interest, to the government.[4] Once the payback obligation is met, the wealthy could conceivably transfer the remainder of their estates to heirs of their choosing. If stakeholders lead economically prosperous lives and are able to pay back their grants, the institution of a social inheritance might one day, after the death of enough stakeholders, become self-financing, thus obviating the need for an ongoing wealth tax.

Ackerman and Alstott's stakeholding proposal, if modified slightly, offers an attractive institutional structure to achieve socialist distributive justice while also promoting worker self-management and socialist appropriative justice. While Ackerman and Alstott use possession of the means to attend college as the standard proxy for equality of opportunity, labor-managed market socialism might use possession of the means to purchase the average capital stock per worker as the standard measure of equal opportunity. This would raise the amount of the stake to around one hundred thousand dollars.[5] This revision of Ackerman and Alstott's proposal is based on a view of the stakeholder grant as a share of the accumulated capital stock of the society into which a person is born. Stakeholding would then cost a little over $310 billion. Edward Wolff (2002) notes that if the United States were to adopt the Swedish wealth tax with a progressive tax rate structure and a top marginal wealth taxation rate of 3 percent, the U.S. government could have raised an additional $330 billion in 1989.

Another modification to Ackerman and Alstott's proposal follows from the capability approach to justice. Ackerman and Alstott would place no limit on how people could use their social inheritance, because they accept the liberal belief that there are plural conceptions of the good life. They argue that once the government provides individuals with the means to achieve opportunity, it is up to those individuals to decide the best use of their grant. A capability approach, in contrast, does not value wealth for its own sake and believes that policies should have specific, capability-enhancing purposes. A socialist interpretation of the capability approach maintains that people should have equal opportunity to enter into nonexploitative work arrangements, through self-employment or by joining a labor-managed firm. A socialist, stakeholder society should therefore promote nonexploitative forms of good living. It would do so by providing a social inheritance to finance investments in human and physical capital: postsecondary education, vocational training, equipment to become an independent contractor, and potential membership fees to join a labor-managed firm. Perhaps the stake could also be used to purchase real estate, since it could readily be used as collateral to finance self-managed work opportunities. But using the stake to buy a car or to travel around the world—options permitted by Ackerman and Alstott's liberal stakeholding proposal—would be prohibited by a socialist stakeholder society.

Providing a substantial capital account that could be used to finance participation in a self-managed enterprise would go a long way toward solving the two major problems I have identified in worker self-management. First, giving potential members of cooperatives a capital account should reduce the risk aversion generally displayed by the asset poor. A regular criticism of worker self-management is that asset-poor collectives will invest less than their capitalist counterparts. If risk-taking is a function of wealth holding, giving all adults a capital account equal to the average capital stock per worker should encourage individuals and collectives to take more productivity-enhancing risks (although perhaps still not as much risk as a rich person under capitalism would be willing to bear).

Second, a socialist stakeholder society would reduce the difficulties faced by a collective of asset-poor workers in trying to obtain credit to start up or expand a new self-managed enterprise. The power of concentrated financial wealth in financial markets would be diminished if all workers gained access to a capital account at the beginning of their working lives. Any collective of workers would now be able to combine their individual stakes into an amount large enough to purchase capital equipment directly or to serve as collateral in pursuit of external finance for the equipment. Credit rationing would be less prevalent. Instituting a social inheritance should therefore facilitate the entry of new self-managed enterprises, producing a more robust market process. Backward-bending market supply curves and perverse employment reductions in response to price increases should not appear. By facilitating the market process in the context of worker self-management, stakeholding serves the goal of socialist distributive justice while also supporting the viability and the positive economic consequences of socialist appropriative justice.

HAYEK AND THE STAKEHOLDER SOCIETY

How does socialist stakeholding fit into the Hayekian vision? Inasmuch as it would be implemented via abstract, well-announced rules and would redistribute wealth outside of the market process, this system of social inheritance would not directly interfere with the market allocation of resources and distribution of income. In Ackerman and Alstott's proposal, the wealth tax is a proportional tax that levies all wealth at the same rate, above the stakeholder exemption of eighty thousand dollars (or one hundred thousand dollars). It does not seek to reward or punish any particular productive activity. Thus it should not disrupt the ability of the market process to coordinate the activities of diverse people with diverse knowledge. In the context of worker self-management, stakeholding might even strengthen the effectiveness of the market process by encouraging entry of new self-managed firms.

One might argue that wealth taxation reduces the incentive to save, thereby restricting the funds available for investment in real capital equipment and lowering the rate of economic growth. If so, stakeholding will make future generations less wealthy than they might otherwise be. On one level, this objection has a perverse quality in that it implicitly assumes that it is better to reduce equality of opportunity today in order to benefit the future population. But future generations will presumably be enriched by any economic growth, great or small, and by the expanded opportunities growth will bring. Why, then, deny potential opportunity to the poor today to the advantage of the relatively rich tomorrow?

On another level, it is not apparent that the incentive to save and to accumulate wealth is significantly impaired by modest levels of wealth taxation. A flat 2–3 percent wealth tax is a comparatively small marginal tax rate on savings and might not act as much of a disincentive to accumulate.[6] A brief reading of the evidence appears to support this conjecture. Savings rates in developed countries without a wealth tax range from 3.6 percent for the United Kingdom to 5.7 percent for the United States to 11.6 percent for Japan. Savings rates in the European countries with a wealth tax range from 4 percent for Spain to 10.5 percent for Switzerland (Wolff 2002, 71). Many European countries with a wealth tax have a higher savings rate than the United States. So it is not readily apparent that wealth accumulation and economic growth would be adversely affected by implementing wealth taxation and redistribution. If it is true that the ability to seize entrepreneurial opportunities is limited by the possession of wealth, then providing all adults with a wealth stake might end up encouraging entrepreneurial activity more widely, thereby producing such a positive impact on the rate of economic growth that it outweighs any negative impact that a wealth tax might have on aggregate saving.

Hayek also raises a moral objection to notions of equal opportunity that call for redistributions of wealth and income. He maintains that just because one person enjoys an inherited advantage, whether genetic or cultural, does not mean that someone else is entitled to the same advantage. No one argues, for example, that in the interest of equality of opportunity, we should compensate the ugly for their social and economic disadvantages relative to the attractive. Hayek asks why the situation should be any different with regard to inherited wealth and family connection. The advantage of the rule of law and equal treatment under the law is that all individuals—the smart and the handicapped, the risk-lovers and risk-averters, and the wealthy and the poor—are all regarded as alike by the coercive state apparatus that enforces universally applicable rules. In Hayek's mind, equal treatment under the law and unequal treatment by the market are both necessary in order for markets to work effectively. Disproportionately large or small market rewards signal the greater or lesser degree to which one's product or service satisfies the interest of others. Thus "the acquisition by any member of the community of additional capacities to do things which may be valuable must always be regarded as a gain for that community" (Hayek 1960, 88). Hayek therefore thinks that the only justification "for insisting on further advantages," beyond already living in a rich society (like the United States) in which people with talent and entrepreneurial vision have the incentive to make their contributions available in markets, "is that there is much private wealth that the government can confiscate and redistribute and that men who constantly see such wealth being enjoyed by others will have a stronger desire for it then those who know of it only abstractly, if at all" (ibid., 100–101). For Hayek, notions of equal opportunity that call for redistribution are just another form of envy.

The capabilities perspective on economic justice does not appeal to envy. It is, as I have shown, a perspective that develops an intersubjective account of good human functioning and human flourishing and asks about the institutional structure that best promotes good functioning for all people. Although they do not explicitly advocate a capability approach to justice, it is in the context of promoting good human functioning that Ackerman and Alstott's justification for wealth redistribution makes the most sense. To work effectively, markets require people to respect others' property and to engage in trustworthy behavior. Ackerman and Alstott thus reason:

> Given the continuing dependence of the wealthy on the cooperation of their fellow citizens, stakeholding does not involve coercive "gifts" to strangers. It represents a suitable act of recognition by the wealthy of the role played by fellow Americans in creating the conditions for the very system necessary for their own success. . . . [P]rivate property is legitimate only when it is rendered compatible with the larger political order created by free and equal citizens. (Ackerman and Alstott 1999, 32)

To this interpretation, I would add that private property is legitimate to the extent that it enhances human capabilities and to the extent that it is compatible with a political order created by people with the means to function well. It is Hayek's rule-utilitarian conception of the common good that eschews an intersubjective account of good living and leads him to think that "[t]here is no obvious reason why the joint efforts of the members of any group to ensure the maintenance of law and order and to organize the provision of certain services should give the members a claim to a particular share in the wealth of this group" (Hayek 1960, 101). This is so because his liberal subjectivism harbors a relativism that cannot make interpersonal comparisons of well-being.

Worker self-management has not evolved into a widespread organizational form, despite the potential efficiency advantages and desirable moral qualities examined in chapter 6 of this book. The most compelling explanation for this situation is that most workers lack enough wealth to buy the necessary productive equipment and to collateralize needed loans. This problem dovetails with the substantive inequalities that motivate the capability theory of justice. Thus, at the same time that worker self-management is not prevalent due to unequal access to resources, people have markedly unequal capacities to achieve good human functioning. For many people, easily achievable functions are not obtained at all, because of poverty and an institutional structure—including schooling, medicine, and prenatal care—that directs its benefits based on wealth and income rather than need. An ethically and economically viable socialism therefore requires a capabilities-enhancing, redistributive institution.

This redistributive institution might be a social democratic welfare state, as Nussbaum (1990) argues. But a welfare state, however desirable, is not a distributive institution that necessarily contributes to the feasibility of worker self-management. Neither, it turns out, is Roemer's market socialist idea to equalize profit income—the annual social surplus. What would make worker self-management feasible is a mechanism to promote entry of new self-managed enterprises. While Roemer's model could be a workable vision of socialism after Hayek if it were stripped of its element of investment planning and pared down to a coupon stock market, the resulting egalitarian distribution of profits would not directly encourage worker self-management. Although Roemer's market socialism might achieve a kind of socialist distributive justice, it would not enable or cultivate socialist appropriative justice.

By comparison, the redistribution of wealth—the accumulated social surplus—might support a socialist form of both appropriative and distributive justice. It is in this light that Ackerman and Alstott's provocative vision of a stakeholder society deserves our attention. By promising all young adult citizens a share of national wealth, stakeholding expands the real opportunities individuals can seize. By restricting the stake to certain capabilities-enhancing uses, it might also facilitate the competitive entry and systemic efficiency of self-managed enterprises. If we take seriously the Hayekian concern to make the market process work effectively, then the redistribution of wealth might be a necessary prerequisite to the implementation of Vanek's worker self-management amendment. To achieve socialist appropriative justice, it may first be necessary to realize socialist distributive justice.

CHAPTER 8

Socialism after Hayek

★

Traditional understandings of socialism have been antimarket. These views generally underestimate or ignore what I have called Hayek's "applied epistemological postmodernism." Because I accept many aspects of this applied postmodernism, I agree with Hodgson when he claims that socialism "must overcome its congenital *agoraphobia*" (Hodgson 1999, 61). Post-Hayekian socialism is necessarily market socialism. National economic planning, whether authoritarian or democratic, is a dubious ambition for the future of socialism. Postmodern Marxism gives market socialism a reachable goal: the abolition of exploitative class processes in which nonproducers appropriate the fruits of workers' labor. At the same time, the postmodern moments of Hayek's economics and the Austrian theory of the market process give postmodern Marxists and other socialists the intellectual tools to overcome their residual market phobia. Together, these Austrian and Marxist perspectives help all of us to recognize that the abolition of class exploitation and the abolition of markets are not isomorphic objectives, since worker appropriation is entirely consistent with worker cooperatives operating in the context of private ownership and free exchange of consumer and capital goods.

For the last century and a half, Marxists have called for an end to the exploitation of labor in order to usher in a postcapitalist, socialist future. But contrary to much of the Marxist tradition that has made changing ownership rights to the capital stock the linchpin of a future without exploitation, worker appropriation in self-managed firms can achieve the primary objective of class emancipation. Jossa (2005) provides textual evidence that Marx himself explicitly advocated worker cooperatives as a socialist form of economic organization. Labor appropriation (in democratic, self-managed firms) is a necessary feature of what I have called "socialist appropriative justice" (see chap. 6). Prohibiting wage labor and capitalist appropriation and replacing them with worker self-management and labor appropriation will end the legal alienation of workers' factual responsibility for production. Worker appropriation in cooperative enterprises fosters human dignity and is consistent with Marx's call to abolish the wages system. If labor-appropriating cooperatives operate in an environment where separate individuals own productive property and markets are effectively free, then, in principle at least, a system of labor-appropriating firms can be a socialist form of economic organization that avoids Hayekian knowledge problems. The specter of labor-appropriating cooperatives in a market economy in which the means of production are privately owned gives us, to combine the phrases of Cullenberg (1992) and Prychitko (1998), a thin vision of Hayekian socialism.[1]

Most socialists will probably find this Hayekian socialism thin soup. They will insist, correctly, that while worker cooperatives may enhance the capability of laborers to work with dignity and responsibility, the larger system of competitive markets is unlikely to yield a distribution of resources that effectively satisfies human needs. Yet this traditional socialist concern is precisely the focus of Nussbaum and Sen's capability theory of justice. Contrary to the postmodern fatalism characteristic of subjectivist, utilitarian, and Hayekian approaches to normative questions, the capability theory of justice believes that it is possible (and desirable) to specify basic human needs in a universal, yet open-ended, intersubjectivist way through comparative, cross-cultural conversations. A biologically essentialist, morally objectivist, or otherwise transcendent, "outside" perspective on human nature is not required. Further, Nussbaum and Sen's approach places a positive value on the equality of capabilities to satisfy these needs. This commitment to capabilities equality leads Nussbaum to argue that some form of social democracy or an elaborate welfare state is generally necessary to address the persistently unmet needs that arise in connection with free market economies.

Here we need to bear in mind Hayek's arguments about the socially constituted, tacit, and limited nature of individual human knowledge. The subjectivity of knowledge means that welfare state officials confront an insuperable knowledge problem: how are they to know whether the implementation of a particular policy will actually enhance the capabilities of any unique individual? This is not a problem derived simply from plural conceptions of good living. It a problem of how to achieve, in particular cases, an intersubjective standard of good living among diverse and dispersed individuals, each of whom possesses unique knowledge of the circumstances of time and place that affects his or her ability to live well. This is a factual knowledge problem, not an ethical knowledge problem. Socialists must have some humility regarding the knowledge that government officials can acquire to implement welfare-enhancing policies successfully.

This book does not aim to figure out how far or in what directions a welfare state can go before it confronts intractable Hayekian knowledge problems.[2] Rather, the aim here has been to explore which sets of institutions might make a system of labor cooperatives function well in a market economy. One reason that labor cooperatives have not evolved widely in modern societies, despite their potential superior efficiency, is that the typical worker lacks wealth and has no access to credit at competitive interest rates—or, in many instances, at any interest rate. The distribution of income and wealth in modern capitalist economies makes it very difficult for workers to establish labor-directed enterprises. Simply abolishing wage labor, as proposed by Jaroslav Vanek's amendment (cited in chap. 6), would do nothing to facilitate the entry of new labor-managed enterprises in the postcapitalist economy. Since the potential entry of new firms is necessary for the discovery and creation of economic opportunities, worker cooperatives in a private property economy may not work effectively—and hence may not provide the means to achieve other aspects of good human functioning—unless income or wealth is redistributed at the same time. Socialist distributive justice aims to create an institutional structure that effectively enhances the ability of people to form new worker-managed, labor-appropriating enterprises. Establishing a stakeholder society—that is, taxing wealth and redistributing it in equal citizens' grants at the age of maturity—is one way to achieve this essential goal.

If some version of Ackerman and Alstott's stakeholder society were adopted and if some form of Vanek's amendment were in place, worker self-management might work well in the context of a competitive market process. A well-functioning, competitive system of worker cooperatives would have other desirable distributive characteristics: profits would accrue to the manual and mental workers who participate in their creation, entry of new firms would tend to compete away economic profits, and incomes would reflect entrepreneurial alertness rather than prior access to wealth. In addition, the ongoing redistribution of wealth through a stakeholding right would likely lead to the enhancement of capabilities other than access to dignified workplaces—for instance, access to education. While wealth, from the capability perspective, is not an intrinsic good, the all-purpose nature of wealth makes it a useful tool for enhancing capabilities in a flexible manner. This is especially so if we restrict stakeholder grants to specific, capability-enhancing uses.

Some socialists, though, still resist the conclusion that markets are a necessary component of a modern, complex society. While there is little support for top-down national economic planning, many socialists today advocate what they call decentralized, participatory planning.[3] Michael Albert and Robin Hahnel are perhaps the best-known advocates of this approach. For them, the achievement of socialism means that workers "would finally seize control of their destinies by consciously and democratically planning their interconnected labors" (Albert and Hahnel 1992, 39).[4]

Albert and Hahnel's model of participatory planning bears some similarity to Oscar Lange's model of socialism, discussed in chapter 2 of this book. Like

Lange, Albert and Hahnel would abolish private ownership and market exchange of capital goods and create what they call an Iteration Facilitation Board (IFB). The IFB would announce prices for all goods and services to both producers and consumers. Producers and consumers would use these prices to formulate their respective production and consumption plans. Unlike Lange's model, Albert and Hahnel's IFB would have no oversight function of the production units: firms would be democratically self-managed.

Albert and Hahnel's model also differs from Lange's in that consumer goods markets would be eliminated. Instead, individuals would belong to local consumers' councils that would gather their members' consumption preferences based on the prices announced by the IFB and report these consumption intentions back to the IFB. The IFB would take these consumption plans and compare them with the production plans announced by the democratically managed firms, looking for any potential shortages or surpluses. If any exist, the IFB would then adjust the array of "indicative" prices, ask for a report on revised consumption and production plans, and look again for shortages and surpluses. This process would continue until a set of mutually consistent prices was reached. Production would then commence, and goods would be shipped to the consumer councils for subsequent distribution to their members, according to individuals' consumption plans.

In Albert and Hahnel's model, individual incomes would be calculated according to a person's effort and "sacrifice for the social benefit" (Albert and Hahnel 1992, 54). A person's coworkers would be responsible for rating his or her work effort. The effort rating of one's peers establishes a budget constraint when a person reports his or her consumption plan to the consumer council. But consumer councils would have the power to adjust the effort ratings of their members, if the councils felt that some people's needs would not be adequately met by the "purchasing power" indicated by their work ratings (ibid., 55). Thus, in this model, market exchange would have no role in determining the allocation and distribution of resources. All production decisions and consumption bundles would be determined by participatory conversations at the various workplaces and consumer councils.

For Albert and Hahnel, such a participatory planning system would serve to correct what they see as three fundamental defects in free market capitalism. First, market participants normally do not consider social costs and benefits when implementing their production and consumption plans. Nor do markets provide an adequate level of public goods, since people have little incentive to express their preferences for these goods in a market setting. Participatory planning may not allocate resources perfectly either, but "the estimates of social costs and benefits that emerge from [a process of participatory planning] will be less imperfect than the estimates that emerge from [market exchange]" (Albert and Hahnel 2002b, 27). As a result, Albert and Hahnel believe that participatory planning is better equipped to incorporate neighborhood effects and to deliver public goods. Second, capitalist firms generally give workers no role in decision making. Albert and Hahnel make the Hayekian claim that hierarchical firms result in a loss of their employees' tacit, practical knowledge, since workers have little incentive to utilize it (Albert and Hahnel 2002a, 155). They believe that participatory planning in the workplace would correct this flaw. Finally, market economies are inequitable in that they do not reward people "according to effort interpreted as personal sacrifice in work and training toward the public benefit" (Albert and Hahnel 1992, 41). Albert and Hahnel argue that a more equitable distribution of goods would be achieved if one's coworkers were responsible for determining the degree of one's efforts and sacrifices for the public good and one's resulting share of consumption goods. A market distribution of payment according to the productivity of one's labor and property is flawed, in the minds of Albert and Hahnel, because actual productivity is not only a function of effort but also the arbitrary and unmerited inheritance of traits and property.

Most of Albert and Hahnel's criticisms of free market capitalism are consistent with this book's argument for post-Hayekian market socialism. Nearly all economists, including Hayek, recognize that markets, in order to function well, must be embedded in an institutional framework that includes a government to provide public goods and to establish a set of rules or policies to internalize social costs and benefits into individual decision making. One purpose of my critique, in chapter 4, of Hayek's legal theory was to highlight the importance of democratic processes in the determination of this institutional structure. A post-Hayekian socialism would give democratic processes a larger role in determining the nature of the institutions in which markets should be embedded in order to promote the common good.

Socialists, such as Albert and Hahnel, who advocate decentralized planning in the absence of private property face a critical question: are social costs and benefits better captured by democratic local, regional, and national planning agencies in the absence of markets or by markets embedded in a set of property rights assignments, rules, and regulations determined by democratic local, regional, and national governments? Pre-Hayekian socialists would be strongly inclined to imagine that participatory planning, without markets, would be a superior method of grappling with social costs and benefits. But socialists who have absorbed the significance of Hayek's discussion of the fragmented, dispersed, inarticulate, and intersubjective nature of human knowledge would surely be more circumspect and more mindful of the cost-benefit knowledge—its discovery and creation—that would be lost if market processes, profit incentives, hard budget constraints, and individual property rights were replaced by dialogues in democratic firms and consumers' councils.

A parallel contrast emerges with respect to labor-managed firms. Albert and Hahnel's critique of the forgone tacit knowledge in hierarchical firms resonates with the argument that this book presents for worker cooperatives. It may well be the case that worker cooperatives or firms that are planned by workers' councils would elicit more tacit knowledge from their members than the typical capitalist enterprise is able to extract from its employees. However, labor-appropriating cooperatives that are subject to the market discipline of profit and loss would in all likelihood offer better incentives for workers to discover and act on their intuitive insights and tacit knowledge than would Albert and Hahnel's system of participatory planning, which could only rely on moral suasion—in the form of wanting to be a good team player—to get individuals to contribute their unobservable (and costly to express) personal knowledge to the benefit of the group. Since the post-Hayekian market socialist firm would offer its members both material rewards and moral suasion, it is likely to be more productive of socially beneficial knowledge than is an Albert-Hahnel participatory enterprise operating in a democratically planned economy.

Albert and Hahnel are certainly right that a free market distribution of wealth, income, and opportunity would leave much to be desired, even in an economy of worker-appropriating firms. This is why post-Hayekian market socialism would include a capabilities-enhancing welfare state. The question is whether an ethic of capabilities equality is preferable to Albert and Hahnel's distributive maxim, "To each according to effort and personal sacrifice towards the common good." Both ethics share the view that ongoing democratic dialogue about justice is important—to determine, for example, the nature of capabilities equality or the extent of an individual's socially beneficial sacrifice. But whereas the capabilities ethic admits a role for market exchange in the interest of justice, Albert and Hahnel's effort ethic allows markets no such role.

There are thus two major defects in Albert and Hahnel's effort ethic. First, in the absence of market prices, estimates of an individual's sacrifices for the common good will be problematic, because they rest entirely on the judgments of one's workmates. These assessments are confounded by two sorts of knowledge problem: (1) a person's capacity to exert effort—and hence the actual sacrifice involved in a person's labor—is largely unobservable, even by one's workmates; and (2) the social benefits of an individual's performance are difficult to judge in the absence of market prices. The second major difficulty with Albert and Hahnel's effort ethic is that it does not recognize the existence of certain "process" aspects of human flourishing, one of which is the freedom to exchange. The capability theory of justice associated with post-Hayekian, postmodern socialism offers a multidimensional account of the material and procedural requirements of a flourishing life that supports both markets and a governmental guarantee of the means to achieve basic need satisfaction. Following Nussbaum and Sen, a post-Hayekian socialism sees the freedom to exchange as a fundamental capability to facilitate the achievement of a flourishing life that should be tempered only insofar as it conflicts with other essential capabilities (e.g., the ability to work in a dignified, nonexploitative labor process). Participatory planning, inasmuch as it seeks to abolish market exchange entirely, is not a promising model for post-Hayekian socialism.

Though they eschew the socialist label, Samuel Bowles and Herbert Gintis (1998) propose a vision of market socialism similar to the one advanced in this book: they advocate workplace democracy and asset redistribution. They do not, however, support a rule banning the capitalist firm, such as Vanek's amendment, or a substantial universal wealth grant, such as Ackerman and Alstott's citizens' stakeholder grant. They seek to encourage worker self-management through government provision of credit to self-managed enterprises at competitive interest rates, government provision of insurance to labor-managed firms that face bankruptcy due to a hostile economic environment (as measured by some set of variables exogenous to the decisions taken by individual firms), and a high level of unemployment insurance (whose benefits are likewise triggered by the behavior of exogenous, macroeconomic variables). Under such a policy regime, Bowles and Gintis argue that worker self-management would evolve naturally in cases where it was more efficient than capitalist enterprises. To promote equality of opportunity, they support asset redistribution through such policies as government-funded vouchers for education, government-subsidized construction of low-income housing, and government enforcement of children's claims on the income streams of their divorced parents.

Bowles and Gintis's strategy is to reduce inequality and increase efficiency by targeting specific problems between principal and agent that arise from information asymmetries. For instance, the capitalist firm is often less efficient than workplace democracy because capitalists (the principals) devote excessive resources to monitoring the effort given by workers (the agents) whose work characteristics are not easily observable when the labor contract is struck. Likewise, poor renters (the agents) have superior information about neighborhood events and normal wear and tear of their dwellings, which may reduce the value of the rental property, yet they have little motivation to report this information to the landlords (the principals) who have the incentive to address these problems. Finally, school administrations (the agents) have superior knowledge about how the educational process might be improved but less incentive to act on their knowledge if children and their families (the principals) are more or less a captive audience, as in many U.S. public school systems today. In each of these cases, a problem between the principles and the agents arises because the agents have superior access to relevant information and hence the power to take actions contrary to the interests of the principals. Bowles and Gintis encourage the redistribution of assets in order to align the incentives of property owners more closely with the incentives of property users. This, they argue, would enhance equality of opportunity while also improving economic efficiency. They describe their goal as "competition on a level playing field" (Bowles and Gintis 1998, 57). Although they nowhere argue this point, Bowles and Gintis's policy proposals would each serve to enhance a certain set of capabilities to achieve well-being.

The question we need to ask is which vision offers more hope for a post-capitalist society: the asset redistributions advocated by Bowles and Gintis or a post-Hayekian socialism comprised of Ackerman and Alstott's stakeholder grant and Vanek's amendment? On the one hand, Bowles and Gintis's policy suggestions might be more politically feasible than the post-Hayekian socialism sketched in this book. Governments are already involved in the provision of insurance and the subsidization of some types of credit and production but generally are not engaged in the distribution of universal cash grants or the prohibition of capitalist work relations. On the other hand, Bowles and Gintis's policies often depend on price-fixing—that is, on government officials altering the prices faced by asset-poor individuals in competitive markets in an attempt to achieve greater equity and efficiency. Hayekians would surely ask how government officials are supposed to know what the right prices should be. Many socialists would question Bowles and Gintis's emphasis on economic efficiency as a central normative goal—for example, their willingness to let workplace democracy evolve only where it is more efficient than capitalist firms. Such arguments are not likely to be compelling to socialists, for whom the ability to participate in dignified, capabilities-enhancing, labor-appropriating workplaces outweighs any potential efficiency losses experienced in moving away from capitalism. For socialists, making capitalist exploitation a thing of the past is an overarching goal (as long as it can be done in ways that do not lead to an overall diminution of other capabilities to lead a flourishing life).

The preceding Hayekian and socialist points give a theoretical edge to the model of post-Hayekian socialism defended in this book. However, it is important to note the complementarity of the two visions. The democratic implementation of Vanek's amendment and a stakeholder society would require a cultural and political sea change in the United States and other wealthy nations. Most people in these countries are not ready to vote to abolish wage labor or to establish sizable, universal wealth grants. It thus seems prudent for practical socialists to be open to market-friendly, evolutionary proposals—such as those advanced by Bowles and Gintis—that promise to move us toward more extensive worker appropriation and the expansion of capabilities equality. Policy experiments to encourage workplace democracy and other capabilities-enhancing forms of asset redistribution or property rights redefinition need not take us anywhere near Hayek's "road to serfdom."

Notes

CHAPTER 1

1. For instance, in the *Manifesto of the Communist Party*, Marx and Engels explicitly call for "abolition of property in land" and the "extension of factories and instruments of production owned by the State" (Marx and Engels 1978, 490). In *Socialism: Utopian and Scientific*, Engels laments the anarchy of the market while describing socialism as a state in which "[s]ocialized production upon a predetermined plan becomes henceforth possible" (Engels 1978, 717).

2. Other important contributions to the Amherst school include, among others, Amariglio 1988, 1990; Amariglio and Ruccio 1998; Callari and Ruccio 1996; Chakrabarti and Cullenberg 2003; Cullenberg, Amariglio, and Ruccio 2001; DeMartino 2000, 2003; Resnick and Wolff 2002; Ruccio 1991; Ruccio and Amariglio 2003; Wolff and Resnick 1987.

CHAPTER 2

1. In the following discussion, my use of the term *constituents* (or the term *constitution*) is intended to capture the idea that a "thing" or an "act"—for instance, in Hayek's work, either the critical act of perception or human action more generally—is the effect of a potentially infinite set of factors, none of which is the essential, ultimately determinant cause of the "thing." Moreover, if one of these constitutive factors is removed, the constituted "thing" ceases to be the same as it was, because the "thing" itself has no essential nature.

2. Resnick and Wolff have made a similar point in a discussion of theoretical differences among economists. They suggest that theoretical disagreements are often constituted by the different organizing concepts, or "entry points" (Resnick and Wolff 1988, 53–54), employed by economists from different schools of thought. If anything separates Hayek's theory of "categories" from Resnick and Wolff's theory of "entry points," it is the tendency for Hayek to treat the classification schemes people use as removed from theoretical struggle. He implies we all share certain categories because they have contributed to our survival as a human community. Resnick and Wolff, on the contrary, believe these categories are "overdetermined" (ibid., 49–54) and thus contain an irreducible element of theoretical, political, and cultural contestation.

3. Historical time is lived time. The concept expresses the notion that the past is irrevocable and the future unknowable. It is an active constituent of human experience. We can contrast historical time with logical time. Logical time is conceived as space, as homogeneous points on a number line. As such, it is reversible and homogeneous; each temporal point is an empty space, waiting to be filled with events on

which time exerts no influence. See O'Driscoll and Rizzo 1985 for a summary exposition of different notions of time in economic theory. In contemporary economics, notions of logical time are more prevalent than notions of historical time.

4. See Sugden 1989 for a defense of a Hayekian understanding of rules and conventions against various rational choice models.

5. See Ebeling 1986 for a brief discussion on the market as a "hermeneutical process." For Ebeling "the economic problem can usefully be understood as a hermeneutical problem, i.e., as a problem of interpreting and understanding what another means and intends in his words and deeds" (ibid., 40).

6. Hayek adds another criticism that bears less directly on the aspects of his subjectivism I pursue here but that will become relevant when I explore models of worker self-management as a form of post-Hayekian socialism in chapters 6–7. Hayek argued that Lange's market socialism discourages risk taking because plant managers lack the property to cover losses from failed ventures.

CHAPTER 3

1. This interpretation of Adam Smith follows Overton Taylor (1955). More recent commentators on Smith's work suggest that perhaps Smith postulated the existence of a universal human nature more as a methodological device than as an empirical fact. See, for example, Fleischacker 2004.

2. Walter Block (1996) nicely demonstrates that Hayek is not a deontological, natural rights libertarian. Block laments Hayek's acceptance of many policies that a natural rights libertarian finds offensive for their violation of a Nozickian sanction against involuntary transfers or for their prohibition of voluntary transfers—that is, minimum wage laws, laws restricting the length of the working day, income maintenance programs, social insurance, antitrust laws, and regulation of externalities. Various degrees of support for all of these policies can be found in Hayek's work, to Block's chagrin. Chapter 5 of the present book addresses whether Hayek can successfully support these kinds of policies with his rule utilitarianism.

3. See Thomson 1991 for a good discussion of Hayek's position in liberal jurisprudence.

CHAPTER 4

1. Kuhn (1970) and Rorty (1979) are two well-known philosophers who have made this point. But see also Hayek 1967e, 54 (emphasis added): "So far as the recognition of the particular conditions is concerned to which a theoretical statement is applicable, we always have to rely on *interpersonal agreement*, whether the conditions are defined in terms of sensory qualities such as 'green' or 'bitter', or in terms of point coincidences, as is the case where we measure."

2. It is clear that Hayek understands the mind to be socially constituted. According to Hayek, "what we call mind is essentially a system of . . . rules conjointly determining particular actions" (Hayek 1978d, 42). These rules are acquired through experience with particular objects, people, languages, and human cultures. Although the mind is a socially constituted system of rules that generates particular actions, the "various combinations of abstract propensities [or rules] ... makes it possible for a causally determined structure of actions to produce ever new actions it has never pro-

duced before" (ibid., 48). As Hayek notes, "[e]ven a relatively limited repertory of abstract rules that can thus be combined into particular actions will be capable of 'creating' an almost infinite variety of particular actions" (ibid., 49).

3. We can also challenge Hayek's legal thought by noting how the subjectivity of rules and facts blurs the line between facts and rules. Kim Lane Scheppele (1990) draws on the legal realist literature to argue that the distinction between law and fact is impossible to uphold because interpretation of facts necessarily involves interpretation of law and vice versa. The radical legal historian Morton Horwitz describes how the emergence of a supposed distinction between law and fact at the turn of the nineteenth century in the United States was due, in part, to the desire of judges to limit the ability of juries to decide the law of a case (M. Horwitz 1977, 28–29). Judges wanted to retain the authority to pass judgment on the law relevant to a case, so that they could encourage economic growth through the legal system. The distinction between law and fact limited the power of juries to the determination of legal facts, thereby minimizing a jury's ability to reach decisions hostile to commercial and industrial interests.

4. James Gordley illustrates how theories of justice have shaped the development and structure of modern law. His work thus disputes Hayek's claims about the apolitical, atheoretical evolution of the common law, as well as Hayek's claims that theories of justice (i.e., the rule of law) are derived from the practice of common law jurists. Gordley notes that some legal theorists, such as Hayek, think that "the 'great elementary conceptions, ownership, possession, contract, tort and the like,' seemed to have emerged without benefit of theory from an English legal tradition that stressed the practical and particular." Gordley contends: "it did not happen that way. The great elementary conceptions of contract law came out of a Greek philosophical tradition grafted on to Roman law by moral philosophers" (Gordley 1991, 246). Gordley concludes that theory saturates both a court's determination of the validity of any contract and a court's rulings more generally.

5. See Kirzner 1985, 116, for his distinction among arbitrage, speculation, and productive creativity.

6. In a response to my critique of his application of the finders-keepers rule to a theory of just distribution (Burczak 2002), Kirzner (2002) does not recognize or acknowledge the importance that a notion of equality (i.e., of opportunity to be an entrepreneur) plays in his defense of that rule.

7. The Austrian literature is generally critical of Stiglitz's work. See, for instance, Thomsen 1992, 29–62. But Thomsen does observe that "individuals in a Hayekian world could attempt to infer information from prices if it were profitable for them to do so" (ibid., 43). This observation is one of the central building blocks of the credit rationing literature. Zappia's interesting 1997 essay develops the theme that the recent Post-Walrasian microtheory literature that includes Bowles and Gintis (1990a, 1993, 1998) and Stiglitz and Weiss (1981) is compatible with a Hayekian perspective.

8. Because voluntary self-enslavement is not permissible in Western society, individuals who lack financial assets but who possess considerable human capital are not able to use their human capital as collateral. As Bowles and Gintis (1990a, 193) remind us, not all forms of wealth may be pledged as collateral in financial transactions.

9. McCloskey (1990) puts forth the identical argument in a critique of Bowles and Gintis 1990a.

10. Ionnides (1993) develops a related perspective on Kirzner's theory of profit.

11. For ease of exposition, the following paragraph makes no distinction between the ethic of reaping where one sows—arguing that a person may legitimately appropriate the product created by the sweat of his or her brow—and the fruit-of-the-tree ethic.

12. See Boettke 1997 for a discussion of Hayek's use of market equilibrium as an ideal type that parallels diZerega's understanding of the common good as an ideal type.

13. Hasnas believes that public choice economists expose real-world political processes to produce inferior results when compared to real-world markets (Hasnas 1995a, 112–32). Yet his conclusion misses the point, insofar as the standard one uses to evaluate markets is precisely what is called into question by the realist critiques of legal neutrality and of a disinterested determination of the common good by the common law.

14. The legal process also institutes a forum to air disputing parties' competing legal arguments and perspectives on justice. But the disputants do not attempt to persuade each other of the merits of their views, and the judge has sole authority to decide who presents a better argument. The legal process, in other words, offers a quite constrained arena for the articulation of competing visions of justice. See, however, Levi 1964, 280–81, for a more favorable evaluation of courts as a site to debate political and moral issues.

CHAPTER 5

1. See Nussbaum 1992a, 222, for a more complete list of essential human functions and the capabilities necessary to achieve those functions. Nussbaum identifies the following basic capabilities one must possess in order to be able to choose a flourishing life. Not all of these are easily influenced by public policy.

1. Being able to live to the end of a complete human life, as far as is possible; not dying prematurely, or before one's life is so reduced as to be not worth living.
2. Being able to have good health; to be adequately nourished; to have adequate shelter; having opportunities for sexual satisfaction; being able to move from place to place.
3. Being able to avoid unnecessary and nonbeneficial pain and to have pleasurable experiences.
4. Being able to use the five senses; being able to imagine, to think, and to reason.
5. Being able to have attachments to things and persons outside ourselves; to love those who love and care for us, to grieve at their absence, in general, to love, grieve, to feel longing and gratitude.
6. Being able to form a conception of the good and to engage in critical reflection about the planning of one's own life.
7. Being able to live for and with others, to recognize and show concern for other human beings, to engage in various forms of familial and social interaction.
8. Being able to live with concern for and in relation to animals, plants, and the world of nature.
9. Being able to laugh, to play, to enjoy recreational activities.

10. Being able to live one's own life and nobody else's; being able to live one's own life in one's very own surroundings and context.

2. Boettke suggests that although Hayek himself was not a libertarian, if Hayek's subjectivism is followed consistently, one is led to libertarian policy conclusions (Boettke 1995a, 22 n. 1). If an implicit account of well-being were (hypothetically speaking) not to be found in Hayek's work, Boettke's conclusion would be correct. Hayekian libertarianism, though, would be libertarianism without normative or empirical foundations, since Hayek's evolutionary legal and social theory is incompatible with notions of natural rights that lie at the heart of classic libertarian thought, such as Nozick's and Rothbard's, and since there is no libertarian tradition of empirical work showing that well-being is enhanced by free market institutions (see Friedman 1997).

3. This is not to suggest that people who inhabit capability-rich environments might not, nevertheless, make choices the Aristotelian would find to be opposed to human flourishing.

4. According to Hayek, the argument for liberty "insists that these individual differences provide no justification for government to treat them differently" (Hayek 1960, 85–86). In traditional classical liberal doctrine, "the duty of government was not to ensure that everybody had the same prospect of reaching a given position but merely to make available to all on equal terms those facilities which in their nature depended on government action" (ibid., 92).

5. Block (1996) is relentless in making this point from the libertarian perspective.

6. In their book *Liberty and Nature: An Aristotelian Defense of Liberal Order* (1991), Douglas Rasmussen and Douglas Den Uyl go so far as to claim that an Aristotelian concern for human flourishing is best realized by libertarianism. In his review of their book, Richard Kraut responds that "any political philosophy that seeks a foundation in an Aristotelian conception of well-being will be naturally and reasonably lead to conclusions that give the state a far larger role to play than the one that Rasmussen and Den Uyl assign it" (Kraut 1997, 372). Since strong separateness is only one of the functional capabilities from an Aristotelian perspective, it is hard not to conclude that there might be ethical limitations on the market.

CHAPTER 6

1. Resnick and Wolff (1987, 121) note: "Marx repeatedly emphasizes the difference between commodity exchange and the production/appropriation of surplus value. The former is strictly an exchange of values; it is not the site or source of surplus value. Commodity exchange is an economic process, but it is not [exploitation]. When the capitalist buys the commodity labor power, this commodity exchange is not the source of surplus value."

2. This list of the possible reasons for a normative critique of capitalist exploitation might usefully be contrasted with the lists of Roemer (1986, 261–62) and Cohen (1995, 195).

3. Resnick and Wolff are not the only Marxists who have insisted that the Soviet Union was an example of state capitalism. See, for instance, the discussion in Bettelheim 1976. However, Resnick and Wolff's interpretation of the Soviet economy as state capitalist is based on their investigation of who appropriates surplus labor,

while other authors, such as Chattopadhyay (1992) and Yaghmaian (1994), call the Soviet Union state capitalist because, despite the state ownership of capital, the labor process did not assume a socialist, nonhierarchical form.

4. Husami 1980 and Roemer 1988 contain two plausible rejoinders to Wood's position. Geras 1985 surveys the literature on the relationship between Marxism and justice and provides an extensive bibliography. Geras 1992 updates that bibliography and treats the continuing debate. Lukes 1985 and Peffer 1990 offer extensive assessments of the contending perspectives. West 1991 constructs a postmodernist alternative on the relationship between Marxism and justice. McCarthy 1992 consists of an edited collection of essays on the relationship between Marx and Aristotle, several of which suggest that Marx's apparent condemnation of exploitation is linked to an Aristotelian perspective on justice.

5. In Wood's reading of Marx, capitalism may be condemned for nonmoral reasons, because it denies the nonmoral goods of "self-actualization, security, physical health, comfort, community, [and] freedom" to all members of society (Wood 1981, 129). Against Wood, Peffer (1990, 179–v85) argues persuasively that it is not easy to distinguish between a concern for self-actualization, security, physical health, comfort, community, and freedom and a concern for fairness and justice.

6. Miller (1983) does not share this conclusion with Gilbert and me.

7. Bowles and Gintis (1993) note that proper maintenance of the capital stock is also difficult to monitor. That is one reason capital owners are often the appropriating agents in the firm. Simply transferring rights of appropriation to workers, as Ellerman (1992) advocates, may result in an inefficient level of capital maintenance. As a result, Bowles and Gintis, unlike Ellerman, believe that the democratically appropriating firm may also need to place significant ownership of the capital assets employed by the firm in the hands of the workers in order to realize a socially efficient amount of maintenance of the capital stock.

8. Vanek (1996) presents a set of other categories (beyond economic efficiency) that we might use to evaluate the performance of a system of labor-managed firms against the performance of firms operating under capitalism. He suggests that worker self-management is superior to capitalism with regard to distributive justice, job security, pollution abatement, the quality of educational institutions, and social harmony. Because I do not have the space here to evaluate all of these consequentialist claims regarding the desirability of worker self-management, I will simply note that reasons besides the Marxist concern to eliminate exploitation can animate a call for the labor-managed firm.

CHAPTER 7

1. That Roemer has never completely grasped the nature of the Austrian perspective on the market process is evident in the title of his review of Joseph Stiglitz's book *Whither Socialism?* In the book, Stiglitz uses the concept of asymmetric information carefully to dismantle general equilibrium theory. Roemer mistakenly believes that Hayek's defense of the market economy relies on general equilibrium arguments. Hence, in his review title, Roemer calls Stiglitz's book "an anti-Hayekian manifesto" (Roemer 1995).

2. Consistent with my argument in chapter 5, democratic government might still adopt targeted capability-enhancing policies that apply "outside" the market.

3. Bowles and Gintis (2002) attempt to quantify the degree to which inheritance impacts economic opportunity.

4. Using a 2 percent real interest rate (roughly equal to the average rate of productivity growth), recipients of an eighty-thousand-dollar stake would have to pay back $250,000 to the state treasury forty years later.

5. This number comes from Bowles and Gintis (1998, 64 n. 48), who claim that the average value of the capital stock per U.S. worker is a little less than one hundred thousand dollars.

6. If the U.S. income tax were replaced by a consumption tax, a change both consistent with a vision of socialism after Hayek and advocated by many economists, any disincentive to save by the wealth tax could be countered by making saving exempt from income taxation.

CHAPTER 8

1. Some of these ideas are debated in Burczak 1996–97, Boettke 1998, Burczak 1998, Cullenberg 1998, and Prychitko 1998.

2. Appreciating Hayek's factual knowledge problem means that when we search for ways to enhance human capabilities, we should probably first investigate alternative sets of capability-enhancing rules that can be applied universally. Jaroslav Vanek's worker self-management amendment (cited in chap. 6) is one example. Then we might ask what kind of goal-oriented, capability-enhancing policies government can provide outside the market. Some sort of government-funded (although not necessarily government-run) educational system would seem to be appropriate in this regard. The provision of national health insurance is another possibility that comes to mind here.

3. Conceptions of decentralized, participatory planning are extensively debated in "Building Socialism Theoretically" (2002), a special issue of the journal *Science and Society*. For another discussion of participatory planning that situates itself against the Austrian critique of central planning, see Adaman and Devine 1996. Cottrell and Cockshott (1993) are a notable exception to the socialist trend toward supporting decentralized, democratic planning; see S. Horwitz 1996 for an Austrian critique of their position, to which I would add little.

4. Prychitko 1988 provides an Austrian critique of an earlier presentation of Albert and Hahnel's model of participatory planning.

References

Ackerman, B., and A. Alstott. 1999. *The Stakeholder Society*. New Haven and London: Yale University Press.

Adaman, F., and P. Devine. 1996. "The Economic Calculation Debate: Lessons for Socialists." *Cambridge Journal of Economics* 20 (September): 523–37.

Albert, M., and R. Hahnel. 1992. "Participatory Planning." *Science and Society* 56 (spring): 39–59.

———. 2002a. "Comment." *Science and Society* 66 (spring): 154–56.

———. 2002b. "Reply." *Science and Society* 66 (spring): 26–28.

Alchian, A., and H. Demsetz. 1972. "Production, Information Costs, and Economic Organization." *American Economic Review* 62 (December): 777–95.

Amariglio, J. 1988. "The Body, Economic Discourse, and Power: An Economist's Introduction to Foucault." *History of Political Economy* 20 (winter): 583–613.

———. 1990. "Economics as a Postmodern Discourse." In *Economics as Discourse*, ed. W. Samuels, 15–46. Boston: Kluwer.

Amariglio, J., and D. Ruccio. 1998. "Postmodernism, Marxism, and the Critique of Modern Economic Thought." In *Why Economists Disagree*, ed. D. Prychitko, 237–73. Albany: State University of New York Press.

Aristotle. 1998. *Nicomachean Ethics*. Mineola, NY: Dover.

Arnold, N. S. 1996. "The Monitoring Problem for Market Socialist Firms." In *Advances in Austrian Economics*, vol. 3, ed. P. Boettke and D. Prychitko, 41–58. Greenwich, CT: JAI Press.

Barone, E. 1908. "The Ministry of Production in the Collectivist State." In Hayek 1935, 245–90.

Bettelheim, C. 1976. *Class Struggles in the USSR: First Period, 1917–1923*. Trans. B. Pearce. New York: Monthly Review Press.

Blair, M. 1995. *Ownership and Control: Rethinking Corporate Governance for the Twenty-first Century*. Washington, DC: Brookings.

Bloch, E. 1986. *Natural Law and Human Dignity*. Trans. D. J. Schmidt. Cambridge, MA: MIT Press.

Block, W. 1996. "Hayek's Road to Serfdom." *Journal of Libertarian Studies* 12 (fall): 327–50.

Boettke, P. 1990. "Interpretive Reasoning and the Study of Social Life." *Methodus* 2 (December): 35–45.

———. 1995a. "Hayek's *The Road to Serfdom* Revisited: Government Failure in the Argument against Socialism." *Eastern Economic Journal* 21 (winter): 7–26.

———. 1995b. "Why Are There No Austrian Socialists? Ideology, Science, and the Austrian School." *Journal of the History of Economic Thought* 17 (spring): 35–56.

———. 1997. "Where Did Economics Go Wrong? Modern Economics as a Flight from Reality." *Critical Review* 11 (winter 1): 11–64.

———. 1998. "Rethinking Ourselves: The Individual, the Community, and the Political Economy of Postcommunism." *Rethinking Marxism* 10 (summer): 85–95.

Bowles, S., and H. Gintis. 1986. *Democracy and Capitalism*. New York: Basic Books.

———. 1990a. "Contested Exchange: New Microfoundations for the Political Economy of Capitalism." *Politics and Society* 18 (June): 165–222.

———. 1990b. "Reply to Our Critics." *Politics and Society* 18 (June): 293–315.

———. 1993. "The Democratic Firms: An Agency-Theoretic Evaluation." In *Markets and Democracy: Participation, Accountability, and Efficiency*, ed. S. Bowles, H. Gintis, and B. Gustafsson, 13–39. Cambridge: Cambridge University Press.

———. 1998. *Recasting Egalitarianism*. London and New York: Verso.

———. 2002. "The Inheritance of Inequality." *Journal of Economic Perspectives* 16 (summer): 3–30.

Buchanan, J., and V. Vanberg. 1991. "The Market as a Creative Process." *Economics and Philosophy* 7 (October): 167–86.

"Building Socialism Theoretically: Alternatives to Capitalism and the Invisible Hand." 2002. Special issue, *Science and Society* 66 (spring).

Burczak, T. 1996–97. "Socialism after Hayek." *Rethinking Marxism* 9 (fall): 1–18.

———. 1998. "Appropriation, Responsibility, and Agreement." *Rethinking Marxism* 10 (summer): 96–105.

———. 2002. "A Critique of Kirzner's Finders-Keepers Defense of Profit." *Review of Austrian Economics* 15 (January): 75–90.

Caldwell, B. 1994. "Hayek's Scientific Subjectivism." *Economics and Philosophy* 10 (October): 305–13.

———. 2004. *Hayek's Challenge*. Chicago and London: University of Chicago Press.

Callari, A., and D. Ruccio, eds. 1996. *Postmodern Materialism and the Future of Marxist Theory: Essays in the Althusserian Tradition*. Hanover, NH: University Press of New England for Wesleyan University Press.

Carling, A. 1990. "In Defense of Rational Choice: A Reply to Ellen Meiksins Wood." *New Left Review* 184 (November–December): 97–109.

Chakrabarti, A., and S. Cullenberg. 2003. *Transition and Development in India*. London and New York: Routledge.

Chattopadhyay, P. 1992. "The Economic Content of Socialism: Marx vs. Lenin." *Review of Radical Political Economics* 24 (September and December 3–4): 90–110.

Christainsen, G. B. 1990. "Law as a Discovery Procedure." *Cato Journal* 9 (winter): 497–530.

Cohen, G. A. 1995. *Self-Ownership, Freedom, and Equality*. Cambridge: Cambridge University Press.

Cohen, M., T. Nagel, and T. Scanlon. 1980. *Marx, Justice, and History*. Princeton, NJ: Princeton University Press.

Cottrell, A., and W. P. Cockshott. 1993. "Calculation, Complexity, and Planning: The Socialist Calculation Debate Once Again." *Review of Political Economy* 5 (January): 73–112.

Crocker, D. 1992. "Functioning and Capability: The Foundations of Sen's and Nussbaum's Development Ethic." *Political Theory* 20 (November): 584–612.

Crowley, B. L. 1987. *The Self, the Individual, and the Community: Liberalism in the Political Thought of F. A. Hayek and Sidney and Beatrice Webb*. Oxford: Oxford University Press.

Cullenberg, S. 1992. "Socialism's Burden: Toward a 'Thin' Definition of Socialism." *Rethinking Marxism* 5 (summer): 64–83.

———. 1998. "Exploitation, Appropriation, and Exclusion." *Rethinking Marxism* 10 (summer): 66–75.

Cullenberg, S., J. Amariglio, and D. Ruccio, eds. 2001. *Postmodernism, Economics, and Knowledge*. London and New York: Routledge.

DeMartino, G. 2000. *Global Economy, Global Justice: Theoretical Objections and Policy Alternatives to Neoliberalism*. London and New York: Routledge.

———. 2003. "Realizing Class Justice." *Rethinking Marxism* 15 (January): 1–31.

de Ste. Croix, G. 1981. *The Class Struggle in the Ancient Greek World: From the Archaic Age to the Arab Conquests*. Ithaca, NY: Cornell University Press.

diZerega, G. 1989. "Democracy as a Spontaneous Order." *Critical Review* 3 (spring): 206–40.

Drèze, J. 1993. "Self-Management and Economic Theory: Efficiency, Funding, and Employment." In *Market Socialism*, ed. P. Bardhan and J. Roemer, 253–65. New York and Oxford: Oxford University Press.

Ebeling, R. 1986. "Toward a Hermeneutical Economics: Expectations, Prices, and the Role of Interpretation in the Theory of the Market." In Kirzner 1986, 39–52.

Ellerman, D. 1988. "The Kantian Person/Thing Principle in Political Economy." *Journal of Economic Issues* 22 (December): 1109–22.

———. 1992. *Property and Contract in Economics*. Oxford, UK, and Cambridge, MA: Basil Blackwell.

Engels, F. 1978. *Socialism: Utopian and Scientific*. In *The Marx-Engels Reader*, 2nd ed., ed. R. Tucker, 683–717. New York and London: W. W. Norton.

Fleischacker, S. 2004. *On Adam Smith's Wealth of Nations: A Philosophical Companion*. Princeton, NJ: Princeton University Press.

Fleurbaey, M. 1993. "Economic Democracy and Equality: A Proposal." In *Market Socialism*, ed. P. Bardhan and J. Roemer, 266–78. New York and Oxford: Oxford University Press.

Frank, J. 1970. *Law and the Modern Mind*. Gloucester, MA: Peter Smith.

———. 1973. *Courts on Trial*. Princeton, NJ: Princeton University Press.

Friedman, J. 1997. "What's Wrong with Libertarianism." *Critical Review* 11 (summer): 407–67.

Friedman, M. 1953. *Essays in Positive Economics*. Chicago: University of Chicago Press.

Gabriel, S. 1990. "Ancients: A Marxian Theory of Self-Exploitation." *Rethinking Marxism* 3 (spring): 85–106.

Geras, N. 1985. "The Controversy about Marx and Justice." *New Left Review* 150 (March–April): 47–85.

———. 1992. "Bringing Marx to Justice: An Addendum and Rejoinder." *New Left Review* 195 (September–October): 37–69.

Gilbert, A. 1992. "Marx's Moral Realism: Eudaimonism and Moral Progress." In McCarthy 1992, 303–28.

Gordley, J. 1991. *The Philosophical Origins of Modern Contract Doctrine*. New York and Oxford: Oxford University Press.

Hasnas, J. 1995a. "Back to the Future: From Critical Legal Studies Forward to Legal Realism, or How Not to Miss the Point of the Indeterminacy Argument." *Duke Law Journal* 45 (October): 84–132.

———. 1995b. "The Myth of the Rule of Law." *Wisconsin Law Review*, (January–February): 199–223.

Hayek, F. 1931. *Prices and Production*. London: Routledge and Sons.

———, ed. 1935. *Collectivist Economic Planning*. London: Routledge and Sons.

———. [1944] 1976. *The Road to Serfdom*. Chicago: University of Chicago Press.

———. 1948a. "Economics and Knowledge." In Hayek 1948c, 33–56.

———. 1948b. "The Facts of the Social Sciences." In Hayek 1948c, 57–76.

———. 1948c. *Individualism and Economic Order.* Chicago: University of Chicago Press.

———. 1948d. "Individualism: True and False." In Hayek 1948c, 1–32.

———. 1948e. "The Meaning of Competition." In Hayek 1948c, 92–106.

———. 1948f. "Socialist Calculation II: The State of the Debate." In Hayek 1948c, 148–80.

———. 1948g. "Socialist Calculation III: The Competitive 'Solution.'" In Hayek 1948c, 181–208.

———. 1948h. "The Use of Knowledge in Society." In Hayek 1948c, 77–91.

———. 1952. *The Sensory Order.* Chicago: University of Chicago Press.

———. 1960. *The Constitution of Liberty.* Chicago: University of Chicago Press.

———. 1961. "Freedom and Coercion: Some Comments and Mr. Hamowy's Criticism." *New Individualist Review* 1 (April): 28–30.

———. 1967a. "Degrees of Explanation." In Hayek 1967f, 3–21.

———. 1967b. "Kinds of Rationalism." In Hayek 1967f, 82–95.

———. 1967c. "The Non Sequitur of the Dependence Effect." In Hayek 1967f, 313–17.

———. 1967d. "Notes on the Evolution of Systems of Rules of Conduct." In Hayek 1967f, 66–81.

———. 1967e. "Rules, Perception, and Intelligibility." In Hayek 1967f, 43–65.

———. 1967f. *Studies in Philosophy, Politics, and Economics.* Chicago: University of Chicago Press.

———. 1973. *Law, Legislation, and Liberty.* Vol. 1, *Rules and Order.* Chicago: University of Chicago Press.

———. 1976. *Law, Legislation, and Liberty.* Vol. 2, *The Mirage of Social Justice.* Chicago: University of Chicago Press.

———. 1978a. "Competition as a Discovery Procedure." In Hayek 1978c, 179–90.

———. 1978b. "The Confusion of Language in Political Thought." In Hayek 1978c, 71–97.

———. 1978c. *New Studies in Philosophy, Politics, Economics, and the History of Ideas.* Chicago: University of Chicago Press.

———. 1978d. "The Primacy of the Abstract." In Hayek 1978c, 35–49.

———. 1979a. *The Counter-Revolution of Science.* 2nd ed. Indianapolis: Liberty Press.

———. 1979b. *Law, Legislation, and Liberty.* Vol. 3, *The Political Order of a Free People.* Chicago: University of Chicago Press.

———. 1988. *The Fatal Conceit.* Chicago: University of Chicago Press.

Hodgson, G. 1999. *Economics and Utopia.* London and New York: Routledge.

Holmes, S., and C. Sunstein. 1999. *The Cost of Rights: Why Liberty Depends on Taxes.* New York and London: W. W. Norton.

Horwitz, M. 1977. *The Transformation of American Law, 1780–1860.* Cambridge, MA: Harvard University Press.

Horwitz, S. 1992. "Monetary Exchange as an Extra-Linguistic Social Communication Process." *Review of Social Economy* 50 (summer): 193–214.

———. 1996. "Money, Money Prices, and the Socialist Calculation Debate." In *Advances in Austrian Economics,* vol. 3, ed. P. Boettke and D. Prychitko, 59–77. Greenwich, CT: JAI Press.

Husami, Z. 1980. "Marx on Distributive Justice." In Cohen, Nagel, and Scanlon 1980, 42–79.

Ionnides, S. 1993. "Comment on I. Kirzner's Notion of Pure Profit." *Journal des Economistes et des Etudes Humaines* 4 (June–September): 329–33.

Jameson, F. 1984. "Postmodernism, or The Cultural Logic of Late Capitalism." *New Left Review* 146 (July–August): 53–92.

Jossa, B. 2005. "Marx, Marxism, and the Cooperative Movement." *Cambridge Journal of Economics* 29 (January): 3–18.

Kain, P. 1992. "Aristotle, Kant, and the Ethics of the Young Marx." In McCarthy 1992, 213–42.

Kamenka, E. 1972. *The Ethical Foundations of Marxism.* 2nd ed. Boston and London: Routledge and Kegan Paul.

Kant, I. 1964. *Groundwork of the Metaphysic of Morals.* Trans H. J. Paton. New York: Harper Torchbooks.

———. 1977. *Prolegomena to Any Future Metaphysics.* Indianapolis: Hackett.

Keynes, J. [1944] 1971. "Letter to Hayek." In *The Collected Writings of John Maynard Keynes*, 27:385–88. New York: St. Martin's.

Kirzner, I. 1979a. "Capital, Competition, and Capitalism." In Kirzner 1979c, 91–106.

———. 1979b. "Knowing about Knowledge: A Subjectivist View of the Role of Information." In Kirzner 1979c, 137–53.

———. 1979c. *Perception, Opportunity, and Profit.* Chicago: University of Chicago Press.

———. 1985. *Discovery and the Capitalist Process.* Chicago: University of Chicago Press.

———, ed. 1986. *Subjectivism, Intelligibility, and Economic Understanding.* New York: New York University Press.

———. 1989. *Discovery, Capitalism, and Distributive Justice.* Oxford: Basil Blackwell.

———. 1992. *The Meaning of Market Process: Essays in the Development of Modern Austrian Economics.* London and New York: Routledge.

———. 1995. "The Nature of Profits: Some Economic Insights and Their Ethical Implications." In *Profits and Morality*, ed. R. Cowan and M. Rizzo, 22–47. Chicago: University of Chicago Press.

———. 2002. "Comment on 'A Critique of Kirzner's Finders-Keepers Defense of Profit.'" *Review of Austrian Economics* 15 (January): 91–94.

Klamer, A., and D. McCloskey. 1989. "The Rhetoric of Disagreement." *Rethinking Marxism* 2 (fall): 140–61.

Koppl, R., and D. G. Whitman. 2004. "Rational-Choice Hermeneutics." *Journal of Economic Behavior and Organization* 55 (November): 295–317.

Kraut, R. 1997. "Aristotelianism and Libertarianism." *Critical Review* 11 (summer): 359–72.

Kuhn, T. 1970. *The Structure of Scientific Revolutions.* 2nd ed. Chicago: University of Chicago Press.

Kukathas, C. 1989. *Hayek and Modern Liberalism.* Oxford: Oxford University Press.

Lachmann, L. 1986. *The Market as an Economic Process.* New York and Oxford: Basil Blackwell.

Lange, O. [1936] 1966. "On the Economic Theory of Socialism." In Lippincott 1966, 55–143.

Lavoie, D. 1985. *Rivalry and Central Planning: The Socialist Calculation Debate Reconsidered.* Cambridge: Cambridge University Press.

———. 1986a. "Euclideanism versus Hermeneutics: A Reinterpretation of Misean Apriorism." In Kirzner 1986, 192–210.

———. 1986b. "The Market as a Procedure for Discovery and Conveyance of Inarticulate Knowledge." *Comparative Economic Studies* 28 (spring): 1–19.

———. 1989. "Economic Chaos or Spontaneous Order? Implications for Political Economy of the New View of Science." *Cato Journal* 8 (winter): 613–35.

————, ed. 1990. *Economics and Hermeneutics*. London and New York: Routledge.

————. 1994. "A Political Philosophy for the Market Process." In *The Market Process: Essays in Contemporary Austrian Economics*, ed. P. Boettke and D. Prychitko, 274–84. Aldershot, UK, and Brookfield, VT: Edward Elgar.

Levi, E. H. 1964. "The Nature of Legal Reasoning." In *Law and Philosophy*, ed. S. Hook, 263–81. New York: New York University Press.

Lippincott, B., ed. 1966. *On the Economic Theory of Socialism*. New York: McGraw Hill.

Llewellyn, K. 1960. *The Bramble Bush*. New York: Oceana Publications.

Lucas, R. 1981. "Understanding Business Cycles." In *Studies in Business-Cycle Theory*, 215–39. Cambridge, MA: MIT Press.

Lukes, S. 1985. *Marxism and Morality*. Oxford: Oxford University Press.

Madison, G. B. 1989. "Hayek and the Interpretive Turn." *Critical Review* 3 (spring): 169–85.

————. 1990a. "Getting Beyond Objectivism: The Philosophical Hermeneutics of Gadamer and Ricoeur." In Lavoie 1990, 34–58.

————. 1990b. "How Individualistic Is Methodological Individualism?" *Critical Review* 4 (winter–spring): 41–60.

Marx, K. 1964. *The Economic and Philosophic Manuscripts of 1844*. Ed. D. Struik. New York: International Publishers.

————. 1965. *Wages, Price, and Profit*. Peking: Foreign Languages Press.

————. 1967. *Capital*. Vol. 3. New York: International Publishers.

————. 1973. *Grundrisse*. Trans. M. Nicholas. New York: Vintage.

————. 1975. "Contribution to the Critique of Hegel's Philosophy of Law: Introduction." In *Karl Marx-Frederick Engels Collected Works*, 3:175–87. New York: International Publishers.

————. 1976. *Capital*. Vol. 1. Trans. B. Fowkes. New York: Vintage.

————. 1978. "Critique of the Gotha Program." In *The Marx-Engels Reader*, 2nd ed., ed. R. Tucker, 525–41. New York and London: W. W. Norton.

Marx, K., and F. Engels. 1970. *The German Ideology*. New York: International Publishers.

————. 1978. *Manifesto of the Communist Party*. In *The Marx-Engels Reader*, 2nd ed., ed. R. Tucker, 469–500. New York and London: W. W. Norton.

McCann, C. R., Jr. 2002. "F. A. Hayek: The Liberal as Communitarian." *Review of Austrian Economics* 15 (January): 5–34.

McCarthy, G. 1992. *Marx and Aristotle*. Savage, MD: Rowan and Littlefield.

McCloskey, D. 1990. "Their Blackboard, Right or Wrong: A Comment on Contested Exchange." *Politics and Society* 18 (June): 223–32.

————. 1992. "Minimal Statism and Metamodernism: Reply to Friedman." *Critical Review* 6 (winter): 107–12.

Miller, R. 1983. "Marx and Morality." In *Nomos*, vol. 26, *Marxism*, ed. J. R. Pennock and J. Chapman, 3–32. New York and London: New York University Press.

————. 1992. "Marx and Aristotle: A Kind of Consequentialism." In McCarthy 1992, 275–302.

Mises, L. von. 1920. "Economic Calculation in the Socialist Commonwealth." Trans. S. Adler. In Hayek 1935, 87–103.

————. 1936. *Socialism: An Economic and Sociological Analysis*. Trans. J. Kahane. London: Jonathan Cape.

Nozick, R. 1974. *Anarchy, State, and Utopia*. New York: Basic Books.

Nussbaum, M. 1990. "Aristotelian Social Democracy." In *Liberalism and the Good*, ed.

R. B. Douglass, G. M. Mara, and H. S. Richardson, 203–52. London and New York: Routledge.

———. 1992a. "Human Functioning and Social Justice: In Defense of Aristotelian Essentialism." *Political Theory* 20 (May): 202–46.

———. 1992b. "Nature, Function, and Capability: Aristotle on Political Distribution." In McCarthy 1992, 175–211.

———. 1995. "Aristotle on Human Nature and the Foundation of Ethics." In *World, Mind, and Ethics,* ed. J. E. J. Altham and R. Harrison, 86–131. Cambridge: Cambridge University Press.

O'Driscoll, G., and M. Rizzo. 1985. *The Economics of Time and Ignorance.* New York and Oxford: Basil Blackwell.

Okun, A. 1975. *Equality and Efficiency: The Big Tradeoff.* Washington, DC: Brookings.

Peffer, R. 1990. *Marxism, Morality, and Social Justice.* Princeton, NJ: Princeton University Press.

Prychitko, D. 1988. "Marxism and Decentralized Socialism." *Critical Review* 2 (fall): 127–47. Reprinted in Prychitko 2002, 17–34.

———. 1995. *Individuals, Institutions, Interpretations: Hermeneutics Applied to Economics.* Brookfield, VT: Avebury.

———. 1996. "The Critique of Workers' Self-Management: Austrian Perspectives and Economic Theory." In *Advances in Austrian Economics,* vol. 3, ed. P. Boettke and D. Prychitko, 5–25. Greenwich, CT: JAI Press. Reprinted in Prychitko 2002, 70–88.

———. 1998. "Hayekian Socialism: Rethinking Burczak, Ellerman, and Kirzner." *Rethinking Marxism* 10 (summer): 75–85. Reprinted in Prychitko 2002, 89–99.

———. 2002. *Markets, Planning, and Democracy.* Cheltenham, UK, and Northampton, MA: Edward Elgar.

Putterman, L. 1996. "Coupons, Agency, and Social Betterment." In Roemer 1996, 139–58.

Rasmussen, D., and D. Den Uyl. 1991. *Liberty and Nature: An Aristotelian Defense of Liberal Order.* La Salle, IL: Open Court.

Rawls, J. 1971. *A Theory of Justice.* Cambridge, MA: Harvard University Press.

Resnick, S., and R. Wolff. 1987. *Knowledge and Class.* Chicago: University of Chicago Press.

———. 1988. "Marxian Theory and the Rhetoric of Economics." In *The Consequences of Economic Rhetoric,* ed. A. Klamer, D. McCloskey, and R. Solow, 47–63. Cambridge: Cambridge University Press.

———. 1993. "State Capitalism in the USSR? A High-Stakes Debate." *Rethinking Marxism* 6 (summer): 46–68.

———. 1994. "Between State and Private Capitalism: What Was Soviet 'Socialism'?" *Rethinking Marxism* 7 (1): 9–30.

———. 2002. *Class Theory and History: Capitalism and Communism in the U.S.S.R.* London and New York: Routledge.

Roberts, B. 1988. "What Is Profit?" *Rethinking Marxism* 1 (spring): 136–51.

Roemer, J. 1986. "Should Marxists Be Interested in Exploitation?" In *Analytical Marxism,* ed. J. Roemer, 260–82. Cambridge: Cambridge University Press.

———. 1988. *Free to Lose.* Cambridge, MA: Harvard University Press.

———. 1994. *A Future for Socialism.* Cambridge, MA: Harvard University Press.

———. 1995. "An Anti-Hayekian Manifesto." *New Left Review* 211 (May–June): 112–29.

———. 1996. *Equal Shares: Making Market Socialism Work,* ed. E. O. Wright. London and New York: Verso.

Rorty, R. 1979. *Philosophy and the Mirror of Nature.* Princeton, NJ: Princeton University Press.

Ruccio, D. 1991. "Economics and Postmodernism." *Journal of Post Keynesian Economics* 13 (summer): 495–510.

Ruccio, D., and J. Amariglio. 2003. *Postmodern Moments in Modern Economics.* Princeton, NJ: Princeton University Press.

Samuelson, P. 1957. "Wages and Interest: Marxian Economic Models." *American Economic Review* 47 (December 6): 884–912.

Scheppele, K. L. 1990. "Facing Facts in Legal Interpretation." *Representations* 30 (spring): 42–77.

Sciabarra, C. M. 1995. *Marx, Hayek, and Utopia.* Albany: State University of New York Press.

Sen, A. 1992. *Inequality Reexamined.* Cambridge, MA: Harvard University Press.

———. 1999. *Development as Freedom.* New York: Anchor Books.

Stigler, G. 1967. "Imperfections in the Capital Market." *Journal of Political Economy* 75 (June): 287–92.

Stiglitz, J., and A. Weiss. 1981. "Credit Rationing in Markets with Imperfect Information." *American Economic Review* 71 (June): 393–410.

Sugden, R. 1989. "Spontaneous Order." *Journal of Economic Perspectives* 3 (fall): 85–97.

———. 1993. "Welfare, Resources, and Capabilities: A Review of *Inequality Reexamined* by Amartya Sen." *Journal of Economic Literature* 31 (December): 1947–62.

Tarascio, V. 1972. "Vilfredo Pareto and Marginalism." *History of Political Economy* 4 (fall): 406–25.

Taylor, F. [1929] 1966. "The Guidance of Production in a Socialist State." In Lippincott 1966, 41–54.

Taylor, O. 1955. *Economics and Liberalism.* Cambridge, MA: Harvard University Press.

Thomsen, I. 1992. *Prices and Knowledge: A Market-Process Perspective.* London and New York: Routledge.

Thompson, F. 1996. "Would Roemer's Socialism Equalize Income from Surplus?" In Roemer 1996, 170–83.

Thomson, A. 1991. "Taking the Right Seriously: The Case of F. A. Hayek." In *Dangerous Supplements: Resistance and Renewal in Jurisprudence,* ed. P. Fitzpatrick, 68–101. Durham, NC: Duke University Press.

Vanberg, V. 1986. "Spontaneous Market Order and Social Rules: A Critical Examination of F. A. Hayek's Theory of Cultural Evolution." *Economics and Philosophy* 2 (April): 75–100.

Vanek, J. 1996. "The Austrians and Self-Management: A Positive Essay." In *Advances in Austrian Economics,* vol. 3, ed. P. Boettke and D. Prychitko, 27–40. Greenwich, CT: JAI Press.

West, C. 1991. *The Ethical Dimensions of Marxist Thought.* New York: Monthly Review Press.

White, L. H. 1984. *Methodology of the Austrian School.* Auburn, AL: Ludwig von Mises Institute.

Williams, J. 1997. "Hayek, Democracy, and the Rule of Law." *Critical Review* 11 (winter): 101–20.

Wolff, E. 2002. *Top Heavy: The Increasing Inequality of Wealth in America and What Can Be Done about It.* New York: New Press.

Wolff, R., and S. Resnick. 1987. *Economics: Marxian versus Neoclassical.* Baltimore, MD: Johns Hopkins University Press.

Wood, A. 1980a. "The Marxian Critique of Justice." In Cohen, Nagel, and Scanlon 1980, 3–41.

———. 1980b. "Marx on Right and Justice: A Reply to Husami." In Cohen, Nagel, and Scanlon 1980, 106–34.

———. 1981. *Karl Marx*. London and New York: Routledge.

Yaghmaian, B. 1994. "Socialist Labor Process Revisited." *Review of Radical Political Economics* 26 (June): 67–91.

Yeager, L. 1985. "Utility, Rights, and Contract: Some Reflections on Hayek's Work." In *The Political Economy of Freedom: Essays in Honor of F. A. Hayek*, ed. K. R. Leube and A. H. Zlabinger, 61–80. Munich: Philosophia Verlag.

Zappia, C. 1997. "Private Information, Contractual Arrangements, and Hayek's Knowledge Problem." In *Austrian Economics in Debate*, ed. W. Keizer, B. Tieben, and R. van Zijp, 264–84. London and New York: Routledge.

Index

coercion, 55, 81, 90–91, 92, 93, 135; freedom from, 46–47, 49, 90
Cohen, G. A., 8, 101, 115, 120
collateral, 73, 75, 126
collective interest, 80, 83. *See also* common good
commodities, appropriation of, 107–8, 109
common good: Hayek on, 14, 36–37, 38–57, 79, 136; democracy and, 78–81; evolution and law in, 50–54, 58; knowledge problems and, 54–57; rule of law and social order, 45–50; spontaneous order and evolution in, 40–45, 51, 92; thick notion of, 54
common law, 3, 13, 45, 50, 56; legal realism and, 14, 58, 59, 61, 64; non-neutrality of, 59–66; precedent and, 50, 52, 64; rule of law and, 38, 39, 51, 54, 57, 82
common stock, 122
competition, 26, 28–29, 31
constitutional amendment. *See* Vanek, Jaroslav
Constitution of Liberty, The (Hayek), 90
constructivist rationalism, 6
consumer preferences, 27–28, 33. *See also* individual choice
consumer's councils, 141, 143
cooperative enterprises, 138, 139–40
cosmos concept, 40–41, 44, 53
cost-benefit analysis, 26, 49, 69, 141, 142
Cost of Rights, The (Holmes and Sunstein), 93
Counter-Revolution of Science (Hayek), 20
coupon stock market, 15, 124–30; market process critique of, 127–30
credit rationing, 58–59, 106, 120, 126, 127; asset poor and, 14, 67, 72, 73, 75, 76, 124, 134; entrepreneurship and, 67–73, 75; inequality of opportunity and, 66–77, 82; interest rates and, 73–76, 140, 144; labor-managed firms and, 123, 128–29; transaction costs and, 75, 76
Crowley, Brian L., 81
Cullenberg, Stephen, 8–9, 10, 11, 139
cultural relativism, 87, 88

debt financing, 129–30
decision-making, 20, 117. *See also* judicial decision-making
DeMartino, George, 9–11, 88, 99, 100
democracy, social, 97–98, 139
democratic legislation, 53, 59–60, 82. *See also* rule of law
democratic process, 14, 78–81, 142. *See also* workplace democracy
Discovery, Capitalism, and Distributive Justice (Kirzner), 70–71
dispersed knowledge, 26, 30, 34, 95. *See also* knowledge problem
distributive justice, 37, 55, 67, 78, 99; Roemer model, 124–30; socialist type of, 4, 9–10. *See also* social justice
dividend income, 125
diZerega, Gus, 80
Drèze, Jacques, 123

Ebeling, Richard, 11
economic planning, 13. *See also* central planning
efficiency, 95, 119, 126, 128, 145
effort ethic, 141, 143–44
Ellerman, David, 101, 118–19; on appropriation, 104–5, 107, 109–10; labor theory of property, 111–14, 115–16, 117, 120–21
Engels, Friedrich, 1, 98, 110
entrepreneurship, 26, 28, 32, 67–73, 128; arbitrage and, 67, 68, 76, 77; bias against asset poor and, 67, 72, 73, 75, 76; capacity for, 131, 135; finders-keepers ethic and, 67–68, 70, 72–73, 77, 89; profit and, 69, 70, 72, 76, 140; risk in, 71–72, 76; speculation in, 69, 77; subjectivism and, 33
epistemological postmodernism, 1–2, 5–12, 13, 40; class and, 6–8. *See also* knowledge problem
equality, liberty and, 89–90, 95
equality of opportunity, 55, 66–77, 124, 132–33, 135; asset redistribution and, 144, 145; capability theory and, 96–97; credit rationing and, 82; entrepreneurship and, 67–73; finders-keepers ethic and, 67–68, 70, 72–73, 131

equilibrium, 27, 32, 73, 76, 120; in Roemer model, 127–28
essentialism, 6, 84, 87–88
estate tax, 132
eudaimonism, 116
"everythingism," 6
evolution. See social evolution
experience, perception and, 21–22
exploitation, 7, 101, 103–9, 120; abolition of, 8–9, 12, 98, 138; ancient, 106; in capitalism, 103–4, 107–9, 115, 121; defined, 103; injustice in, 103–4, 110, 114–15; self-exploitation, 105–7. See also class exploitation

factor valuation tables, 31, 35
factual knowledge problem, 2, 56, 93, 94–98, 99, 153n2. See also knowledge problem
finders-keepers theory, 67–68, 70, 72–73, 77, 89, 131
Fleurbaey, M., 123–24
flourishing life, 15, 88, 97, 117, 136; capability theory and, 84, 85, 144. See also good life
Frank, Jerome, 61–62, 65
freedom, 4, 8, 90–92, 131; from coercion, 46–47, 49, 90–91; economic justice and, 86; process aspects of, 97; rule of law and, 40, 53, 94
freedom of contract: property rights and, 39
free market system, 2, 28, 67, 85, 120, 141. See also market economy
Friedman, Milton, 55
fruit-of-the-tree ethic, 77

Gabriel, Satya, 106, 107
German Ideology, The (Marx), 10
Gilbert, Alan, 102, 116
Gintis, Herbert, 16, 73–74, 75, 119, 144–45, 146
Global Economy, Global Justice (DeMartino), 9–11
good life, 81, 85, 91, 133, 139; thin theory of, 86–87. See also flourishing life
government action, 14, 57, 96, 129, 142; arbitrariness of, 39; coercive power of, 46–47, 54–55, 90–91, 92, 93; financial regulation and, 126; limited,

38; public policy and, 44–45, 84, 85, 144; rule of law and, 45, 55; stakeholder proposal and, 132. See also public policy
government officials, 2, 56, 129, 145. See also central planning
"Great Society," 85
group interest, 61, 65. See also common good
group selection, 42–43

Hahnel, Robin, 16, 140–44
Hasnas, J., 79, 150n13
Hayek, Friedrich, 1, 121, 129, 148n2; on central planning, 13–14; on market discovery, 26–29, 67, 70, 127–28; and Marx compared, 4; on perception, 20–24; on rule of law, 90–91; on stakeholder society, 134–36; on worker self-management, 117–21. See also common good, Hayek on; knowledge problem; rule of law
Hayek, Friedrich, works of: The Constitution of Liberty, 90; Counter-Revolution of Science, 20; The Mirage of Social Justice, 55, 91, 98; The Political Order of a Free People, 80–81; The Road to Serfdom, 38–39, 54, 91, 98
hermeneutical process, 11, 84
Hodgson, Geoffrey, 12–13, 138
Holmes, Stephen, 93
Horwitz, Morton, 65, 149n3
Horwitz, Steven, 11
human action, 17, 62; constituents of, 20–26; perception and, 20–24; public policy and, 44–45; social evolution and, 40, 41–42; social rules and, 24–25; spontaneous order and, 40–45; subjective knowledge and, 33–34
human capital, 119–20
human dignity, 117, 121, 138
human nature, 84, 86, 116
Husami, Z., 101, 108, 120

impartiality, 57, 58–61, 66, 72, 82
imputation principle, 112–14
incentives, 119; central planning and, 34, 36; managerial, 127, 129; market, 10, 28; social welfare policy and, 94. See also profit incentive

income, entrepreneurial profit and, 70–71

income redistribution, 4, 32, 55, 106–7, 121; in coupon stock market, 124, 125, 130; minimum income, 91–92, 95; wealth redistribution and, 9, 82, 137

individual choice, 26, 27–28, 36, 58, 90–91, 142; choice-worthy decisions and, 95, 96–97; constraints on, 77; Nussbaum on, 88–89, 98; prices and, 32–33; rational choice in, 42–43; responsibility and, 94, 118–19. *See also* human action

individual initiative. *See* entrepreneurship

individualism, 40, 46; methodological, 17–20, 42–44

individual responsibility, 48, 118–19

industrialization, law and, 65

Inequality Reexamined (Sen), 89–90

information: asymmetric, 58–59, 74; in stock markets, 126

inheritance, 125; social, 131–34, 135

institutional welfarism, 97–98. *See also under* welfare

interest rates, 123–24, 129, 130, 132; credit access and, 73–76, 140, 144

interpretive community, 88

intuition, of judges, 61, 62

investment, 32, 123, 126, 127, 129–30; capital, 133

invisible hand, 48

Iteration Facilitation Board (IFB), 141

Japanese economic system, 126, 128

Jossa, B., 138

judicial decision-making, 60–66; efficiency in, 79; impartiality, 60–61; intuition in, 61, 62; precedent in, 50, 52, 63–64; subjective knowledge in, 64, 78

justice: appropriative, 10–11, 101, 102, 138; in common law, 53; exploitation and, 103–4, 110, 114–15; sense of, 50. *See also* distributive justice; social justice

Kain, P., 102

Kamenka, E., 102

Kant, Immanuel, 21, 52, 102, 115

Keynes, John Maynard, 38–39, 57

Kirzner, Israel, 27–28, 75–77; on entrepreneurship, 67–73; finders-keepers theory of, 67–68, 70, 72–73, 77, 89, 131

knowledge problem, 2–3, 9, 13, 117, 142; capabilities equality and, 85–94; common good and, 78; dispersed knowledge and, 26, 30, 34; factual, 2, 56, 93, 94–98, 99, 153n2; Marxist socialism and, 11; rule of law and, 48; social justice and, 54–57, 82–100; social order and, 51. *See also* subjective knowledge

Koppl, R., 11

Kukathas, Chandran, 52

labor cooperatives, 138, 139–40, 143

labor-managed firms, 101–21, 123; appropriation in, 104–5, 107–11, 113–14; capability theory and, 114–17; Hayek on, 117–21; imputation principle and, 112–14; property theory and, 111–14, 115, 116–17; responsibility of labor in, 111–12; self-exploitation and, 105–7

labor theory of property, 111–14, 115, 116–17, 120–21

labor theory of value, 107–9, 115

Lachmann, Ludwig, 11

Lange, Oscar, 17, 29, 73, 129, 140–41; on central planning, 30–33, 35

language, perception and, 22

Lavoie, Don, 2, 11, 12, 34; on cosmos, 44

Lee Kuan Yew, 87

legal realism, 14, 58, 59, 61, 64

Levi, Edward, 65–66

liberalism, 36, 52, 55, 80; good life and, 85, 86; individual choice and, 88–89

libertarianism, 4, 90, 92, 148n2

living standards, 33, 131

Llewellyn, Karl, 61, 62–64, 65

location, perception and, 23–24

Locke, John, 102, 105, 111–12

Lucas, Robert, 17, 18

McCloskey, D., 84, 88

Madison, G. B., 19–20

management, 128–29; central planning

public policy, 39, 44–45, 54, 85, 144; capability theory and, 84; democratic, 59–60, 79; voluntary consent and, 80. *See also* government action

Putterman, Louis, 130

quality of life, 83. *See also* well-being

rational action, 20, 41
rational choice, 11, 42–44
rationalism, 6–7
rational principle, 21, 51–52
Rawls, John, 51, 57, 86–87, 89, 96
redistribution. *See* income redistribution; wealth redistribution
reductionism, 18–19
residual claimants, 119, 128
Resnick, Stephen, 6–7, 8, 99, 101, 120, 147n2; on appropriation, 104, 109, 110; on exploitation, 103, 107
responsibility, 86, 94, 117, 121; individual, 48, 118–19; of labor, 111–14
risk, 74, 123, 133–34; entrepreneurial, 71–72, 76
Road to Serfdom, The (Hayek), 38–39, 54, 91, 98
Roberts, Bruce, 107–8
Roemer, John, 17, 29, 100, 101, 120, 137; coupon stock market and, 15, 124–30; on distributive justice, 124–30; on exploitation, 103, 104, 106–7
Ruccio, David, 7
rule of law, Hayek on, 3, 13, 48, 79; common law and, 38, 39, 51, 54, 57, 82; equality under, 73, 90–91, 135; as evolutionary concept, 14, 50–54, 64; freedom vs. coercion in, 46–47, 49; impartiality in, 57, 82; perception and, 24; precedent and, 52; property rights and, 92; social order and, 45–50; subjectivity of, 62–64
rule utilitarianism, 49, 93, 136. *See* utilitarian theory

Samuelson, Paul, 107
Sciabarra, C. M., 7, 14
science, postmodern, 44
Scottish Enlightenment, 19
self-exploitation, 105–7
self-management, 99, 122, 134, 141. *See*

also labor-managed firms; workplace democracy
Sen, Amartya, 8, 13, 14–15, 72, 83, 95, 120; on essentialism, 87–88; on flourishing life, 117; on individual choice, 88–89, 94; on well-being freedom, 91–92. *See also* capability theory
sensory perception. *See* perception
Smith, Adam, 41, 85
social democracy, 97–98, 139
social evolution, 19; cosmos concept in, 40–41; human action and, 40, 41–42; rule of law and, 45–54, 65–66; spontaneous, 40–45, 51, 53
social inheritance, 131–34, 135
socialism, 1, 3, 12; class justice and, 98–100; market phobia in, 12–14; post-Hayekian, 12–16; thin notion of, 8–9, 10, 11. *See also* market socialism
socialist appropriative justice, 101, 138
socialist calculation debate, 29–36
social justice, 67, 94; knowledge problems and, 54–57, 82–100; in labor-managed firm, 101–21; property rights and, 93. *See also* capability theory; distributive justice
social welfare, 41, 81, 94. *See also under* welfare
Soviet Union, 12, 36; famine in, 55; state capitalism in, 7, 109
speculation, 69, 77
spontaneous order, 40–45, 51, 53, 55, 80, 92
stakeholder society, 15–16, 130–36, 137, 140, 146; Hayek and, 134–36; social inheritance in, 131–34, 135; wealth tax in, 124, 132, 134
standard of living, 33, 131
state capitalism, 7, 30, 109
state ownership, 118
Stigler, George, 75
Stiglitz, Joseph, 74, 75
subjective knowledge, 2, 13, 30, 94, 139; discursive, 60; entrepreneurship and, 67; good life and, 87; in judicial decisions, 62, 63–64, 78; legal realism and, 58, 59. *See also* knowledge problem
subjectivism, 18, 20, 25, 136; central planning and, 33–34, 36; distributive

justice and, 37; rule of law and, 50, 62–64

Sugden, Robert, 89–90

Sunstein, Cass, 93

surplus labor, 103–11; appropriation of, 104–5, 107–11; class and, 4, 98–99; labor theory of value and, 107–9; self-exploitation and, 105–7

synoptic delusion, 3, 7

Tarascio, V., 27

taxis and cosmos, 40–41, 53

tax revenue, 93, 125. See also wealth taxation

Taylor, Fred, 31

Thatcher, Margaret, 1

Thompson, Frank, 129

Thomson, I., 51–52

time, perception and, 24

totalitarian democracy, 39

totalitarianism, 97

transaction costs, 75, 76

universal rules, 45, 49, 51–52, 78, 81, 87–88. See also common law

utilitarian theory, 4, 49, 83, 91, 92

value, labor theory of, 107–9, 115

Vanberg, Viktor, 36–37, 42–43

Vanek, Jaroslav, 124, 140, 145, 146; on worker self-management, 118, 122, 137, 152n8

voluntary consent, 80

wage-for-labor-time exchange, 65, 99, 102; abolition of, 3, 9, 104; Ellerman on, 112–13, 115, 117, 121; exploitation in, 110–11

wage incentives, 119

wage labor, 102, 122, 140

wage slavery, 118

wealth redistribution, 9, 82, 127, 137; in stakeholder society, 16, 124, 131–36. See also distributive justice

wealth taxation, 124, 132, 134–35, 140. See also stakeholder society

Weiss, Andrew, 74, 75

welfare: policy, 83, 97–98; rights, 93; state, 123, 137, 139, 143

well-being, 4, 17, 78, 83; freedom in, 91–92. See also good life

West, Cornel, 116

Whitman, D. G., 11

Williams, Juliet, 80

Wolff, Edward, 133

Wolff, Richard, 6–7, 8, 99, 101, 120, 147n2; on appropriation, 104, 109, 110; on exploitation, 103, 107

Wood, Allen, 108, 114–15, 116

worker appropriation, 138–39; responsibility and, 113–14

workers' councils, 143

worker self-management, 99, 100, 124, 138; capability theory and, 114–17; coupon stock market and, 126–27; Hayek and, 117–21; monitoring in, 119, 126, 128–29, 144; stakeholder society and, 133–34; Vanek's proposal for, 118, 122, 137, 152n8. See also labor-managed firms

workplace democracy, 4, 10, 15, 122, 144, 146. See also labor-managed firms

Yeager, Leland, 49